Beijing
Tianjin
Dalian
Qingdao
CHINA
Suzhou
Shanghai
Hangzhou
Ningbo
Delhi
INDIA
Kolkata
Mumbai
Guangzhou
Zhongshan
Shenzhen
Hong Kong
Hanoi
VIETNAM
Bangalore
Chennai
Ho Chi Minh City
SINGAPORE

India Briefing

The Practical Application of India Business

Series Editor

Chris Devonshire-Ellis

For further volumes:
http://www.springer.com/series/10356
http://www.asiabriefingmedia.com

Dezan Shira & Associates is a specialist foreign direct investment practice, providing business advisory, tax, accounting, payroll and due diligence services to multinationals investing in China, Hong Kong, India and Vietnam. Established in 1992, the firm is a leading regional practice in Asia with nineteen offices in four jurisdictions, employing over 170 business advisory and tax professionals.

We also provide useful business information through our media and publishing house, Asia Briefing.

Dezan Shira & Associates
Chris Devonshire-Ellis
Editors

Doing Business in India

Third Edition

Springer

DEZAN SHIRA & ASSOCIATES

Dezan Shira & Associates
Kowloon
Hong Kong SAR

Chris Devonshire-Ellis
Dezan Shira & Associates
Asia Briefing Ltd.
Kowloon
Hong Kong SAR

ISBN 978-3-642-27617-0 e-ISBN 978-3-642-27618-7
DOI 10.1007/978-3-642-27618-7
Springer Heidelberg New York Dordrecht London

Library of Congress Control Number: 2012933320

Printed on acid free paper

Springer is part of Springer Science+Business Media (www.springer.com)

Preface

This book is a timely introduction to foreign direct investment in India, coming as it does on the cusp of massive increases of foreign capital and cash flows into the country. Although over the past 20 years India has been seen to lag behind the phenomenal growth story that is China, that period has now come to an end. The era of a resurgent, confident India is now at hand.

The future success of India lies in its people—India has a massive population of 300 million aged 15 and under, and the work force strength the nation now possesses will turn it into one of the great economic powerhouses of this century, perhaps even surpassing China. That inherent intellect, and the realization by Indians that their destiny is on their own hands, has unleashed a wave of entrepreneurial spirit and can-do attitudes that it is hard to match anywhere else.

I also hear often about India's decayed infrastructure, the chaos in transportation and the inefficient bureaucracy. Yet looking back, the same was also true of China 15 years ago. The road to Beijing airport used to be populated by the occasional donkey and cart. Now it is an eight lane tollway, with locally made sedans cruising the highway en route to international flights. I am reminded of how recent the Beijing donkey episode was when I see the road sign on Mumbai's impressive new Bandra–Worli Sealink: "No Buffalo Carts." Just as China made the transition from agricultural base to urban renewal, so India is doing as well. It is also true that within the infrastructure problems, great opportunities abound for the foreign investor. Millions of dollars are to be made by the private sector by working with the Indian government in public–private partnerships, and as expertise and experience are required to bring the nations transportation, energy, communications and many other sectors into the modern world, many more will be created.

Another factor in India's favor is the local resilience. While shocked and still mourning the dead after the horrific Mumbai terrorist attacks, the reality is that after the blood was mopped up and remembrances held, society just got on with life as always. It's a bold reminder of a people long able to cope with difficulties and to move on. In an emerging market, which will undoubtedly experience its own economic and financial bumps in the road, such resilience is a vital commodity.

This book signals not just how to do business in India (although I hope our readers will join this lucky band who do so) but also the beginning of a new India: confident, welcoming, and part of the global community. I hope you will find the information within these pages of use.

Welcome to business in India.

Yours faithfully
Chris Devonshire-Ellis

About Asia Briefing's India Business Guide

Thank you for buying this book. Asia Briefing's publications are designed to fill a niche in the provision of information about business laws and taxes in Asia. Produced by the foreign direct investment practice Dezan Shira & Associates, we started this series of guides several years ago with the knowledge that much of the intelligence regarding Asia was expensive, or contradictory. Much also did not adequately address the real on the ground issues faced by multinational businessmen—the practical knowledge that must be part of the armory of any business operating in emerging markets.

India Briefing is designed to deal with this gap and is aimed at providing both the regulatory background as well as detailed information concerning Asia business with a firm eye on the practicalities of turning a profit and remaining in compliance on the mainland. Accordingly, we have tried to make this guide informative, easy to read and inexpensive. We have drawn on the experience and practical knowledge of Dezan Shira & Associates, Asia's largest independent business and tax consultancy with offices in China, Hong Kong, India and Vietnam.

This book is a window into one of the fastest growing economies in the world, providing an overview of India, its history, key demographics and overviews of the states and union territories highlighting business opportunities and infrastructure in place in each region. We have also included information on FDI trends, business establishment procedures, labor and tax considerations as well as commentary on Indian business etiquette and culture. The guide also details procedural, operational and tax differences between India and its economic and geographical neighbor, China. The materials within this guide have been researched and written by professionals familiar with the issues that face foreign investors in India.

Contributors to the original version of this guide include: Seema Rani Bhendi, Chris Devonshire-Ellis, Mark Hannant, Peter Higgins, Joyce Roque, Linda Tjoa and Vikas Srivastava. The cover was designed by Chris Wei, the book was designed and laid out by Becky Jian and Chris Wei and edited by Andy Scott, Mark Hannant, and Chris Devonshire-Ellis. Updates for 2011 were led by Jennifer Park, with contributions by Dezan Shira & Associates Shanghai and India offices.

At India Briefing, our motto is "The practical application of India business"—we hope that's the information you find within these pages.

With best regards,
Asia Briefing

A note on sourcing: Data for net state domestic product (NSDP) is provided by the 2010–2011 Union Budget and Economic Survey from the Government of India, http://indiabudget.nic.in. In certain cases, the most recent figures in this survey are from several years ago (as far back as 2006), but were included nonetheless to ensure consistency of sources.

Contents

Chapter 1
An Introduction to India

Stretching from the frigid mountains of the Northern Himalayas to the tropical greenery of Kerala in the South, and from the sacred Ganges River to the dusty sands of the Thar Desert, India's geographic landscape offers an incomparable variety. Daily life includes crowded bazaars, obsession with Bollywood movies and music, fiery cooking spices, and dust and cow dung, all of which engulf a person the moment he or she steps off the plane.

With over 1.1 billion citizens, India is the second most populous nation in the world (after China), the largest democracy, and thoroughly unique in its diverse set of cultures, religions, races and languages. While this sometimes bewildering country is full of paradoxes and frustrations, India is coming of age. Spurred by the free-market and trade liberalization reforms of the early 1990s, the economic revolution of the last 20 years has transformed India with new consumer goods, technologies and ways of life. While poverty remains a harsh reality for approximately 40% of India's citizens, a stone's throw away from the massive slum settlements of Delhi, Mumbai and Kolkata are wealthy sub-societies valuing status, pedigree, and copious amounts of luxury jewelry.

Since 2000, India's amazing growth has allowed it to leapfrog over intermediary stages of development. This is especially impressive given the anemic growth rate India had in the past several decades. After the 2008 global slowdown, India managed to display resilience and impressive growth compared to other developing countries. The country's economy is expected to grow at 8.6% in 2010–2011 and is considered one of the worlds' best performing economies in the last quarter century. Today, the land where the Buddha lived and taught, and whose religious customs are as old as the rivers that sustain them, is the second-largest producer of computer software in the world.

Furthermore, the Indian government is shaping laws and regulations to make the country an utterly compelling destination for investment. Since 1991, when former Finance Minister Manmohan Singh introduced liberal and deregulating economic reforms, India has lowered its trade barriers and tax rates, broken state-run industries and encouraged competition. In addition to government policies

Dezan Shira & Associates and C. Devonshire-Ellis (eds.), *Doing Business in India*,
India Briefing, DOI: 10.1007/978-3-642-27618-7_1,

favorable to investment, India boasts rich reserves of raw materials, booming domestic demand (the fifth largest economy in the world in terms of purchasing power parity), and an abundant, young, English-speaking workforce that is relatively low-cost (one of the lowest labor costs per hour in the world). Furthermore, a pervasive air of entrepreneurship, a well-developed banking system and a liberal policy on technology collaboration abounds in the country. The World Investment Prospects Survey 2010–2012 report by the United Nations Conference on Trade and Development ranked India as the second most attractive FDI destination for the year 2010 (China was ranked number one and Brazil number three).

Yet the dramatic changes that have occurred in the last few decades have involved huge internal realignments of India's laws and business environment. As a result, the foreign business and investment community are often confused or misinformed—a reality that we aim to remedy. This book aims to provide a basic overview of all topics related to doing business in India–history, business etiquette and culture, and how to invest into the country, in addition to a demographic and geographic overview and a brief comparison with China.

India key facts and figures
Population: 1,210,193,422
Capital: New Delhi
Borders: Bhutan, China, and Nepal to the northeast, Bangladesh and Myanmar to the east, and Pakistan to the west.
Area: 3,287,263 km^2
Major languages: Hindi and English
Major religions: Hinduism, Islam, Christianity, Sikhism, Buddhism, Jainism
Life expectancy: 65.77 (men) 67.95 (women)
Monetary Unit: 1 Indian Rupee = 100 paise
Main exports: Agricultural products, petroleum products, gems and jewelry, machinery, iron and steel, chemicals, vehicles, textile goods, leather products.
GNI per capita: US $1,180 per capita in PPP dollars, current prices (World Bank 2009)
Internet domain:.in
International dialing code: +91

Why India Now?

India has been widely considered an attractive FDI destination since 1991 for the following four reasons:

1. Traditional manufacturing markets in China are becoming more expensive
2. Increasing relaxation of FDI laws

3. The growing young domestic market
4. India's democratic political system.

But to leave the reason for Indian investment at these four points would be unrepresentative of the real opportunities in the country. Additional compelling reasons include:

1. *Strong Congress Party*—In May 2009, the Congress Party registered a monumental, landslide victory and the new government has indicated a strong desire to ease FDI regulations to promote development in key industries such as infra-structure, energy and telecommunications to quickly drive the country to devel-oped nation status. The liberalization of FDI regulations is a deliberate strategy on the part of the new Indian government to develop infrastructure, offering significant opportunity for foreign engineering and construction companies.
2. *Demographic "dividend"*—While traditionally thought of as a burden, India's large population will actually begin to yield the country some cost savings and drive economic growth. India is rated best destination for outsourcing by A.T. Kearney, and, according to Foreign Affairs magazine, 125 of the Fortune 500 now have research and development bases in India—a testament to India's high-quality human capital. Furthermore, it is projected that the working population of India is estimated to add 120 million within the next decade and another 100 million by 2030. India's median age is 26.2 and its young population provides an expansive low-cost workforce. In China, where the median age is nearly 35.5, the ratio of workers to retirees will start to drop, causing workforce and production challenges.
3. *Pervasive entrepreneurial spirit*—India's people are known to be self-reliant, with a tenacious capitalist spirit. Many of the world's top billionaires come from India and manage best-in-class companies such as Reliance Industries, Arcelor Mittal and Bharti Airtel. The country has generated a huge number of students with management degrees over the past decade and these young graduates are an integral part of India's business growth. These young Indian professionals no longer hold the protectionist ideals of their grandfather's generation—they are eager to partner with foreign companies. Moreover, given the country's strong pool of scientific and technical manpower (over 100,000 IT professionals added each year) combined with India being the second largest English-speaking population in the world, India is an entrepreneurial hotbed.
4. *High domestic demand*—India has relied on its domestic market more than exports for many years. Unlike its other Asian neighbors who rely on exporting labor intensive, low-priced manufactured goods, India's growth is based on its demanding domestic consumer. According to a study conducted by McKinsey Global Institute, by 2025 India will become the fifth largest consumer market in the world and aggregate consumer spending is projected to quadruple to approximately US $1.5 trillion. Research from the McKinsey Global Institute indicates that within the next two decades, the size of the middle class in India

will be more than quadrupled to nearly 147 million and Indian incomes are likely to grow fourfold in the coming two decades. The Associated Chambers of Commerce and Industry of India predicts that by 2011, 315 hypermarkets will come into existence in first and second tier cities across India, riding on the boom of the retail sector and high domestic demand.

Top Reasons to Invest in India Now

Strong Economic Indicators

- Fifth largest economy in terms of purchasing power parity (2010)
- GDP growth rate of 8.6% (2010–2011)
- Liberal and transparent foreign investment regime
- Well developed banking system and vibrant capital market
- Strong and independent judicial system.

Excellent Human Capital Skills

- Strong pool of engineers, researchers and scientists, many India Institute of Technology and India Institute of Management graduates
- Second largest English-speaking population in the world
- Median age of working population will be 30 by the year 2025.

Easy Industrial Licensing Policy

- Under the Industries (Development and Regulation) Act of 1951, an industrial license is only needed for items that fall under compulsory licensing, are reserved for small-scale sector, or in a location that is restricted
- No approval is required, only notification needed.

Financial Sector Reforms

- Stable tax regime; only three rates of indirect tax and trade facilitation measures have been introduced
- The 1999 Foreign Exchange Management Act provides a liberal regime; foreign exchange procedures are straightforward
- Stocks can be sold on without prior approval

- Profits, dividends and capital investment can be repatriated
- Royalties can be paid by wholly owned subsidiaries to parent companies.

Trade Policy Reforms

- Trade policy liberalized and most items are on an open general license
- Policies fully compatible with the WTO
- Functioning of the Directorate General of Foreign Trade is computerized: all 33 locations are web-enabled, 70% of the total transactions of exporters and importers are web-enabled, transaction times have been reduced to just 6 hours and on-line banking fully integrated.

Proactive FDI Policy

- FDI under automatic route, except in a few areas
- Investors can bring automatic route cases for Foreign Investment Promotion Board approval
- Foreign Investment Implementation Authority helps solve foreign investors' problems and meets periodically with investors to facilitate and sort out operational difficulties
- An empowered sub-committee of the National Development Council was set up to create an investor friendly climate and remove regulatory barriers to investments
- Foreign technology collaborations freely allowed under automatic and government approval routes
- Global competitive report ranks India in first place in terms of prevalence of foreign technology licensing
- Modernization of legislations on intellectual property; all IPR laws are TRIPS compliant and the Intellectual Property Appellate Tribunal is functional.

Infrastructure Development

The Indian government's emphasis on investment in the infrastructure sector is evident in its preliminary assessment on the next Five Year Plan (2012–2017), which plans to allocate $1,025 billion for infrastructure development with at least half of its investment coming from the private sector.

Some facts and figures for recently completed and anticipated infrastructure developments:

Roads

- India has second largest road networks in the world totaling 4.2 million kilometers
- The National Highways Development Project (NHDP), the largest highway project ever undertaken by the country estimated to cost US $13.2 billion, is being implemented by the National Highway Authority of India.

Railway

- Indian Railways has long been regarded as the backbone of India's socio economic growth and the country has the world's fourth largest rail network and the second largest in Asia after China
- Indian Railways has recently attracted immense global media and corporate attention due to its turnaround to profitability, and has been consistently recording buoyant growth rates over the last few years as India's population continues to increase
- New generation fuel efficient, recyclable, low emission trains, with certified emission reduction credits are being introduced
- Increases of freight and cargo in both domestic and international routes have placed considerable stress on capacity on the two main Delhi-Mumbai and Delhi-Kolkata lines, so construction of a dedicated freight corridor is planned, with an investment of US $614.40 million in 2009–2010
- Renewal of over 2,941 km of rail, which will require 3.39 million tons of rail steel, and the renewal of over 2,382 km of pre-stressed concrete sleepers
- Previously, containerization was operated under a state monopoly, CONCOR, but this sector has now been liberalized and is open to competition; private sector entities may now either partner with or compete with CONCOR.

Airports

- Major upgrade of airport at New Delhi was completed in 2010 and upgrade of airport at Mumbai is expected to end in 2012. Other major cities are also given significant increase in business and leisure air travel.

Ports

- India has approximately 12 major and 200 minor ports, through which roughly 95% of the country's trade is conducted
- A major program aimed at developing the ports and shipping sector at an estimated investment of US $22 billion is underway

- Government incentives include automatic approval of up to 100% foreign equity participation with regard to the construction of ports and harbors.

Telecommunications

- India is one of the fastest growing telecom markets with the third largest telecom network and second largest wireless network in the world.

Urban Planning

- Development of townships for the rapidly growing and increasingly affluent urban middle class
- City level infrastructure is needed in drinking water supply, sewerage and sanitation, drainage and solid waste management and urban transport; approximately US $1.2 trillion would be needed over next two decades.

Power

- The power sector is a high priority given the sheer size of market and the returns available on the investment capital; so the Indian government has an ambitious mission of "power for all by 2012," which would require that installed generation capacity be at least 200,000 MW by 2012, and plans to double its goal to 400,000 MW by 2020.

Chapter 2
A Brief History of India

Civilization in India began around 2500 B.C. when the inhabitants of the Indus River Valley began commercial and agricultural trade. Around 1500 B.C., the Indus Valley civilization began to decline, likely due to environmental changes. At this time, Aryan tribes migrated into the Indian subcontinent and flourished in the Ganges River valley. Throughout ancient and medieval India, a number of kingdoms ruled the country and specifically in the fourth and fifth centuries AD, Northern India was unified under the Gupta Dynasty and this period is referred to as "India's Golden Age," where Hindu culture, language and politics reached unprecedented growth. Islam expanded across India over the next 500 years and in the tenth and eleventh centuries, Turks and Afghans invaded India and established capitals in Delhi.

In the sixteenth century, successors of Genghis Khan swept across the Khyber Pass and established the Mughal Dynasty, which lasted for over 200 years in India. South India was dominated by Hindu Chola and Vijayanagar Dynasties between the eleventh and fifteenth centuries. The Hindu and Muslim systems of North and South India mingled and culturally influenced each other, leaving a lasting impact in the region.

The first British colony of India was established in 1619 in Surat (in present day Gujurat). Later in the century, the East India Company opened trading stations at Madras (present day Chennai), Bombay (present day Mumbai), and Calcutta (present day Kolkata). For the next 200 years, the British expanded their influence and by the 1850s, Britain controlled most of India, Pakistan, and Bangladesh. In 1857, a rebellion in North India, referred to as India's First War of Independence led by mutinous Indian soldiers (it is also called the Sepoy Rebellion) caused the British Parliament to transfer all political power from the East India Company to the British Crown. Great Britain began controlling most of India directly while managing the rest through treaties with local rulers.

Dezan Shira & Associates and C. Devonshire-Ellis (eds.), *Doing Business in India*,
India Briefing, DOI: 10.1007/978-3-642-27618-7_2,

Indian Independence

In the late 1800s, Indian counselors were appointed to advise the British viceroy and participate in legislative councils, enabling Indians to take initial steps towards self-government. Around 1920, independence advocate Mohandas K. Gandhi (also called Mahatma or Great Soul) transformed the India National Congress Party by organizing mass civil disobedience movements to protest continued British colonial rule. For his role in India's independence, Gandhi is officially honored as the Father of the Nation and his birthday, October 2, is a national holiday.

On August 15, 1947, India became independent from British rule along with Pakistan. Hostility between Hindus and Muslims had led the British to partition British India, creating East and West Pakistan, where there were Muslim majorities.

Pakistan's independence sparked unprecedented and prolonged riots across India and Pakistan, resulting in millions of Indian Muslims migrating to Pakistan and millions of Pakistani Hindus and Sikhs migrating to India. Approximately 500,000 people died as a result of a riot that broke out between Sikhs, Hindus, and Muslims when pre-partition Punjab and Bengal was divided. Furthermore, disputes arose over several states including Kashmir and Jammu whose ruler had illegally entered India following an invasion by Pashtun tribesmen from Pakistan. This led to the First Kashmir War in 1948 that ended in Pakistan administrating one-third of the state.

In 1971, Bangladesh, formerly East Pakistan and East Bengal, seceded from Pakistan and became its own country.

Post Independence

Jawaharlal Nehru became the country's first prime minister and India became a republic within the Commonwealth after disseminating its constitution on January 26, 1950. After independence, the Congress Party, the party of Mahatma Gandhi and Jawaharlal Nehru, primarily ruled India under the leadership of Nehru and then his daughter, Indira Gandhi, and grandson, Rajiv Gandhi, with the exception of two brief periods in the 1970 and 1980s.

Prime Minister Nehru governed India until his death in 1964. He was succeeded by Lal Bahadur Shastri, who also died in office. In 1966, power passed to Nehru's daughter, Indira Gandhi, who served as PM from 1966 to 1977. In 1975, with an onslaught of serious political and economic problems in the country, Mrs. Gandhi declared a state of emergency and suspended many civil liberties.

Seeking justification from the public for her policies, she called for elections in 1977, only to be defeated by Moraji Desai, who headed the Janata Party, a coalition of 5 opposition parties. In 1980, Indira Gandhi returned to power. In June 1984, under her order, the Indian army forcefully entered the Golden Temple in

Punjab, the most sacred Sikh shrine, to remove armed insurgents present inside the temple. She was assassinated on October 31, 1984 in retaliation for this operation. She was India's first and, to date, only female prime minister. Her son Rajiv was chosen by the Congress Party to take her place and his government was eventually brought down in 1989 on allegations of corruption. In the 1989 elections, the Congress party lost to the Janata Dal, a union of opposition parties including the Hindu-nationalist Bharatiya Janata Party (BJP) and the Communist Party. This loose coalition collapsed shortly afterwards and national elections were held again in 1991.

Present Day

On May 27, 1991, while campaigning in Tamil Nadu on behalf of the Congress Party, Rajiv Gandhi was assassinated, reportedly by Tamil extremists from Sri Lanka. In the elections, Congress returned to power by putting together a coalition under the leadership of Prime Minister Narasimha Rao. This Congress-led government served a full 5 year term and initiated the 1991 economic liberalization and reform that opened India to global trade and investment.

The 1991 elections gave no single political party a majority; the India National Congress (INC) formed a minority government under Prime Minister P.V. Narasimha Rao who completed a five-year term. Between 1996 and 1998 there was instability in the federal government. The BJP formed a government briefly in 1996, followed by the United Front coalition that excluded the BJP and the INC. In 1998, the BJP formed the National Democratic Alliance (NDA) with several other parties and became the first non-Congress government to complete a full 5 year term run under the leadership of Prime Minister Atal Bihari Vajpayee. In 2004, the INC won the largest number of Lok Sabha (the directly elected lower house of Parliament) seats and formed a coalition called the United Progressive Alliance (UPA). Prime Minister Manmohan Singh was sworn in on May 22, 2004, and is currently serving his second five-year term. In the 2009 Lok Sabha elections, the INC party won again with an unprecedented majority.

Family Politics

While democracy is built on the ideal that any man or woman can be elected, in India, political analysts suggest it helps to be part of a political family to win an election. The Nehru-Gandhi dynasty that has governed the Congress Party since independence is India's version of the iconic American political dynasty, the Kennedy family.

India's politics can sometimes be seen as democracy to a fault with frequent elections, leadership changes and over 1,000 registered national and regional political parties. But internally most of the major parties, especially the Congress Party, are not quite democratic with party leaders selecting candidates, often their own relatives, and not holding primary elections and many argue that nepotism has deeply infiltrated India's political system. Political families are deep-rooted at every level of government. According to the New York Times, "at least nine of the 32 members of Prime Minister Manmohan Singh's cabinet either descended from political families or have children seeking or holding office."

Even though Indian politicians have a high turnover rate, analysts suggest Indian voters prefer a familiar family pedigree, due to cultural reverence for the family name and also because the political landscape is so overcrowded that voters prefer to vote for a "brand" name they are familiar with. Several of the royal families who ruled over feudal states are still today heavily evolved into political families.

Political System

According to India's constitution, the country is a "sovereign socialist secular democratic republic" with a parliamentary system of government. India is governed by a constitution, which was adopted in 1949 and came into force in 1950. There are 28 states and seven Union territories in the country. The system of government in states resembles that of the Union. In the states, the governor, as the representative of the president, is the head executive, but real executive power rests with the chief minister who heads the Council of Ministers. The Council of Ministers of a state is collectively responsible to the elected legislative assembly of the state.

President: The president is the constitutional head of the Union and is elected by members of an electoral college consisting of elected members of both houses of parliament and legislative assemblies of the states. However, real executive power lies with the Council of Ministers lead by the prime minister. The Council of Ministers is collectively responsible to the Lok Sabha, the house of the people.

Vice-president: The vice-president is elected by the Electoral College and holds office for 5 years. They are ex-officio chairman of the Rajya Sabha.

Council of Ministers: The Council of Ministers is comprised of cabinet ministers, ministers of states and deputy ministers. The prime minister communicates all decisions of the Council of Ministers related to administration of affairs of the Union to the president. Generally, each department has an officer or secretary that advises the ministers on policy matters and general administration.

Cabinet Secretariat: The Cabinet Secretariat plays an important coordinating role in decision-making at the highest level and operates under the supervision of the prime minister. The legislative arm of the Union, the Parliament, consists of the President, Rajya Sabha and Lok Sabha. All legislation requires consent of both houses of Parliament. In the case of financial legislation, the Lok Sabha has the ruling vote.

Rajya Sabha: The Rajya Sabha consists of 245 members, of which 233 represent states and union territories and 12 members are nominated by the president. Elections to the Rajya Sabha are indirect—members are elected by the elected members of legislative assemblies of the concerned states.

Lok Sabha: the Lok Sabha is composed of representatives of the people chosen by direct election. The term of the Lok Sabha is 5 years.

Party recognition: If a political party is recognized in four or more states, it is considered a national party. The most prominent national parties in India include: the Congress Party, Bharatiya Janata Party, Janata Dal, and the Communist Party of India. There are over 1,000 registered national and regional parties in the country.

Chapter 3
India Business Etiquette and Culture

India is one of the oldest civilizations in the world and is a complicated mixture of old and new traditions from the West and East. For those doing business in the country, it is vital to gain a basic understanding of the country's cultural customs. The country is defined by its cultural and linguistic diversity—unmatched by any other country. If you are planning to do business with or in India, it is important to understand this vibrant culture.

India is better thought of as a continent, composed of many different cultures and languages. Behavior, etiquette and approach may need to be modified depending on whom you are working with.

Making Appointments

English is the business language of India. While Hindi is the official language of India and there are more than 29 regional languages spoken in the country, English is spoken by all middle class Indians and many less-skilled workers have basic speaking skills.

Date format in India is expressed in the British manner of day, month, and year; so August 15, 2009 is written 15 August 2009 or 15/08/09. The business calendar year is from April to March and there are multiple holidays throughout the year that vary dependent upon region and religion.

E-mail is the preferred and easiest method for setting up meeting appointments with Indian contacts. The postal service is considered to be unreliable, but if you do use written communication the style often used is based on British pre-war colonial, using phrases such as "Dear Sir" or "Yours faithfully."

Dezan Shira & Associates and C. Devonshire-Ellis (eds.), *Doing Business in India*, India Briefing, DOI: 10.1007/978-3-642-27618-7_3,

Indian names are comprised of given name and family name, similar to the Western style. It is common for "Mr." or "Ms." to be used in initial communications but once contact has been established the formality decreases.

In any initial communication, be sure to provide a clear overview of who you are, your role, and a brief description of your organization. Also, detail what you would like to discuss in a meeting as it is appreciated when you visit any company's office given the long travel times in cities. If you are setting up a lunch or dinner meeting, it is advisable to check if the guest is vegetarian or prefers Indian or Western food.

It is very normal for meetings to start a few minutes late or have some interruptions and should not be considered a sign of disrespect. Everything takes time in India and things do not always work like clockwork. Indian culture has a slower, informal pace when it comes to business and many Indians believe that schedules are required to be flexible in order to accommodate different people's timetables. It is advisable to keep a margin in your schedule for unexpected delays such as meetings running late or traffic. Furthermore, if you are visiting government officials, be prepared to be kept waiting. Also note that Muslim businessmen may take small breaks during meetings for their prayers.

In India, unlike some East Asian countries, you can be straightforward about what you want to achieve from the meeting or business engagement. There is not the issue of "losing face" and Indian businessmen appreciate being clear and forthright. It is important to be very specific in what you are looking for and have specific tender documents detailing your orders; given the extreme optimism in India and dynamic growing market, smaller start-ups have been known to over-promise. Establish a clear timeline and monitor deliverables.

Greetings

The traditional India greeting is the "Namaste," which you do with hands pressed together, palms touching and fingers pointed upwards, in front of the chest with a slight nod or bow of the head. In a business setting, it is customary to shake a male colleague's hand; shaking hands with women is less common and it is better to wait for a woman's initiative in a handshake out of respect. In the absence of a handshake, you can do a Namaste. It is very common for people, especially those younger than you, to call you "Sir" or "Madam" out of respect.

Many foreigners are perplexed by the common non-verbal signal that Indian's do of shaking their head from side to side. It appears to be a combination of a verbal of yes and no. In India, this gesture is a visual way to communicate to someone that you understand what they are saying or that you agree with them.

Religions and Holidays

India is composed of a multitude of religions coexisting (though not always peacefully) side by side. The dominant religion is Hinduism, but significant numbers of Muslims, Buddhists, Sikhs, Jains, Jews, and Christians also live in the country. In India, religion is a key aspect of life and must be respected in order to maintain successful business relationships. Despite the elimination of the traditional caste system that derives from Hinduism, attitudes still remain and aspects of the system still influence the hierarchical structure of business practices in India today.

Holidays in India come in all shapes and sizes and vary in terms of religion and region. It is important to check online before scheduling appointments if there are any conflicts. The three largest national holidays of India are:

- Jan 26 Republic Day
- 15 Aug Independence Day
- 2 Oct Mahatma Gandhi's Birthday.

Below is a list of additional government holidays for 2010 (dates will vary year by year):

- Feb 16 Milad un Nabi (Shia)
- April 16 Mahavir Jayanti
- April 22 Good Friday
- May 17 Budha Purnima
- Aug 13 Raksha Bandhan
- Aug 30 Eid ul-Fitr (end of Ramadan)
- Oct 6 Dussehra (Way Dashmi)
- Oct 26 Diwali (Deepavali)
- Nov 6 Idu'l Zuha/Bakrid
- Nov 10 Guru Nanak's Birthday
- Dec 5 Al-Hijra/Muharram
- Dec 25 Christmas Day.

Diwali—Known as the Festival of Lights, this national holiday typically occurs between the end of September and early November. It is common for people to light small clay lamps filled with oil to signify the triumph of good over evil within an individual. During Diwali, many people wear new clothes and share sweets and other snacks with each other. Some Indian businesses may start their financial year by opening new accounting books on the first day of Diwali for good luck the following year.

In Hinduism, Diwali marks the return of Lord Rama to his kingdom, Ayodhya, after defeating the demon King Ravana, the ruler of Lanka in the epic story of Ramayana. It also celebrates the slaying of the demon King Narakasura by Lord Krishna. Both stories signify the victory of good over evil.

The notion of Karma—that everything happens for a reason—is a significant aspect of the culture and decision-making process of many Indians. Indians have a strong sense of community and define group orientation through hierarchical structure. Given the large population, there is a noticeable lack of privacy and a smaller concept of personal space, with several generations of families often living together under one roof. Given this, interpersonal relationships are critical in business practices.

Eid ul-Fitr—Islam is India's second-most practiced religion after Hinduism. More than 13.4% of the country's population (over 138 million as per 2001 census and 160.9 million per 2009 estimate) identify themselves as Muslims; India's Muslim population is the world's third largest behind Indonesia and Pakistan. Eid ul-Fitr (Eid) is a Muslim holiday that marks the end of Ramadan, the Islamic holy month of fasting. Eid means "festivity" in Arabic, while Fitr means "to break fast." Celebrated on the first day of Shawwal, Eid ul-Fitr lasts for three days of celebration.

In India, the night before Eid is called Chand Raat, which means "night of the moon." People often visit shops and malls with their families for last minute Eid shopping. Women often paint their hands with traditional "henna" and wear colorful bangles.

During Eid, the traditional greeting is "Eid Mubarak" and frequently includes a formal embrace. Gifts are given—new clothes are traditional—and it is also common for children to be given small amounts of money (Eidi) by their elders. It is common for children to "salam" parents and adult relatives. After the Eid prayers, it is common for families to visit graveyards and pray for the salvation of departed family members.

Making Conversation

It is not uncommon for Indians to ask questions which can be seen as too personal or intrusive. Discussing one's family and personal life is normal among Indians and enquiring about the other person's family is seen as a sign of friendliness and interest.

There are many topics of conversation that Indians find engaging such as politics, cricket, films and most recently, India's economic reforms and growth. Bollywood, India's film industry, produces the largest number of films annually [around 800–1,000] in the world. There are more than 13,000 movie theaters in the country and many Indians also keep abreast of the latest movies through TV, videos and DVDs. Like cricket players, film stars are considered national icons and are the subject of a lot of social discussion and gossip.

In general, Indians are very tolerant and accepting of religious and cultural differences, given the country's vast diversity. As religious practices and rituals play a major role in Indian life, a genuine enquiry into a certain religious practice will normally be met with an enthusiastic response. India's relationship with its neighboring country, Pakistan, has historically never been a very amiable one. Some educated Indians view this as a failure on the part of politicians on both sides. However, many Indians can be very biased, emotional and one-sided when discussing Pakistan. In general, it is advisable to avoid discussing Pakistan/India issues.

In addition, it is hard to not notice the large rich-poor divide that exists in India. It is common to find wealthy, extravagant homes next to sprawling slums. Some Indians may be sensitive and defensive about the poverty as they are very proud of the economic growth the country has seen. While Indians do openly discuss the country's poverty, if a foreigner initiates a discussion on this topic, it may be interpreted as an impolite criticism.

Hierarchy (Names and Titles)

Indians are accustomed to old British customs of hierarchy and there is a higher degree of formality between colleagues than in the West; for example, it is normal to use "sir" when talking upwards. It is recommended to use last names upon meeting someone for the first time and mention any higher academic or other titles.

The influences of Hinduism and the ancient tradition of the caste system have created a culture that emphasizes established hierarchical relationships. Indians are quite conscious of social order and their status relative to other people, whether they are family, friends, or strangers. All relationships involve hierarchies. For example, teachers are called gurus and are viewed as the source of all knowledge. The patriarch, usually the father, is considered the head of the family. The boss is seen as the source of ultimate responsibility in business. Every relationship has a well-defined hierarchy that must be observed for the social order to be maintained.

Business Attire

For men, the normal business attire is a button-down shirt, trousers and a jacket or tie depending on the formality of the meeting or industry (in the banking sector suits are more prevalent). Also, given that India has a warm climate, a full-sleeved shirt with a tie is acceptable. In the IT sector, however, the dress code is much more casual. It is common to find employees wearing T-shirts and jeans with sneakers.

In recent years, the dress code for women in Indian business settings has undergone a significant transformation. Earlier, most women would wear traditional Indian clothes such as the Salwar Kameez (long tunic and loose pants) or simple saris to the office. Now, women often wear pant-suits or long skirts, which cover the knees. The neckline of the blouse or the top should be high. For women, a salwar-suit is also acceptable for business dress. Jeans with a T-shirt or short-sleeved shirt are acceptable as casual wear in informal situations for both men and women.

It is ok to wear casual dress if invited to a social gathering. However, if a foreigner wears an Indian costume [kurta-pajama for men, and sari or salwar-suit for women], this kind of dress is also appreciated, and often seen as a gesture of friendship or keenness to understand the Indian culture. If invited to a formal event such as a wedding, formal attire is recommended.

Negotiating a Deal

There are as many salesmen as buyers in India; the average India businessman has a lot of experience "wheeling and dealing" so it's important to be patient during the negotiating process. Decision-making is a slow process and final decisions are typically reached by the person with the most authority. Delays are frequent and to be expected, especially when dealing with the government.

Entertaining Clients

It is common for foreigners to be invited for dinner or a meal at the home of an Indian business contact. Indians take great pride and joy in hosting guests, especially those from abroad, and serving home-cooked traditional meals.

If you are invited to an Indian's home for dinner, it is highly recommended to take some kind of gift, such as a box of sweets or flowers. If your host has children, carrying a small gift for the child such as a toy or a book is also appreciated. If you are visiting an Indian during a festival, it is customary to carry a box of sweets, known as "mithai."

In many Indian homes, people remove his or her shoes before entering. Observing this custom is particularly important so if you notice your host without shoes on you should remove yours as well. However, if the host insists you keep your shoes on, this is ok as well.

If you are attending a wedding and giving money as a gift, note that the Indian custom is to add an extra rupee for good luck (101, 501, 1,001, etc.). The adding of one is considered auspicious and your gift would be more appreciated if it is in these denominations.

Drinking alcohol is culturally not accepted in some parts of India and many Indians do not drink at home. However, if your host drinks and keeps drinks at home, then drinking will be acceptable.

Food

Eating and drinking are intrinsic aspects of Indian culture and there is great variety based on local customs and religions. It is common practice for hosts to offer beverages such as tea, coffee or soft-drinks with some light snacks or refreshments to a guest, even in business meeting settings.

If you ask for or are offered water, it is ok to ask if the water is filtered or from a bottle. Most Indians use only filtered water and will understand your need to clarify this before drinking. If you are doing several meetings in a day or are feeling full, it is ok to decline the first offer for food and drink. It is customary [though not mandatory] to refuse the first offer, but to accept the second or third. It would be considered a breach of etiquette not to accept something small to eat or drink at all. Even if you don't want to have the refreshments/snacks, it is advisable to accept them and leave them untouched or slightly consumed.

For a large number of Indian Hindus, eating meat is a religious taboo. While planning a meal for your Indian guests [or placing an order in a restaurant], it is recommended to ask if they are vegetarians or non-vegetarians. Much Indian food is eaten with the fingers and it is customary to eat with the right hand only.

In terms of drinking, it is better to ask your guest "What would you like to drink?" rather than "Can I get you a beer?" Even guests who drink will not drink alcohol on certain occasions such as religious festivals or if there is an older, highly respected relative present. Therefore, it is prudent to have fruit-juices or soft-drinks available.

Tipping

In India, excessive tipping is not common, but a certain amount of tip is expected. In most restaurants, 10% is a sufficient tip. You can, however, give an additional tip by leaving the change to show your appreciation. For taxis, it's ok to round up to the nearest amount.

Travel

All foreigners visiting India need a visa. When applying for a visa, you may need a letter from your Indian contact explaining the purpose of the meeting. It is important to visit your doctor before your trip to check which vaccinations or boosters you require and it is common for visitors to take anti-malaria drugs which begin typically one week prior to travel.

It is advisable if you negotiate a rate with a taxi driver, to confirm the amount before getting into the car and to check your change thoroughly.

Safety

Since the November 2008, Mumbai terrorist attacks, the city has taken many steps to regain security and safety in the city. These attacks are similar to the train and bus bombings that occurred in Madrid and London in the past decade and indicate that all modern metropolises are at risk and when visiting India, visitors should take the same precautions they would in any large city.

Bridging Cultural Divides and Institutional Voids are Key to Success

By Mark Hannant

Everyone, it seems, wants a piece of the "India story." The sense of ambition and the scale of the opportunities make it an exciting place to do business and increasingly you don't even have to be in India to be doing business in India. But cultural differences as well as the absence of soft infrastructure mean India is not for the faint hearted.

India's GDP growth for 2011–2012 is predicted to remain around 9%, in line with performance in the previous year. Massive investment in infrastructure means new power stations, ports, airports, roads and whole new cities to house the millions of people who move from rural areas in search of a better life. The rapidly growing urban middle class is demanding access to products and services. More than half a billion mobile phone numbers are already allocated and the telecom companies are racing to get the next 500 million potential users signed up. Demand is strong for everything from cars and flat screen TVs to pharmaceuticals and banking services. Financial inclusion is also growing as the banks penetrate deeper into rural India, creating new markets.

General Business Challenges

For all the "India Shining" hyperbole, there are plenty of impediments—none insurmountable, but each significant enough to be factored into an India strategy. Many of the institutions, the soft infrastructure that businesses take for granted in the developed world, don't exist in emerging markets. Market information can be absent, difficult to come by or lack credibility. Accreditation systems, such as the measures to grade prospective contractors' credentials for example, may not exist or may be unreliable. The regulatory environment often doesn't offer a "level playing field." The legal system can be inefficient to say the least—there's a joke in India that you bring proceedings in court and your grandchildren inherit them. These institutional voids manifest themselves on many levels. They are obstacles for some, but opportunities to others.

In its annual 2010 Doing Business rankings, the World Bank rates India the 134th easiest place to do business out of 183 countries. Within the individual measures on which this ranking is based, India ranks 165th in terms of starting a business and scores well in terms of credit availability (32nd) and the protection it affords investors (44th). However, it's a difficult place to close a business, with India ranking 134th (the process takes on average seven years) and enforcing a contract can be extremely difficult—on this measure India comes in second to bottom ahead of only East Timor.

Graft in India remains a fundamental and insidious problem; Transparency International ranks India 87th in its report on corruption. A key example of this is the 2G spectrum scam, in which government ministers illegally undercharged telecom companies for licences, allegedly costing the exchequer close to US $40 billion in lost revenues over the past three years. The affair has claimed the jobs of several ministers, and CEOs of some of India's largest conglomerates with telecom interests have been summoned to Delhi for questioning. But not all corruption comes on such a grand scale. Indian bureaucracy can be stultifying and thus the paying of small sums to officials to 'oil the wheels' is endemic. Graft and corruption create multiple inefficiencies and add hidden costs to doing business.

The pool of well-educated, English-speaking workers is often spoken of as one of India's advantages, particularly over its regional rival, China. Both the education and the English language are basic truths, but the reality is more complex. The Indian education system largely trains people to pass exams and take instruction. The language skills that will get a student through an advanced engineering exam may be a long way from the standard of English you'd expect from a client manager representing your business. The talent pool is also limited and wage inflation is rife. Liberalization also means the old "job for life" career model is morphing and people often move for relatively small salary increases. Attracting and retaining good staff can be a real challenge.

Cultural Challenges

One area where in-bound investors often struggle is in responding to the many cultural differences that exist in India. These include social hierarchies, religious beliefs and the ownership structures of businesses.

India is a very hierarchical country and has what sociologists refer to as a high "power distance." Power distance is a measure not of the absolute levels of inequality in a society but of the degree to which individuals—be they at the top or bottom of the pile—accept and expect that inequality. Levels of inequality are extreme in India. This inequality is sharply illustrated by the newly built billion-dollar 27-storey private residence of Indian's richest individual, the chairman of Reliance Industries, Mukesh Ambani, in downtown Mumbai. This glass and steel palace exists in a city with a population of 20 million, half of whom is estimated to have a monthly income of less than US $150. Vast numbers live in slums. Yet people are highly accepting of this acute inequality. Western European countries on the other hand exhibit low power distances and are by many measures more equitable. Before doing business in India, it is necessary to understand the scale of the inequality and how hierarchy impacts personal and business decision-making.

Another cultural hurdle for western investors is connected to religious belief. The vast majority of Indians are Hindus who believe in reincarnation and this has a bearing on people's ambition and life expectations. Concepts of what can be achieved in "three score years and ten"—the striving for goals and landmark achievements—don't have the same pull if you believe this isn't your only chance. Why stress in this life if you have more lives to come? Senior HR experts and professionals involved in organizational development in large Indian companies tell me how this belief system has an impact on such seemingly mundane things as company appraisal systems: it means that people you engage with in India—whether they are employees, business partners or indeed customers—may bring a fundamentally different set of ideas to the table to the ones you have.

The family-owned enterprise structure can also be a challenge for business in India. The primary model for businesses, from the smallest street stall to the largest multinational conglomerate, in India is still the family-owned enterprise. The large, multi-billion dollar businesses are usually referred to as "promoter-owned." Even in publicly listed companies the promoter family may own a significant chunk of stock. And while they may not be majority shareholders, they can act as though they are and in some instances show little respect for the views or interests of other shareholders. The Satyam accounting fraud, exposed in 2009, was billed as "India's Enron" and there was a predictable dash to paint Satyam as a one-off. The reality is that family structures and the appointment of close family or caste associates to directorships is inconsistent with generally accepted principles of good corporate governance. It is often difficult to know who the real decision makers are. Just because someone has the title of Group President, Managing Director or even CEO doesn't mean he has the clout that you might expect at that pay grade.

The family ownership structure will not change any time soon. India's continued success is largely vested in the hands of a small group of promoter families. But it is noticeable that some are actively looking for ways in which they can be less opaque and realizing that engaging stakeholders can be a way of differentiating themselves. Some of this new thinking comes from increasing exposure to western business ideas and regulatory regimes. Listing your business on the London or New York stock exchange often demands a new approach to corporate governance and greater transparency than has been the historic norm in India.

Liberalization, Globalization and Change

The liberalization of the Indian economy, which began tentatively in 1991 with the gold crisis, has found its way into almost all spheres of commerce. Few sectors are now closed to foreign investment. The 'favourable' circumstances that existed for the first five post-independence decades—protectionist policies ensuring there was no threat of foreign competition in a nation where demand would always outstrip supply—have gone. Businesses founded in those years of the 'License Raj' found success despite remaining unproductive, inefficient and uncompetitive. They can't survive in the increasingly competitive landscape of a 'euphoric' emerging market.

A generation of MBA graduates with degrees from international business schools and in many cases several years of work experience are coming back to India. Where previous generations settled overseas, this cadre sees huge opportunity in India. They are returning with heads full of new ideas and hard-drives full of innovation models. Armed with a vision and a sense of destiny, these extremely intelligent, (and often scarily young!) men and women realize things can, and in many cases have to, be done differently.

In a liberalized marketplace with foreign competition and customer choice, things are changing. Indian businesses are waking up to the challenges of differentiating themselves domestically. They are realizing the importance of creating sustainable value propositions to attract and retain talent, for example. Indian companies are also beginning to measure themselves not only against their Indian competitors but also to benchmark against international standards. This is particularly evident among Indian businesses seeking to capture global opportunities. They realize the need for new approaches if they are to compete internationally. Businesses creating international footprints are realizing the need to reposition themselves and find new ways to think and talk about themselves. When your stated ambition is to become a "respected global entrepreneur" you need to think of yourself as something more than India's number one.

A combination of macroeconomic factors, opportunity and ambition mean a growing number of Indian companies are becoming global businesses by acquiring assets in other regions of the world. Indian businesses are in large part well capitalized with strong balance sheets and the cash reserves required to make acquisitions without much need for leverage. At the same time many target businesses in the west are either distressed or at historically low valuations. The balance of power is shifting east. But many of those acquirers are learning that their international growth is about more than just having financial clout. "Buying is easy; owning is hard," as the saying goes.

One result of this power shift towards the east is that more and more people across the globe find themselves employed by companies that are Indian-owned. You don't have to be in India to be doing business in India. A prime example is the Tata group, one of India's most respected business houses, seen as clean, trusted and has been an integral part of India's national development. Tata group is huge, with global revenues of over US $60 billion—more than 70% of which come from outside of India—and has invested heavily in the UK and owns such household brands as Tetley Tea and Jaguar Land Rover. Along with other less high profile but large-scale acquisitions of industrial enterprises in the chemicals and steel sectors, Tata group has become the largest manufacturing employer in the UK.

The cultural considerations involved in doing business with India are no longer just challenges for the inbound investors. Increasing numbers of engineers, product developers, HR and IT professionals are finding that their boss sits in India and they're "doing business in India" whether they fly in for a quarterly summit or join a weekly video conference call with their colleagues in Delhi, Bangalore, Pune or Ahmedabad. India—along with the business and cultural challenges it brings—is becoming a part of their reality.

About the Author

Mark Hannant is an entrepreneur, communicator and business strategist living in Mumbai. You can find him on Linked In.

Chapter 4
Key Sectors for FDI

Foreign investment by sector

Rank	Sector	Cumulative inflows		Percentage of total FDI-inflow (%)[a]
		US $ billion	Rs billion	
1.	Services	26.87	1,201.65	21
2.	Computer software and hardware	10.71	476.19	8
3.	Telecommunications	10.34	471.08	8
4.	Housing and real estate	9.62	431.12	7
5.	Construction activities	9.13	405.32	7
6.	Automobile industries	5.92	267.84	5
7.	Power	5.88	266.42	5
8.	Metallurgical industries	4.17	182.23	3
9.	Petroleum and natural gas	3.14	136.84	2
10.	Chemicals (other than fertilizers)	2.88	130.14	2

Source Ministry of commerce and industry, April 2000 to February 2011

[a] In terms of US $

In the past decade, the services sector (financial and non-financial) has received more foreign investment than any other industry, accounting for approximately 23% of total FDI. The services sector has played an integral part in the overall growth of the Indian economy and has seen double-digit growth rates since early 2000. Following the services sector, computer software and hardware (8%), telecommunications (8%), housing and real estate (7%) and construction activities (7%) are the four most invested sectors.

Given that agriculture is well protected under policy regulation and the services sector is well established through IT, business processing offices (BPO) and banking, the infrastructure development sector is a critical area for opportunity.

Dezan Shira & Associates and C. Devonshire-Ellis (eds.), *Doing Business in India*,
India Briefing, DOI: 10.1007/978-3-642-27618-7_4,

The government has clearly indicated infrastructure development remains the nation's top priority. Recognizing that a steady supply of power along with a solid transport infrastructure will help revive the Indian economy and boost productivity, the government has set up plans to increase the gross capital in infrastructure in the next several years, which translates into over US $500 billion worth of investments.

A June 2009 study from First Global indicates the government plans to fund these projects through public private partnership (PPP) investments, respectively at a 70:30 ratio. Infrastructure projects related to power and road sectors will be major beneficiaries of private–public sector projects. Roads, civil aviation, railway components, communications and mining will all have high potential to attract foreign investments and there are a large number of state level PPP projects in the government's pipeline that could be awarded in sectors such as ports, transport, irrigation and urban development.

In addition, the real estate and oil and gas industries present significant opportunities. Given the expanding economy, energy demand is predicted to increase five-fold in the next 25 years, creating a huge potential for returns in investment in the oil and gas industry.

Roads

Within India, roads are the dominant modes of transportation. India has one of the largest road networks in the world, totaling 4.2 million km, carrying almost 90% of the country's customer traffic and 65% of its freight. The density of India's highway network—at 0.66 km of highway per square kilometer of land—is similar to that of the United States (0.65) and much greater than China's (0.16) or Brazil's (0.20). On the other hand, most highways in India are narrow and congested with poor surface quality, and 40% of India's villages do not have access to all-weather roads.

Indian road construction projects have become a lucrative and emerging investment opportunity for numerous international giants. The National Highways Development Project (NHDP), the largest highway project ever undertaken by the country, is being implemented by the National Highway Authority of India (NHAI). The Golden Quadrilateral, essentially a pan-Indian, four-lane highway ring that connects Mumbai, Delhi, Kolkata and Chennai, and the NSW Corridor, from Srinagar in the northwest, south to Kanyakumari in the far south, and from Porbander in the west across to Silchar in the east, collectively add about 13,000 km of four lane highway to India's road network. Other projects also exist that will see India increase its road network by a total of 66,590 km within the next 5 years.

Several multinationals have taken the lead in assisting the growth and reform of India's highway infrastructure. The various international companies to join the league include Berhad (Malaysia), Deutsche Bank, Emirates Trading Agency

(Dubai), the Isolux Corsan Group (Spain), Italthai (Thailand), Baelim (Korea), Dyckerhoff (Russia), Widmann AG (Germany), IJM Corporation, SDN and Road Builders (Malaysia), Kajima and Taisei (Japan). These companies have acquired equity stakes between 10 and 51% in various highway projects floated by the National Highway Authority of India (NHAI) and other state governments. For toll roads, 100% FDI is permitted, with income tax breaks available for periods of up to 10 years, making this sector highly attractive for investment.

Facts and Figures

- Share of FDI inflow: 6.36% (refers to all construction activities not just roads)
- Transport Minister Kamal Nath indicated that India is likely to attract US $10 billion for roads between 2009 and 2011
- Malaysian company IJM Corp. Bhd has embarked on a major highway project worth nearly US $156.7 million in Andhra Pradesh.

Investment Incentives

- Simplified policies with transparent procurement procedures
- Model Concession Agreement (MCA) standardization
- Viability Gap Funding up to 40% of project cost based on competitive bidding for each project
- Tax concessions: complete tax holiday for any ten consecutive years out of 20 years of the concession period
- Retention of toll by concessionaire for BOT (Toll) projects
- Duty free import of high capacity and modern road construction equipment
- Greater equitable allocation of risk
- Strong dispute resolution mechanism
- Robust institutional and legal set up to help investors
- Revenue sharing in the form of negative grant and concession fees
- Protection of the concessionaire from the risks of additional tollway and competing roads.

Investment Opportunities

- Roads, bridges and bypasses
- Consultancy services
- Major highway contracts under international competitive bidding (ICB)
- Collaborations for equipment manufacture
- Equipment leasing
- Design engineering
- New technology
- New management techniques.

FDI Policy

- 100% FDI permitted in road sector.

Key Indian Players

- Gayatri Projects Limited
- IRB Infrastructure Developers Limited
- IL&FS Transportation Networks Limited
- Hindustan Construction Company.

Railway

Investment is needed to improve railway track, rolling stock and delivery times. At present, passenger trains manage an average of 50 kph, while freight trains just 22 kph. Indian Railways has long been regarded as the backbone of India's socioeconomic growth. The country has the world's fourth largest rail network and the second largest in Asia after China. Indian Railways has recently attracted immense global media and corporate attention due to its turnaround to profitability, and has been consistently recording buoyant growth rates over the last few years as India's population continues to increase.

Indian Railways has identified the following initiatives to help transform the viability of Indian rail into a commercially acceptable operational model:

- Increases in income through advertising on all Rajdhani (luxury express coaches), with the cost of advertising being around US $1.26 million per train

- Introduction of new generation trains that would be fuel-efficient, recyclable and have low-emission to generate certified emission reduction credits
- Construction of a dedicated freight corridor, with an investment of US $614.40 million in 2009–2010
- Renewal of 44.5 million pre-stressed concrete (PSC) sleepers set for open line work
- Technological upgrades and modernization for higher operating efficiency
- Development of PPP in new routes, railway stations, logistics parks, cargo aggregation and warehouses
- Development of 100 budget hotels with private participation in the vicinity of railway stations
- Installation of Wi-Fi to provide wireless access at 500 stations
- Introduction of marketing rights for advertising on railway tickets and reservation charts
- Establishment of integrated logistic parks on unused lands
- Development of agri-retail hubs, cold storage houses, multi-purpose warehouses on surplus land with the railways
- Training of railway managers to meet future challenges, Indian Railways is planning to set an international management institute in New Delhi
- Renewal of over 2,941 km of rail, which will require 3.39 million tons of rail steel, and over 2,382 km of pre-stressed concrete sleeper renewal
- Implementation of dynamic pricing policy, tariff rationalization, non-peak season incremental freight discount scheme, empty flow direction freight
- Discount schemes, loyalty discount schemes and long-term freight discount schemes among others to boost capacity utilization levels.

Meanwhile, according to the Ministry of Railways, increases of freight and cargo in both domestic and international routes have placed considerable stress on capacity on the two main Delhi–Mumbai and Delhi–Kolkata lines. The government has decided to build dedicated freight corridors in the Western and Eastern high-density routes to cater for this deficit.

Previously, containerization was operated under a state monopoly, CONCOR. Facing the increasing containerization of cargo and freight, this sector has now been liberalized and is open to competition. Private sector entities may now either partner with or compete with CONCOR.

Airports

India has a total of 454 airports (including grass runways), of which 16 have international status. Of these, the Airports Authority of India (AAI) owns and operates 97. The AAI has stated it aims at upgrading all of these as well as adding new locations to better unify the country within the next 12 years. This requires infrastructure investment in terminals, runways and related construction to full operational and passenger capability at over 500 airports. The government has stated several times its intention to attract private investment into this sector, and many domestic and multinational players have been showing interest in the projected growth of India's aviation sector. Much of this is within airport development and management. Some of these include India's private airlines, among them Jet, Sahara, Kingfisher, Deccan, and Spicejet, who collectively account for about 60% of India's domestic passenger traffic.

India is now poised to meet international standards in the development and infrastructure of its airports as any recent traveler to Delhi, Mumbai or Chennai will testify. The government is planning modernization of the airports to establish a standard, while newly developed airports will help release pressure on the existing airports in the country.

The Delhi, Mumbai, Bangalore and Hyderabad airports are all earmarked for privatization once construction work is completed. Several regional airports are also set for significant upgrading to international standards, including Amritsar, Gutuahati, Ahmadabad, Goa, Chennai and Cochin.

According to the AAI, investment of US $8.5 billion has been planned for the development of Indian airports during the 11th five year Plan. The airports in Mumbai and Delhi have already been privatized and are now being upgraded at an estimated investment of US $4 billion.

The AAI plans to invest an additional US $3.07 billion between 2010 and 2015. From this, 43% will be for the three metro airports in Kolkata, Chennai and Trivandrum. The remainder will be invested in upgrading other non-metro airports and in the modernization of the existing aeronautical facilities, such as radar and related equipment upgrades.

The "open sky" policy of the government and rapid air traffic growth have resulted in the entry of several new privately owned airlines and increased frequency/flights for international airlines; foreign airlines currently have the lion's share of passenger traffic into and out of India as the approvals procedures for obtaining a license to operate in India as a foreign airline is just 5 years, as opposed to five for Indian domestic carriers operating international routes.

The following statistics and figures have been reported by the Ministry of Civil Aviation:

- Passenger traffic is projected to grow at a CAGR of over 15% in the next 5 years;
- Cargo traffic to grow at over 20% per annum
- 100% FDI is permissible for existing airports; FIPB approval required for FDI beyond 74%
- 100% FDI under automatic route is permissible for Greenfield airports
- 49% FDI is permissible in domestic airlines under the automatic route, but not by foreign airline companies
- 100% equity ownership by non-resident Indians (NRIs) is permitted

- AAI Act amended to provide legal framework for airport privatization
- 100% tax exemption for airport projects for a period of 10 years.

Telecommunications

India is the fifth largest telecommunications services market in the world. It has been growing annually at a rate of 25% for the past 5 years and has just overtaken China as the fastest growing market globally. India permits 100% foreign investment for telecommunications equipment manufacturing.

According to the Ministry of Information Technology and Communications, India possesses favorable demographics and socioeconomic factors leading to high growth in telecommunications. These include:

- Growth of disposable income combined with changes in lifestyle
- Increasing affordability, low tariffs, easy payment plans and handset financing
- Increased coverage and availability of mobile services
- Telecom devices and software for internet, broadband and direct to home services, set top boxes, gateway exchange, modem, mobile handsets and consumer premise equipment, gaming devices, EPABX, telecom software
- Telecom services for voice and data via a range of technologies
- Applications and content development ranging from gaming to education.

Facts and Figures

- Share of FDI Inflow: 8.04%
- Nine million phones are being added every month in India, outpacing China's monthly rate of increase (below 8 million a month)
- Industry will generate revenues worth US $43 billion in 2009–2010.

Investment Opportunities

- Manufacturing of equipment and components
- Exports of telecommunications equipment and services
- Setting up a national long distance bandwidth capacity in the country
- Tele-banking, tele-medicine, tele-education, and tele-trading
- E-commerce
- Telecom and value added services.

FDI Policy

- 100% FDI permitted through the automatic route in telecommunications equipment manufacturing
- FDI ceiling in telecommunications services has been raised to 74%
- Introduction of a unified access licensing regime for telecommunications across India.

Key Indian Players

- Bharti Airtel Ltd
- Idea Cellular Ltd
- MTNL
- BSNL
- Reliance Communication Ltd.

Recent FDI

- Vodafone Essar will invest US $6 billion over the next 3 years in a bid to increase its mobile subscriber base from 40 million at present to over 100 million
- Sistema Shyam TeleServices Ltd (SSTL), a joint venture between Russia-based telecom major Sistema and Shyam Group in India, is planning to invest US $5.5 billion by 2015.

Power

India requires an additional 100,000 MW of power by 2012. The country currently has a peak deficit of 18% and an overall deficit of 9%. While India possesses the fifth largest electricity generation capacity in the world, it has low per capita consumption at just 606 units, less than half of China's consumption per head.

While concerns exist over Chinese-managed projects close to India's border areas, opportunities exist for politically neutral energy providers to service the India market.

According to the Ministry of Power, the total installed capacity in India is calculated to be 145,554.97 MW. They also state that:

- Generation capacity of 122 GW; 590 billion units produced (1 unit = 1 kwh) CAGR of 4.6% over the last 4 years
- India has the fifth largest electricity generation capacity in the world with low per capita consumption at 606 units
- Transmission and distribution network of 5.7 million circuit kilometers
- Coal-fired plants constitute 57% of the installed generation capacity, followed by 25% from hydroelectric power, 10% gas-based, 3% from nuclear energy and 5% from renewable sources.

The State Electricity Regulatory Commission has said that India possesses a vast opportunity to grow in the field of power generation, transmission, and distribution. The target of over 150,000 MW of hydroelectric power generation is yet to be achieved. A huge capital investment is required to meet this target. This has resulted in numerous power generation, transmission, and distribution multinationals establishing operations in the country under the PPP program. The power sector is still experiencing a large demand–supply gap, and this has called for the effective consideration of some strategic initiatives. There are excellent opportunities in transmission network ventures—an additional 60,000 circuit kilometers of transmission network is expected by 2012 with a total investment of about US $200 billion.

According to the Ministry of Power, the implementation of key reforms is likely to foster growth in all segments as follows:

- Coal based plants at pithead or coastal locations (imported coal)
- Natural gas/CNG based turbines at load centers or near gas terminals
- Hydroelectric power potential of 150,000 MW is untapped as assessed by the government of India
- Renovation, modernization, upgrading and life extension of old thermal and hydroelectric power plants.

Opportunities exist in:

- Allowing foreign equity participation up to 100% in the power sector under the automatic route
- Encouraging the private sector to set up coal, gas or liquid-based thermal projects, hydroelectric projects and wind or solar projects of any size
- Constitution of independent state electricity regulatory commissions
- Deregulation of the ancillary sectors such as coal
- Introduction of the Electricity Act and national electricity and tariff policies
- Provision of income tax holiday for a block of 10 years in the first 15 years of operation and waiver of capital goods' import duties on mega power projects (above 1,000 MW generation capacity)
- Unbundling of the state electricity boards into generation, transmission and distribution companies for better transparency.

Initiatives the government has introduced to facilitate foreign investment in the sector under the automatic route:

- Unbundling of vertically integrated SEBs
- "Open access" to transmission and distribution network
- Distribution circles to be privatized
- Tariff reforms by regulatory authorities.

Facts and Figures

- Share of FDI inflow: 3.78%.

Investment Incentives

- Generation and distribution power projects of any type and size are allowed
- The Electricity Act of 2003 allows trading in power and provides for further deregulation
- A renewable license period of 30 years
- Return on equity up to 16% is assured at 68.5% PLF for thermal power plants. Similar incentives are provided for hydroelectric power projects
- Import duty at the concessional rate of 20% has been set for import of equipment
- The government allows a 5 year tax holiday for power generating projects with an additional 5 years in which a deduction of 30% taxable profits is allowed.

Investment Opportunities

- Power generation and transmission
- Power distribution
- Power exchange
- Rural electrification
- Hydro power
- National grid program
- Renewable power.

FDI Policy

- 100% FDI permitted in power sector excluding nuclear power.

Key Indian Players

- Tata Power
- Reliance Power
- Torrent Power
- Power Grid Corporation of India.

Oil and Gas

Facts and Figures

- Share of FDI Inflow: 2.83% (petroleum and natural gas)
- Constitutes over 15% of GDP
- The government is considering a series of tax holidays, including a 7 year tax break, to assist with the development of exploration in its oil and gas sectors to lessen its dependence on imports
- The Investment Commission of India states the total opportunity in the oil and gas sector is expected to reach US $35–40 billion by 2012.

Investment Opportunities

- Petroleum products
- Improved oil recovery (IOR) and enhanced oil recovery (EOR) techniques
- Crude oil production from the deepwater block D6 in KG Basin
- Use of improved technology
- Extended oil field acquisition activities
- Capacity utilization of refineries
- Foreign company collaboration
- End-user market and infrastructure development
- Setting up oil and gas courses at universities and training institutes
- Opportunities for world-class service providers.

Foreign Direct Investment

- Allowing 100% FDI in private refineries through automatic route and 26% in government-owned refineries
- 100% FDI is also allowed in petroleum products, exploration, gas pipelines and marketing/retail through the automatic route.

Key Indian Players

- Indian Oil
- Bharat Petroleum
- Oil and Natural Gas Commission (ONGC)
- Reliance Industries
- Essar.

Recent FDI Projects

- BG Energy Holdings will set up three wholly owned subsidiaries in Andhra Pradesh, Karnataka and Tamil Nadu, with around US $28 million investment in each for setting up gas distribution and transmission infrastructures.

Real Estate

Facts and Figures

- Share of FDI Inflow: 6.80%
- Real estate accounts for almost 5% of the country's GDP
- Growth of India's middle class is creating high demand for housing along with increased presence of foreign firms needing commercial space
- A McKinsey report indicates average profit from construction in India is 18% which is double the profitability for a construction project in the United States.

Investment Opportunities

- Residential complexes
- Office and industrial complexes
- Commercial space for organized retailing
- Hotels and hospitality sector
- Special economic zones
- Venture funds.

Foreign Direct Investment

- India permits FDI up to 100% under automatic route in townships, housing, built-up infrastructure and construction development projects
- Limit of FDI in township project reduced from 100 to 25 acres. Minimum capitalization US $10 million (wholly owned subsidiaries) and US $5 million (JV with Indian partner)
- Investment can be repatriated after 3 years of project completion.

Key Indian Players

- DLF Building India
- Eldeco Group
- Mahindra Group
- MGF Developments
- Tata Housing
- Unitech Group.

Recent FDI Projects

- Mexican global multiplex operator Cinepolis plans to invest US $357.7 million in India over the next 7 years to open 500 movie screens
- Morgan Stanley made a US $70 million investment in Mantri, Bangalore
- Hotel chain Marriott International will open 24 new properties in India in coming years
- Jakarta-based Salim group invested US $100 million in Kolkata.

Ports

The ports situation in India offers tremendous scope for the development of international maritime transport both for passenger and cargo handling. There is a notorious delay in turnaround times at Indian ports; in Mumbai it typically takes about three days to turn a container ship around, in Shanghai it takes 8 h. Massive investment is required to combat problems with inadequate berths, road links, and related infrastructure constraints. The major Ports highlighted for redevelopment are: Kandla, Mumbai, Mormugao, New Mangalore on the east coast, Cochin and Tuticorn to the South, and Chennai, Ennore, Vizag, Paradip and Kolkata on the east coast.

With 12 major ports and 187 minor ports, the 7,517 km-long Indian coastline plays a key role in maritime transport amongst international trade capabilities. According to the Department of Shipping, the government of India has targeted an increase in the cargo handling capacity of major ports by 200% to reach 1.5 billion metric tons by the year 2012.

The government aims to achieve this through an investment of US $25 billion through public–private partnerships. An independent Crisil credit rating report focusing on Indian ports and maritime transport estimated that port capacity will grow by 160% over the 2011–2012 periods. Cargo handling at the major ports is projected to grow at 7.7% annually to 2011–2012, while cargo traffic is estimated to reach 877 million tons by 2011–2012. Containerized cargo is expected to grow at 15.5% over 7 years. The new foreign trade policy sees India's share of global exports doubling in the next 5 years to US $150 billion. A large portion of newly generated foreign trade is expected to be via shipping, taking an estimated 95% by volume and 70% by value of India's total trade.

According to the Ministry of Shipping, infrastructure initiatives include:

- Formulation of a national maritime development policy to facilitate private investment, improve service quality and promote competitiveness; US $11.33 billion has been allocated
- An investment of more than US $9.07 billion to be made by 2015 for 111 shipping sector projects
- In 2009, the Ministry of Shipping launched 10 major expansion projects at an estimated investment of US $1.06 billion, 60% of which was allocated for the Chennai mega container terminal
- Permission for 100% foreign direct investment for port development projects under the automatic route
- 100% income tax exemption is provided for a period of 10 years for port developmental projects
- The opening up of all the areas of port operation for private sector participation
- Increase in the rail connectivity of ports with the domestic market.

The experience of operating berths through PPPs at some of the major ports in India has thus far been successful. It has been decided to expand the program and allocate new berths to be constructed through PPPs; a model concession agreement is being formulated for this purpose.

The government has also decided to empower and enable the 12 major ports to attain world-class standards; to this end, each port is preparing a perspective plan for 20 years and an action plan for 7 years. A high-level committee has finalized the plan for improving rail-road connectivity of major ports; the plan is to be implemented within a period of 3 years and further changes in customs procedures are being carried out with a view to reducing the dwell time and transaction costs; the government has also delegated powers to the respective port trusts for facilitating speedier decision-making and implementation, at the same time, several measures to simplify and streamline procedure related to security and customs have been initiated.

The National Maritime Development Program is expected to bring a total investment of over US $120 million into port infrastructure.

Chapter 5
Investment Policy and Procedure

FDI Trends in India

The cumulative amount of FDI equity inflows over the past decade plus (April 2000 to February 2011) stood at US $193.739 billion, according to the data released by the Department of Industrial Policy and Promotion. India has been ranked second for global foreign direct investments in 2010 and will continue to remain among the top five striking places for international investors during the 2010–2012 period, according to the United Nations World Investment Prospects Survey 2009–2012.

Mauritius is currently the highest contributing country of FDI to India—accounting for approximately 42% of the total FDI inflows into the country—due to the special tax treatment that investments that come through Mauritius receive. Singapore is the second largest source of FDI in India, primarily into telecommunications, services, electrical equipment, fuel (power and oil refinery) and transportation. Finally, the third largest investor into India is the United States, which invests largely into fuels (power and oil refinery), telecommunications, electrical equipment, food processing industries and the services sector.

Government Initiatives to Promote FDI

In 1991 under the leadership of then-Finance Minister Manmohan Singh, the Indian government issued an industrial policy that greatly liberalized the country's economy. This policy enabled rapid and substantial growth for India and created a sea of change in the FDI environment where the government began acting as a "facilitator" of private investment by creating a conducive environment. The 1991 policy bridged the gaps in critical infrastructure to encourage investment between the public and private sector to create public–private partnerships and helped

Dezan Shira & Associates and C. Devonshire-Ellis (eds.), *Doing Business in India*, India Briefing, DOI: 10.1007/978-3-642-27618-7_5,

Foreign direct investment into India

Financial year	FDI inflow (in US $ billion)	Percent growth over previous year (%)
2000–2001	4.03	N/A
2001–2002	6.13	52
2002–2003	5.04	−18
2003–2004	4.32	−14
2004–2005	6.05	40
2005–2006	8.96	48
2006–2007	22.83	146
2007–2008	34.86	53
2008–2009	37.84	9
2009–2010	37.76	−0.2

Source Department of Industrial Policy and Promotion, Ministry of Commerce and Industry, per international best practices (not-DIPP)

Foreign investment by country

Rank	Country	Cumulative inflow April 2000 to Feb 2011		Percentage of total income[a] (%)
		US $ billion	Rs billion	
1.	Mauritius	53.88	2411.86	42
2.	Singapore	11.83	525.89	9
3.	United States	9.40	423.16	7
4.	United Kingdom	6.41	283.78	5
5.	Netherlands	5.62	252.55	4
6.	Japan	5.24	237.85	4
7.	Cyprus	4.73	215.95	4
8.	Germany	2.96	132.14	2
9.	France	2.24	101.58	2
10.	U.A.E.	1.88	85.36	1

Source Department of Industrial Policy and Promotion, Ministry of Commerce and Industry
[a] In terms of US $

create a wave of FDI spending, making India one of the most attractive FDI destinations in the world.

In February 2009, the government issued several measures to encourage foreign direct investment in India. The Department of Industrial Policy and Promotion modified the guidelines for calculating foreign investment and the transfer of ownership or control of Indian companies to non-resident entities. This was to create a more investor-friendly environment with more credible regulations in light of the global financial crisis. The amendment in regulation focused on historically sensitive sectors that had high barriers for investment such as aviation, banking, defense, insurance, media, retail and telecommunications. For example, the FDI cap for telecommunications increased from 74–98%. The February policy change also indicated that environmental clearances are not required for projects with an investment of less than Rs 1 billion (nearly US $21 million). Amendments in the policy also introduce a new concept of controls and ownership in the sector. An Indian company that is backed by foreign investments but ultimately controlled and owned by Indians can invest without being subject to the FDI cap.

In August 2009, the Indian government announced it will not be changing the limit on foreign direct investment in the banking and media sectors. Indian law only allows for 74% FDI in private banks and 20% in state-run banks. In the media industry, businesses such as newspapers and periodicals only allow foreign investors to invest by as much as 26%. The Indian parliament previously approved a law to increase the FDI limit in local insurance companies from 26–49%.

In March 2010, India consolidated its FDI policy, pulling all previous FDI-related acts, regulations, press notes, press releases and clarifications issued either by the DIPP or the Reserve Bank of India (RBI) into one document. According to the modified policy, overseas investors can insert their funds through the automatic route in the Indian economy. Such investments do not mandate any prior government permission and the Indian company receiving such investment would simply be required to inform the RBI.

The Indian government has permitted the Foreign Investment Promotion Board (FIPB) to authorize FDI tenders of up to US $358.3 million. Previously all tenders that involved foreign direct investment of more than US $129.16 million were presented in front of the Cabinet Committee of Economic Affairs (CCEA) for authorization. The change was made to encourage incoming FDI and to facilitate the process by which it occurs.

While the government has taken steps to further liberalize and incentivize FDI, even more reform will likely take place in the coming months and years. Given that the majority of initiatives undertaken so far have been policy changes and increases to sector caps, reforms such as tax holidays, concessions and breaks can be expected to help and attract investors.

India's new development sutras

In discussions with Gajendra Haldea, the advisor to the Infrastructure Planning Commission, and with Dhanendra Kumar, the Chairman of the Competition Commission of India, two things stood out as the mantra for the execution of public–private partnerships.

Firstly, that the Indian government knows full well the constraints it is operating under. These arrangements must adhere in both government and private sectors to principals of being cost effective, commercially sustainable and affordable, and having time-bound deliverables.

Secondly, that competition will drive India forward, and that "legal certainty" is a prerequisite of a competitive society. The competition issue is of particular note, as is the government's understanding of the issue at the highest levels. India has gone through a period of stagnation and self interest, with rampant corruption.

Developments in India's booming telecommunications industry—a market that is now growing faster than China's—have led the government to take a stance that competition succeeds where government regulations could not. Despite government regulations to the contrary, without legislation in place to fully open up markets, competitors in India would tend to form cartels and block entrance to other participants, thus resulting in a moribund and underperforming market, despite a government desire to see otherwise. In throwing the market open to outside investors, the Indian telecoms market was able to exponentially expand, and now offers its subscribers many more features and at some of the lowest call costs in the world.

This new, get-government-out-of-commerce sutra is a major driving force for foreign investors in India. Barriers are coming down, and the government wishes to see infrastructure development perform in the same, competitive manner to rebuild the nation. That, coupled with the previously mentioned, sensible fiscal policies regarding affordability and sustainability are the new mantras of Indian government policy. These make for a welcome change.

FDI Policy and Regulations

The Department of Industrial Policy and Promotion provides official information about India's FDI policy and procedures. Overall, among the emerging economies, India has one of the most liberal and transparent policies on foreign investment. Foreign investment up to 100% is allowed under the automatic route in all activities and sectors except the following, which require prior approval of the government:

- Sectors prohibited for FDI
- Activities and items that require an industrial license
- Proposals in which the foreign collaborator has an existing financial/technical collaboration in India in the same field
- Proposals for acquisitions of shares in an existing Indian company in the financial service sector and where the Securities and Exchange Board of India (substantial acquisition of shares and takeovers) regulations, 1997 are relevant
- All proposals falling outside notified sectoral policy or CAPS under sectors in which FDI is not permitted.

According to the International Trade and Development Division of the Indian government, the country's foreign trade policies have been formulated with a view to invite and encourage FDI. The Reserve Bank of India (RBI) manages the administrative and compliance aspects of FDI. Foreign investment can be divided into two broad categories: investment under the automatic route and investment through prior approval of government.

Automatic Route for FDI

Foreign investment in sectors permitted under the automatic route does not require any prior approval either by the government or the RBI. The investors are only required to notify the regional RBI office concerned within 30 days of receipt of inward remittances and file the required documents with that office within 30 days of the issuance of foreign investors' shares. Most sectors fall under the automatic route for FDI. In these sectors, investment can be made without approval of the central government. For sectors that are not in the automatic route, investment requires prior approval of the central government. The approval is granted by the Foreign Investment Promotion Board (FIPB).

After the grant approval for investment by the FIPB or for the sectors falling under the automatic route, FDI can then take place after receiving the necessary regulatory approvals from the state governments and local authorities for activities such as the construction of buildings, water and environmental infrastructure.

FDI Under Government Approval

Foreign investment in activities not covered under the automatic route requires prior government approval. Approvals of all such proposals, including composite bids involving foreign investment and foreign technical collaboration, are granted on the recommendations of the FIPB.

Application for all FDI cases except non-resident Indian (NRI) investments and 100% export oriented units (EOUs) need to be submitted to the FIPB Unit, Department of Economic Affairs, Ministry of Finance. Application for NRI and 100% EOU cases need to be presented to the Secretariat for Industrial Assistance in the Department of Industrial Policy and Promotion.

Prohibited Sectors

The Indian government does not permit FDI in the following sectors:

- Gambling and betting
- Lottery business
- Atomic energy
- Retail trading
- Agricultural or plantation activities of agriculture (excluding floriculture, horticulture, development of seeds, animal husbandry, pisiculture and cultivation of vegetables and mushrooms, under controlled conditions and services related to agriculture and allied sectors) and plantations (other than tea plantations).

Foreign investment in the retail sector is still restricted under Indian laws and does not allow FDI into multi-brand retail. For single-brand retail outlets 51% FDI is allowed. Foreign companies such as Wal-Mart entered the Indian market only for wholesale trading known as "cash and carry" where currently 100% FDI through the automatic route is allowed.

A table with more detail on automatic approval, restricted, and prohibited sectors is available at the end of this chapter.

Industrial Licensing

With progressive liberalization and deregulation of the economy, an industrial license is required in very few cases. Industrial licenses are regulated under the Industries Development and Regulation Act of 1951. At present, industrial license is required only for the following:

1. Industries retained under compulsory licensing
2. Manufacture of items reserved for the small scale sector by larger units
3. When the proposed location attracts local restrictions.

The following industries require a compulsory license:

- Alcoholic drinks
- Cigarettes and tobacco products
- Electronic aerospace and defense equipment
- Explosives
- Hazardous chemicals such as hydrocyanic acid, phosgene, isocynates and di-isocynates of hydro carbon and derivatives.

Industrial Entrepreneurs Memorandum

Industrial undertakings exempt from obtaining an industrial license are required to file an Industrial Entrepreneur Memoranda (IEM) in Part 'A' (as per prescribed format) with the Secretariat of Industrial Assistance (SIA), Department of Industrial Policy and Promotion, Government of India, and obtain an acknowledgement. No further approval is required.

Immediately after commencement of commercial production, Part B of the IEM has to be filled in the prescribed format. The facility for amendment of existing IEMs has also been introduced.

Industrial undertakings are free to select the location of a project. In the case of cities with a population of more than a million (as per the 1991 census), however, the proposed location should be at least 25 km away from the Standard Urban Area limits of that city unless, it is to be located in an area designated as an "industrial area" before the taking of the 25th July, 1991 census. Electronics, computer software and printing (and any other "non-polluting industry") are exempt from such location restriction. Relaxation in the aforesaid location restriction is possible if an industrial license is obtained as per the notified procedure.

The location of industrial units is further regulated by the local zoning and land use regulations in addition to environmental regulations.

Small Scale Undertakings

An industrial undertaking is defined as a small scale unit if the investment in fixed assets in plant and machinery does not exceed Rs 10 million. The small scale units can get registered with the Directorate of Industries/District Industries Centre where the state government is concerned. Such units can manufacture any item including those notified as exclusively reserved for manufacture in the small scale sector. Small scale units are also free from locational restrictions. However, a small scale unit is not permitted more than 24% equity in its paid up capital from any industrial undertaking either foreign or domestic.

Manufacturing of items reserved for the small scale sector can also be taken up by non-small scale units, if they obtain an industrial license. In such cases, it is mandatory for the non-small scale unit to undertake a minimum export obligation of 50%. This will not apply to non small scale EOUs that are engaged in the manufacture of items reserved for the SSI sector, as they already have a minimum export obligation of 66% of their production. In addition, if the equity holding from another company (including foreign equity) exceeds 24%, even if the investment in plant and machinery in the unit does not exceed Rs 10 million, the unit loses its small scale status.

A small scale unit manufacturing small scale reserved item(s), on exceeding the small scale investment ceiling in plant and machinery by virtue of natural growth, needs to apply for and obtain a Carry-on-Business (COB) License. No export obligation is fixed on the capacity for which the COB license is granted. However, if the unit expands its capacity for the small scale reserved item(s) further, it needs to apply for and obtain a separate industrial license.

It is possible that a chemical or a by-product recoverable through pollution control measures is reserved for the small scale sector. With a view to adopting pollution control measures, the government has decided that an application needs to be made for the granting of an industrial license for such reserved items which would be considered for approval without necessarily imposing the mandatory export obligation.

Environmental Clearances

Entrepreneurs are required to obtain statutory clearances relating to pollution control and the environment for setting up an industrial project. A Notification (SO 60(E) dated 27.1.94) issued under The Environment (Protection) Act, 1986 has listed 30 projects in respect of which environmental clearance needs to be obtained from the Ministry of Environment.

This list includes industries like petrochemical complexes, petroleum refineries, cement, thermal power plants, bulk drugs, fertilizers, dyes, paper, etc. However, if investment is less than Rs 1,000 million, such clearance is not necessary, unless it is for pesticides, bulk drugs and pharmaceuticals, asbestos and asbestos products, integrated paint complexes, mining projects, tourism projects of certain parameters, tarred roads in Himalayan areas, distilleries, dyes, foundries and electroplating industries. Further, any item reserved for the small scale sector with investment of less than Rs 10 million is also exempt from obtaining environmental clearance from the Central Government under the Notification. Powers have been delegated to the State Governments to grant environmental clearance for certain categories of thermal power plants.

Setting up industries in certain locations considered ecologically fragile (e.g., Aravalli Range, coastal areas, Doon Valley, Dahanu, etc.) are guided by separate guidelines issued by the Ministry of Environment of the Government of India.

According to the International Trade and Development Division of the Indian government, the country's foreign trade policies have been formulated with a view to invite and encourage FDI. The Reserve Bank of India (RBI) manages the administrative and compliance aspects of FDI. Foreign investment can be divided into two broad categories: investment under the automatic route and investment through prior approval of government.

Establishing Legal Entities

An overseas company setting up business operations in India has the following options:

Joint Venture Companies
Foreign companies may set up a joint venture company that will take on an independent legal status as an Indian company distinct from the parent foreign company. A joint venture can be established either under the automatic route, if the specified conditions are met, or obtain approval from the FIPB.

Wholly-Owned Subsidiaries
Similar to joint venture companies, foreign companies may also set up a wholly-owned subsidiary that will take on an independent legal status as an Indian company distinct from the parent foreign company. A wholly-owned subsidiary can be established either under the automatic route, if the specified conditions are met, or obtain approval from the FIPB.

Trading Companies
Foreign companies may invest in trading companies engaged primarily in exports. Such trading companies are treated on par with domestic trading companies in accordance with trade policy. For setting up trading companies engaged primarily in exports, the RBI accords automatic approval for foreign equity up to 51%. All other proposals can be addressed to the Foreign Investment Promotion Board (FIPB).

Liaison Offices

A foreign company can open a liaison office in India to look after its Indian operations, to promote its business interests, to spread awareness of the company's products and to explore further opportunities. Liaison offices are not allowed to carry on any business or earn any income in India and all expenses are to be borne by remittances from abroad.

Project Offices

The project office, essentially a branch office set up with the limited purpose for executing a specific project, is the ideal method for companies to establish a business presence in India if the business objective is to have a presence for a limited period of time. Project offices are particularly common among foreign companies engaged in turnkey construction or installation.

Branch Offices

Foreign companies engaged in manufacturing and trading activities outside India may open branch offices for the purposes of:

- Representing the parent company or other foreign companies in various matters in India, such as acting as buying and selling agents
- Conducting research in which the parent company is engaged, provided the results of this research are made available to Indian companies
- Undertaking export and import trading activities
- Promoting technical and financial collaborations between Indian and foreign companies.

Foreign companies intending to set up any kind of office for the promotion of exports from India have to obtain a prior approval from the Reserve Bank by submitting an application in the prescribed form to the Central Office of the Reserve Bank. On approval of such cases, permission is granted initially for a period of three years, subject to the condition that expenses of such offices will be met exclusively out of inward remittances; such offices are not permitted to generate any income in India.

Below, we discuss the first three business structural options–liaison offices, project offices and branch offices. Although such offices are permitted to undertake only limited activities, these types of offices are preferred by foreign companies with limited business purposes in India, as they are easy, quick and inexpensive to establish and maintain. Finally, we briefly discuss the benefits of a private limited company (which a wholly-owned subsidiary can be established as) over such offices.

Liaison Office

A liaison office (LO) is set up mainly to investigate and recognize the business and investment ambiance. An LO is not allowed to commence any commercial/trading/industrial activities, directly or indirectly, and is required to sustain itself out of private remittances received from its parent company through usual banking channels.

Permitted Activities:

- Representing the parent company in India
- Promoting export from/import to India
- Acting as a communication channel and promoting technical/financial collaborations between the parent company and Indian companies.

Forbidden Activities:

- Carrying out commercial operations in India
- Borrowing or lending money (all operating costs of the LO must be met through inward bank remittances to the parent company).

Eligibility

An overseas company intending to open an LO in India is required to obtain prior approval from the Reserve Bank of India (RBI), the country's central bank. A request from an overseas entity to establish a LO in India is considered on the basis of this criteria:

Principal Business

RBI Route—The principal business of the foreign entity falls under the sectors where sectoral cap for foreign direct investment under the automatic route is 100%.

Government Route—The principal business of the foreign entity falls under the sectors where the sectoral cap for foreign direct investment under the automatic route is less than 100%. Requests from entities falling under this category are considered by the RBI in consultation with the Government of India, Ministry of Finance, and Department of Economic Affairs (GOI, MoF, DEA).

Net Worth

Net worth (total of paid-up capital and free reserves, less intangible assets as per the latest audited balance sheet or account statement by a certified accountant) not less than US $50,000 or its equivalent.

Track Record
A successful, profit-making track record during the three immediately preceding years in the parent company's home country. Applicants that do not satisfy the eligibility criteria may submit a letter of comfort from their parent company, subject to the condition that the parent company satisfies the prescribed eligibility criteria.

Application
A parent company is normally granted permission from the RBI to open an LO within 2–4 weeks of application.

The following documents are essential for applying to the RBI to set up an LO:

- Form FNC 1* (3 Copies)
- Letter from the principal officer of the parent company*
- Letter of authority from the parent company in favor of the local representative*
- Two copies of the English version of the Memorandum and Articles of Association (Charter Documents) of the parent company, attested by Indian Embassy/Notary Public in the country of registration
- The latest audited balance sheet of the parent company.

**These documents would need to be signed by the principal officer of the company that intends to set up an LO in India.*

Approval is generally given for one to three years and can be renewed upon expiration.

Once consent to set up a LO is given by the three governing bodies (GOI, MoF, DEA), an endorsement letter will be sent to the parent company. The LO will then have to apply for a permanent account number (PAN) and tax deduction and collection account number (TAN) as well as a record with Customs. Visas for overseas staff will also be sought at this time and company bank accounts can also be opened after this. An LO must uphold a QA22C bank account, allowing inflows from abroad.

Tax Liability
An LO is deemed taxable in India if it is seen to constitute a business connection in India or a permanent establishment in India of its foreign parent, which tax authorities have generally found to be the case. Consequently, any receipt from activity in India by the LO or its foreign parent is liable to tax in India (in certain cases without appropriate allowance for expenses). However, only activities in India attributable to operations in India are liable to Indian tax. No income from operations confined to the purchase of goods in India for the purpose of export is taxable in India (under the Income Tax Act).

On an annual basis, LOs have to file an activity certificate by a chartered accountant stating that the LO has undertaken only permitted actions. Once it is confirmed that the governing bodies in India (RBI, income tax department, etc.) do not desire to file an objection certificate for an LO, custom registration procedures can begin.

The LO must file standard returns to the RBI, including audited annual accounts and an activity report for the year.

Winding-up

In the event of winding-up, the LO has to approach designated AD category-1 Bank with the following documents:

- Copy of the RBI's/sectoral regulators' permission-granting documents to establish the office
- An auditor's certificate indicating how the remittable amount arrived
- A statement of assets and liabilities
- A statement of the manner of disposal of assets
- Confirmation that all liabilities in India, including gratuity and other benefits to employees, have been paid or provided for
- Confirmation that no legal proceeding is pending in any court in India
- Confirmation that there is no legal impediment to the remittance
- A report from the registrar of companies regarding compliance with the 1956 Provisions of Companies Act
- Any other documents specified by the RBI while granting approval.

After the above application materials are approved and the designated AD category-1 bank confirms that annual activities certificates have been filed, the RBI will grant approval to close the office.

At the time of closure of the LO, the RBI grants permission to send back the balance in the Indian bank account to the parent company.

Branch Office

An overseas company also has the option of establishing a branch office (BO). Similar to an LO, a BO may undertake only limited activities but the scope of activities are broader than an LO.

Permitted activities:

- Export or import of goods, professional or consultancy services
- Research work in the activities of a parent company
- Technical/financial collaborations with Indian companies
- Acting as a buying or selling agent
- IT and software development services
- Technical support on products sold.

Forbidden activities:

- Retail trading activities
- Manufacturing or processing activities.

Eligibility

Companies engaged in manufacturing or trading activities abroad are permitted to open a BO. Entities from Nepal are not allowed to open BO in India.

Net Worth

Net worth as per the latest audited balance sheet certified by a chartered accountant or equivalent in that country and shall not be less than US $1,000,000 or its equivalent.

Track Record

The profit-making track record of a parent company during immediate preceding five financial years.

Application

An application to the RBI should be made through a designated authorized category-1 (AD category-1) bank along with:

- Certificate of incorporation registration
- Memorandum of association attested by the Indian embassy/notary public in the country of registration
- Latest audited balance sheet
- Letter of comfort from the parent company in the case that an applicant is a subsidiary and does not otherwise satisfy eligibility criteria.

Approval is generally given for a period of three years and an extension is granted on the track record of annual activity certificates, and the record of the account maintained with the designated bank, per the terms and conditions of original approval.

A permanent account number (PAN) should be obtained from the income tax authorities in India. BOs are permitted to open a non-interest bearing INR current account with an AD category-1 bank. Such banks can allow a term deposit not exceeding 6 months out of temporary surplus.

Winding-up

In the event of winding-up, the company has to approach designated AD category-1 bank with the following documents:

- A copy of the RBI's/sectoral regulators permission-granting documents to establish the office
- An auditor's certificates indicating how the remittable amount arrived
- A statement of assets and liabilities
- A statement of the manner of disposal of assets
- Confirmation that all liabilities in India, including gratuity and other benefits to employees have been paid or provided for

- Confirmation that all income accruing from sources outside India has been remitted to India.
- No objection/tax clearance from income tax authorities.

Project Office

A project office is a place of business to represent the interests of the foreign company executing a project in India.

Permissible activities:

- Activities to execute the project under approval.

Forbidden activities:

- Any activities unrelated to executing the project under approval.

Eligibility
Foreign entities from Pakistan, Bangladesh, Sri Lanka, Afghanistan, Iran, Bhutan or China are not allowed to acquire immovable properties in India.

A project office must secure a contract from an Indian company in order to execute a project in India and thus establish a project office. A project must be:

- Funded from remittance from abroad directly
- Funded by a joint or multilateral financing agency
- Cleared by an appropriate authority
- A company or entity in India awarding the contract is funded by a public financial institution or bank in India.

In case the PO does not meet the above criteria, the entity must approach the RBI for approval. A PO is permitted to acquire property for its own use and carry out permitted or incidental activities (said property may not be rented out or leased out).

Banking
Where the contract specifically provides for payment in foreign currency, each project office can open two foreign currency accounts; one in US $ and one in the currency of the parent company. In the same AD category-1 bank permissible debits shall be expenditure related to the project. Credits shall be foreign currency receipts from the parent/group company/sanctioning authority/multilateral/bilateral financing agency. Foreign currency accounts shall be closed on completion of the project.

Application criteria

A PO can be set up under common permission or specific permission. Application in form FNC-1 shall be made to the relevant regional office of the RBI along with the following details:

- Name and address of the parent company
- Reference number and date of letter awarding the contract
- Particular authority awarding contract
- Total amount of contract
- Address and tenure of project
- Nature of project.

A permanent account number (PAN) should be obtained from the income tax authorities in India.

The tenure of the PO shall end with the conclusion of the project. Extra activities are not allowed, except for activities for which the approval is given under that contract.

Winding-Up

On completion of project, the following documents are to be submitted to an AD category-1 bank:

- A certified copy of audited project accounts
- A certified accountant certificate indicating how the surplus arrived
- Evidence of tax payment or a certified accountant certificate to that affect
- An auditors certificate that no statutory liabilities are outstanding.

Intermittent remittance can be made before the completion/pending winding-up, with the following restrictions:

- An auditors certificate is provided stating that sufficient provisions are made to meet the liabilities and taxes
- An undertaking from the PO that remittances will not affect project completion
- In addition, an inter-project transfer of funds needs the prior permission of the RBI.

Private Limited Liability Company

The procedure for establishing a private limited liability company (LLC) in India depends on the intended scope of business. For certain RBI-designated sectors, 100% foreign ownership is allowed and the automatic route of approval is permitted (this process is described in the next article). Other sectors are restricted (RBI approval is required, the automatic route is unavailable) or prohibited by the RBI.

Eligibility

An LLC requires a minimum of two directors, and has from two to fifty shareholders with liability limited to the paid and unpaid capital that is issued as part of the company. Both directors and shareholders can be other legal entities. The minimum paid-up capital for a private company is about US $2,500. Formation takes approximately 6–8 weeks.

In a private limited company, the shareholders' right to transfer shares is restricted and the invitation to the public to subscribe to any shares or debentures is prohibited. No invitation or acceptance of deposits from persons other than members, directors or their relatives is allowed.

Companies must also comply with various requirements relating to the filing of various documents and forms with the Registrar of Companies, including annual returns, a list of directors, and a notice of the creation of charge in its assets or of an increase in its nominal share capital and copies of notices for shareholder meetings. Furthermore, a private limited company must keep a record of accounts, audit its records, and file an annual report or return with the registrar of companies.

Application

Generally, the steps of application for a limited liability company include:

- Obtain the certificate of approval and company incorporation certificate from the local approval authority
- Complete draft application documentation
- Apply for pre–registration of the name with the approval authority
- Draft a memorandum of association and articles of association for the private limited company
- Apply for the incorporation certificate of the company
- Obtain the Director Identification Number (DIN) for each director from the Ministry of Corporate Affairs
- Obtain a digital signature certificate from the Ministry of Corporate Affairs for the directors
- Obtain approval for the registered address of the company
- Obtain a company seal from the state treasury or an authorized private bank
- Obtain Permanent Account Number (PAN) for the company and its directors (if directors are resident in India)
- Obtain a tax account number for the company
- Enroll with the office of Inspector, Shops, and Establishment Act (state/municipal)
- Enroll for value-added tax with the State Commercial Tax Office.

These steps are slightly simplified for the automatic route of approval and slightly more involved for those LLC that fall into a sector designated by the RBI as restricted. For more details, please see the next article on the automatic route of approval and consult a professional.

Private Limited Company vs. LO/BO/PO

A wholly-owned subsidiary can be set up as a private limited company. Such a company is often preferable over other types of offices, as it allows total control over business, provides limited liability, and has fewer restrictions on business activities. The exception to this is when a company needs to raise finances through a public issue.

A private limited company is a company limited by shares in which there can be a maximum of 50 shareholders and a minimum of two. No invitation can be made to the public for subscription of shares or debentures and no deposits can be made or accepted from the public and restrictions are in place for the transfer of shares. The liability of each shareholder is limited to the extent of the unpaid amount of the shares' face value and the premium thereon in respect of the shares held. However, the liability of a director or manager of such a company can at times be unlimited.

Restricted Sectors

RBI Approval Required, Automatic Route Unavailable

- Petroleum sector (except for private sector oil refining), natural gas/LNG pipelines
- Investing companies in infrastructure and services sector
- Defense and strategic industries
- Atomic minerals
- Print media
- Broadcasting
- Postal services
- Courier services
- Establishment and operation of satellites
- Development of integrated townships
- Tea sector
- Asset reconstruction companies.

Prohibited Sectors

- Retail trading (except single brand product retailing)
- Atomic energy
- Lottery business
- Gambling and betting
- Housing and real estate business (exception: development of townships, construction of residential/commercial premises, roads or bridges to the extent specified in RBI Notification)
- Agriculture (excluding floriculture, horticulture, development of seeds, animal husbandry, viniculture and cultivation of vegetables, mushrooms under controlled conditions and services related to agro and allied sectors) and plantations (other than tea plantations)
- Chit funds
- Nidhi companies (mutual benefit financial companies).

General Legal Application Procedures for Incorporating a Company

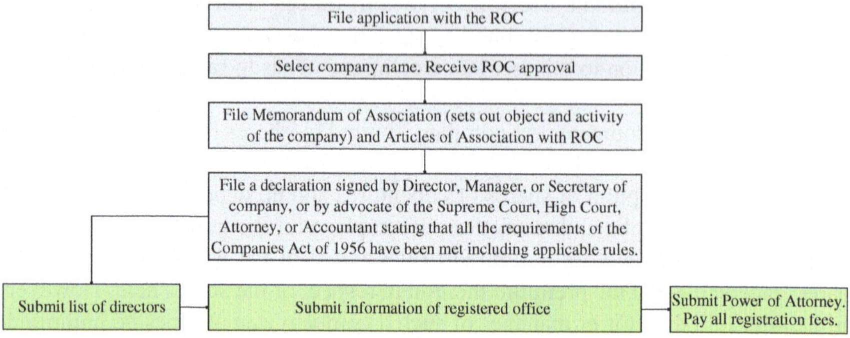

Furthermore, a private limited company faces fewer restrictions in business activities than a other types of offices, such as a liaison office, which is not allowed to commence any commercial, trading, or industrial activities, directly or indirectly, and is required to sustain itself out of private remittances received from its parent company through normal banking channels.

In addition, for private limited companies, the parent company can execute manufacturing activities as well as commercial activities in the country, whereas liaison offices are not allowed to conduct any commercial activities.

Private limited companies nonetheless have a series of possible disadvantages that investors should be aware of, including a governance system many people are unfamiliar with and additional lawyer time in drafting establishment agreements (meaning higher legal bills).

Tax Considerations

India boasts a well-developed tax structure with clearly demarcated authority between central and state governments and local bodies. The central government levies taxes on income, customs duties, central excise and service tax, while the state governments levy value-added tax (which most states have), sales tax in states where VAT is not yet in force, stamp duty, state excise tax, land revenue tax, and tax on professions. Local bodies are empowered to levy tax on properties, octroi (local tax collected on various articles brought into a district for consumption), and for utilities like water supply and drainage.

There are some important tax factors when considering an investment decision in India, including: the tax implications on the return of the investment, realized when the foreign investor exits the investment; the tax liabilities of the Indian company being invested in; the tax liabilities on transactions, such as outsourcing of support services or other trade-related transactions between the foreign investor and the Indian investment company; and the position adopted by Indian tax authorities on past practices and activities relating to foreign investment and the corresponding related points of tax law.

At the time of incorporation of a company, the members/promoters have to pay the registered capital which is also known as authorized capital; this amount is kept fixed. The Minimum Share Capital Requirement for a Private Limited Company in India is Rs 100,000. The authorized capital allows a company to issue shares to its shareholders up to the amount authorized. If a company draws from its authorized capital and fails to maintain the amount of authorized capital it can be subject to penalties. Authorized capital is a kind of "Locked up capital" and during the course of the business, a corporation has to always maintain this amount in a specified bank account and it can only be taken back by the company in the case of liquidation. Authorized Capital of a company can be enhanced by a Resolution at a meeting of Shareholders.

The tax rates for domestic companies and foreign companies differ quite a bit. Domestic companies are taxed at the rate of 33.99%, including a 10% surcharge as well as a 2% education cess and 1% higher education cess, if the taxable income exceeds Rs 10 million (US $235,000), or else 30.90% if the taxable income is Rs.10 million or below.

General tax rates applicable to foreign companies are 42.23% plus a 2.5% surcharge, a 2% education cess and 1% higher education cess. Such rates become applicable mainly where the foreign company has a permanent establishment in India. If the company has no permanent establishment in India, the tax rate depends on the nature of income (capital gains, royalties, etc.) and the provision of the relevant double taxation avoidance agreement.

In case a company's taxable profit as computed under the provisions of the Income Tax Act is less than 10% of its book profit, then it is subject to a minimum alternate tax at the rate of 11.33% (inclusive of surcharge and education cess).

A company is also taxed when it receives a return on investment. Returns on investment in India are realized when the investor exits the investment, selling its shares in whole or in part. In such a case, the investor will realize either a capital gain or business income. Shares situated in India are considered assets, therefore gains from the sale of those assets will be considered taxable in India. The rate on capital gains will vary based on the type of asset (shares, property, debt

Taxes levied by the central government	Indirect taxes	Taxes levied by state governments and local bodies
Tax on corporate income	Excise duty	Sales tax/VAT
Capital gains tax	Customs duty	Property tax
Personal income tax	Service tax	Octroi
Tax incentives	Securities transaction tax	Utilities (water supply, drainage, etc.)
Double taxation avoidance treaty		

Tax overview for foreign companies in India

Tax description	India
Standard VAT rate	–
On specified goods	10%
Sales within the State	Varies
Sales outside the State	2%
Standard CIT rate	40%
Dividend distribution tax	17%
Property tax	20%
Social security (Provident fund)	10–12%
Private income tax (PIT)	0–30%

Also subject to a service tax of 10%

instruments), the length of time the investor has held the asset and whether the transactions have taken place on a recognized stock exchange in India.

Capital gain arises in the previous year in which the transfer of assets takes place, even if the consideration for the transfer is received or realized in the later year. When the income from a sale is classified as business income under Indian law it will be taxable in India, but only if such income accrues or arises in India or is attributable to a "business connection" in India. The rate of corporate tax applicable to business income of non-residents is higher than the rate applicable to domestic entities; approximately 42.23%. It is worth noting that the dividend distribution in India is imposed on the investee, and the investor is not taxed in India.

However, it is worth noting that taxation schemes have undergone tremendous reforms in the past fifteen years. Tax rates have been rationalized and simplified resulting in better compliance, ease of tax payment and better enforcement. The process of rationalizing the tax administration is still ongoing, however. The investor should consider the tax implications on the overall profitability of their business endeavor.

The central and state governments have provided various tax related incentives that can be availed by a foreign investor establishing a company in India. These incentives include: indirect and direct tax incentives, including a reduction in indirect taxes (sales tax and tax depreciation allowance) and a tax deduction for the first ten years of the operation of new industrial units in specific areas; tax holidays; and special tax provisions for those undertakings in which the operations are 100% export oriented.

Corporate Income Tax

A corporate income tax is levied against profits and income under the provisions of the Income Tax Act. Domestic and Foreign companies and Partnership firms pay a flat rate income tax of 30, 40, and 30%, respectively; there is an additional Education fee of 3% on total taxes and surcharges. The Indian tax year runs from April 1 to March 31. Business losses can be carried forward eight years and set off

Capital gains rates

Capital gains category	Short-term capital gains tax	Long-term capital gains tax
Sale transactions of securities attracting STT[a]	15%	N/A
Sale transaction of securities not attracting STT[a]	N/A	N/A
Individuals (resident and non-residents)	Progressive slab rates	20% with indexation; 10% without indexation (for units/zero coupon bonds)
Partnerships (resident and non-resident)	30%	
Domestic companies (resident and non-residents)	30%	
Overseas financial organisations specified in section 115AB	40% (corporate) 30% (non-corporate)	10%
FIIs	30%	10%
Other foreign companies	40%	20% with indexation;10% without indexation (for units/zero coupon bonds)
Local authority	30%	
Co-operative society	Progressive slab rates	

[a] Note: STT stands for Securities Transaction Tax

against future profits. Unabsorbed depreciation is allowed to be carried forward indefinitely to hedge against future business profit.

Other taxes include:

- wealth tax
- central excise duty
- sales tax
- customs duty
- service tax
- withholding tax
- stamp duty on transfer of assets.

Capital Gains Tax

According to the Income-Tax Act of 1961 (amended), a company is also taxed when it receives a return on an investment. In India, returns on investment are realized when the investor exits the investment by selling their all or part of their share. In such case, the investor will realize either a capital gain or some business income. Shares situated in India are considered assets, and as such, gains from the sale of those assets will be considered taxable in India. The rate on capital gains will vary based on the type of asset, the length of time it was held, and if the transaction took place on an Indian recognized stock market.

Equities held for more than one year are considered long-term capital assets along with real estate and other assets which are held for more than three years. Long-term capital gains are taxed at a basic rate of 20%. However, long-term

Taxable income slab (Rs)	Rate (%)
Up to 180, 000	N/A
Up to 190,000 (women)	
Up to 240,000 (65–79 years old)	
Up to 500,000 (80 years old and above)	
180,001–500,000	10
500,001–800,000	20
800,001 upwards	30[a]

[a] A surcharge of 10% of the total tax liability is applicable when the total income exceeds Rs 1 million

capital gains from the sale of equity shares or units of mutual funds that are subject to a securities transaction tax are exempt from a capital gains tax. In the case of securities, a person has the option to either index costs to inflation and pay 20% of indexed gains or pay 10% of non-indexed gains.

Short-term capital gains (securities held for less than one, three years for other assets) are taxed at the normal corporate income tax rate, which is usually 30%.

Individual Income Tax

Individual income tax (IIT) in India is based on resident-status and the source of the income. Residents are taxed on their global income whereas non-residents are only taxed on their income that is sourced, received, or accrued in India. Work done in India, regardless of the employer's international status, will be taxed. As residency determines tax rate, it is important to understand how resident status is itself determined. This is not wildly complicated, just intricate.

Personal Tax Rates

For individuals, Hindu Undivided Family (HUF), Association of Persons (AOP) and Body of Individuals (BOI):

- education fee is applicable at a rate of 3% of income tax, inclusive of any surcharges
- marginal relief may be provided to ensure that the additional IT payable, including surcharges, on excess of income over Rs 1 million is limited to an amount by which the income is more than this mentioned amount
- agricultural income is exempt from income-tax.

Dividend Distribution Tax

Dividend distribution tax (DDT) is levied against the distributing Indian company, not its shareholders. The company is liable to pay a DDT of 16.60875% (inclusive of surcharges and education fees) on such dividends.

Wealth Tax

A wealth tax is imposed at 1% of the value of specified assets held by the taxpayer in excess of the basic exemption of Rs 3 million (US $37,500).

Excise Duty

The term "manufacture" means bringing into existence, a new product having a distinct name, character, use and marketability, including packing, labeling etc. Manufacturing goods in India attracts excise duty under the Central Excise Act 1944 and the Central Excise Tariff Act 1985.

Most products attract excise duties at a rate of 10%. Some products also attract a special excise duty or additional duties at a rate of 8% above the 16% excise duty. A 2% education fee is also applicable on the aggregate of the excised duties. An excise duty is levied on an ad valorem basis or on the maximum retail price in some cases. For the year 2011, 130 items are under the tax net.

Customs Duty

The levy and the rate of customs duties in India are governed by the Customs Act 1962 and the Customs Tariff Act 1975. Imported goods in India attract basic customs duties, additional customs duties, and an education fee. The rates of basic customs duties are specified under the Tariff Act. The peak rate of basic customs duties has been reduced to 10% for industrial goods. Additional customs duties are equivalent to the excise duty payable on similar goods manufactured in India. An education fee of 2% is levied on the aggregate of the customs duty on imported goods. The customs duty is calculated using the transaction value of the goods.

Sales Tax and Value Added Tax

Sales tax is levied on the sale of movable goods. Most States in India have replaced the sales tax with a new value added tax (VAT) since April 1, 2005. A VAT is imposed only on goods, not on services. The VAT is implemented at the state level by State governments. A VAT is applied on each stage of sale with a mechanism of credit to keep track of the VAT paid. There are four tiers of VAT, covering 550 items:

- 1% for essential commodities
- 1% on bullion and precious stones
- 4% on industrial inputs and capital goods and
- items of mass consumption including medicine, drugs, agricultural and industrial inputs, capital and
- declared goods
- all other items 12.5%

- petroleum products, tobacco, liquor etc., attract higher VAT rates that vary from state to state sugar, textile and tobacco products are exempt from VAT for one year.

Every business is required to register their VAT. However, businesses with less than Rs 500,000 turnover are exempt from VAT. A central sales tax of 4% is also levied on inter-state sales but will be eliminated gradually.

Double Taxation Avoidance Agreement
Double taxation occurs when an individual pays two or more taxes for the same asset, income, or financial transaction in different countries, discouraging FDI. Thus, countries enter into tax treaties, known as a Double Taxation Avoidance Agreement (DTAA), to ensure that international trade and services, as well the movement of capital, are not adversely affected and that individuals are not doubly taxed. India has entered into DTAAs with 81 countries, including the U.S., Canada, U.K., Japan, Germany, Australia, Singapore, U.A.E, and Switzerland.

The provisions of Double Taxation are incorporated under the Indian Income Tax Act 1961 which also provides relief for double taxation. India has entered into "Comprehensive Agreements" with most countries and only a few "Limited Agreements." Thirdly, a mandatory transfer pricing audit is required if the related party transaction exceeds Rs 150 million; if below Rs 150 million, there is still a high risk of audit. Last but not least, transfer pricing penalties can be classified into three categories: a penalty of 100–300% of the undercharged tax; a penalty of 2% of the value of the international related party transaction if the required documentation is not maintained or not furnished during an audit; a penalty of Rs 100,000 if the accountant's report is not furnished.

Given the high level of documentation requirements and a high risk of transfer pricing auditing, transfer pricing work can be very complicated in India.

Transfer Pricing Regulations

In India, the five generally accepted methods of transfer pricing are outlined in OECD Guidelines. There are basically two laws supervising four aspects of transfer pricing in India: Finance Act 2001 and Income Tax Rule 1962. Firstly, since the transfer pricing law is exclusively applied to related-party transactions, there is a comprehensive definition of what is a related party in the Finance Act section 92(A.)

Secondly, according to Section 92 of the Finance Act, international transactions between associated enterprises have to be arm's length in nature—independent and on an equal footing. This arm's length nature has to be supported by documentation signed and verified by an accountant. Besides this document, based on Rule 10D of the Income Tax Rule, taxpayers involved in internationally related party transactions are required to maintain a series of more detailed documents showing the ownership structure, property/service involved etc. Apart from all these documentations, another accountant's report is needed to disclose factual information on the international transactions between related parties and to provide an opinion on whether the required documentation has been maintained by the taxpayers before the tax return due date. All the documents mentioned above need to be in English and be furnished by October 31 following the close of the relevant year. Records also need to be maintained for at least eight years from the end of the relevant fiscal year.

The Indian Government amends tax rules regularly, much of which directly impacts foreign investors. Keep in mind that India only has 18 years of experience in open markets. The regulatory environment is still evolving rapidly, and so investors should expect change. Investors will want to choose the state in which they invest carefully, as each has different levels of tax sophistication and varying approaches to market needs.

Relief from certain types of capital gains is often sought through double taxation avoidance treaties between India and Mauritius, Singapore, The Netherlands, Cyprus and the United Arab Emirates, and may allow structuring alternatives for foreign investment that entirely relieves investors of the capital tax liability or significantly mitigates the same.

Trademark and Patent Applications

One of the first issues that needs to be taken care of when investing in India is registration of your trademark. Omission in doing so can prove highly problematic later, yet it is a relatively low cost and simple procedure. India is not yet a signatory to the Madrid Agreement which standardizes international trademark and patent processes and claims between the member countries. However, the country has indicated that it intends to join the Madrid System for the international registration of trademarks. The Union Cabinet gave its approval for India's accession to the Madrid Protocol last year. The next steps taken will be to amend its Trademarks Act 1999 and to introduce a bill in Parliament to start the necessary procedure for accession.

The Madrid Protocol simplifies the registration of trademarks internationally, within its member countries. It allows people or companies who are nationals of, are domiciled in the territory of the a member country, or have a real and effective industrial or commercial establishment in the territory of a member country, to effectively extend their trademark registration within that country to other countries which are members of the protocol.

As India is not yet part of this protocol, it therefore becomes a more pressing need to register your mark in India to cover it through the Indian protocol. The process, which involves several filing procedures, takes about 12 months from commencement to issuance of the certificate, and must be carried out by licensed Indian trademark lawyers.

The Trademarks Act of 1999 provides protection to the owner of a trademark and imposes criminal liabilities for the infringement of the trademark owner's rights. To enjoy protection, the owner of a trademark must apply for registration with the Trademark Registrar of the Registry of Trademarks, India. The Trademarks Act is also applicable to the protection of service marks, certificate marks and collective marks. The Trademark Registry Office performs the statutory duties in connection with the registration of trademark and other activities related thereto. Trademark Registry Offices are located in Ahmadabad, Chennai, Kolkata, Mumbai and New Delhi.

In India, a trademark is defined as a "mark" used or proposed to be used for or in connection with goods or services to distinguish such goods or services from other goods or services. A mark can be any brand, heading, label, ticket, name, sign letter, text, word, numeral, slogan, base line, shape, color or any combination of any of these.

To register the mark as a trademark, the mark must meet the following requirements:

- It must be distinctive
- It must not be identical or similar to a mark already registered or any pending prior application for registration
- It must not be prohibited by law
- It must be owned by the applicant.

Trademark Registration Procedure

1. Trademark search: It is advisable to conduct a trademark search for the relevant classes before filing the application to register a trademark in order to make sure that there is no identical or similar trademark already registered or for which an application for registration has been submitted. Government fees for this are Rs 500.
2. Filing application: The application to register the trademark is filed with the Registrar of Trademarks.
3. Publication in the Trademark Gazette: If after a preliminary examination, the Trademark Registrar considers the mark to be distinctive, it orders the publication of the mark in the Trademark Gazette. If no opposition to the mark is filed within 90 days from the date of publication, or 120 days if a request for an extension of time is given by an opponent and opposition is refused, the mark proceeds for grant of registration certificate.
4. Trademark registration: The trademark is registered and the trademark registration certificate is issued by the Registrar of Trademarks.
5. If there is no objection or opposition raised, the process of registering a trademark usually takes 12–18 months.

Special Economic Zones

India was one of the first countries in Asia to recognize the effectiveness of the export processing zone model in promoting exports, with Asia's first processing zone set up in Kandla in 1965. With the aim of attracting larger foreign investments in India, the government announced their special economic zones policy in April 2000.

Special economic zones are deemed to be "foreign territory" for the purposes of trade operations, duties and tariffs. More than 500 SEZs have been proposed, 114 of which have been created. An SEZ may be set-up in the public, private, or joint sector or by a state government. The minimum size of an SEZ is 1,000 ha. The zones in India closely follow the successful Chinese SEZ model.

With the goals of economic competitiveness and easier exporting, SEZs function as fast growth engines which can boost manufacturing and create new job opportunities at an unprecedented rate. Business entities may be established in SEZs for the manufacturing of goods, the provisioning of services, and other activities including processing, assembling, trading, repairing, reconditioning, in addition to the production of gold, silver, and platinum jewelry. These entities must be net foreign exchange earners, and they are not subjected to any predetermined value addition or minimum export performance requirements.

The functioning of the SEZs is governed by a three-tier administrative set up. The Board of Approval sits at the highest level and is headed by the commerce secretary. The approval committee at the zone-level deals with the approval of units in the SEZs and other related issues. Each zone is headed by a development commissioner, who is the former chairperson of the zone's approval committee.

Special economic zones offer a great many advantages. They may import, or procure from domestic sources, all of their requirements of capital goods, raw materials, consumables and office equipment for the setting up of operations without any license or specific approval. Such duty free goods procured locally can be used over a period of five years. Investors enjoy 100% income tax exemption for the first five years, and 50% for the following two years, exemption from central sales tax, exemption from service tax, and exemption from state sales tax and other levies as extended by the respective state governments. As well, investors benefit from other incentives such as the external commercial borrowing by SEZ units of up to US $500 million a year without any maturity restrictions through recognized banking channels. The Government of India allows 100% FDI in the manufacturing sector in SEZ entities, with the exception of sectors requiring an industrial license (aerospace and defense for example). The setting up of offshore banking accounts for SEZ entities is allowed.

Special economic zone entities also enjoy flexible exchange control regulations, and may borrow up to US $500 million in a year for external commercial borrowing. Beyond the exemption from central sales tax and service tax for SEZ entities, yet another advantage is single window clearance for central and state-level approvals. All post approval clearances such as the granting of importer-exporter code numbers, changes in the name of the company or implementing agency and broad banding diversification are given at the zone-level by the development commissioner.

Permitted Activities in SEZs

Indian SEZs have a fairly loose definition of permitted activities, and they allow activities, such as services, that other Asian countries place restrictions on. India also does not discriminate between manufacturing entities and services entities when it comes to tax breaks and investment incentives, making India an interesting potential destination for foreign investors in the services industry.

Manufacturing

- Make, produce, fabricate, assemble, process or bring into existence a new product having a distinctive name, character or use; including processes such as refrigeration, cutting, polishing, blending, repair, remaking, and re-engineering.

Services

- Trading, warehousing, research and development services
- Computer software services, call centers, data processing, database management
- Insurance claim processing, medical transcription, support centers
- Offshore banking, professional services (excluding law and/tax) rental or leasing services
- Other business services, courier, audio-visual, construction, distribution, educational, financial, hospital, travel and tourism, cultural, transportation, entertainment, recreational, and auxiliary services
- Free trade and warehousing, whereas these are specifically carried out.

Tax Incentives for Investors

The following are applicable to new companies establishing operations within India's SEZs:

- 100% income tax exemption on export income for SEZ units under Section 10AA of the Income Tax Act for first five years
- 50% for next five years thereafter
- 50% of the ploughed back export profit for next five years as credited to "special economic zone reinvestment reserve account" will be available (this special reserve can be utilized for acquiring machinery or plant within three years; until

the acquisition of the machinery or plant, the amount can be utilized for the purposes of the business of the undertaking other than)

- For distribution by way of dividends or profits
- For remittance outside India as profits or
- For the creation of any asset outside India.

Major Indian SEZs

Kandla Free Trade Zone, Gujarat

Kandla, established in 1965, was India's first free trade zone, and provides an internationally competitive duty free environment with low costs for export production. The basic infrastructure facilities include developed land, standard design factory buildings, power, water and customs clearance facilities. The government of Gujarat offers special incentives to units setting up in this zone that are 100% export oriented.

Santa Cruz Electronics Export Processing Zone, Mumbai

The Santa Cruz Electronic Export Processing Zone was established in 1974 in Mumbai with access to commercial, industrial and social infrastructure. It has an efficient communication network and a competent ancillary base. It has a skilled and experienced urban work force and a well developed financial and credit structure.

Falta Export Processing Zone, West Bengal

The Falta Export Processing Zone was approved by the Government of India in 1984 and was declared a customs bonded area on August 16, 1985. Falta provides developed land and built-up space at affordable and attractive rates, a stable power supply, telecommunications, water, and a container handling jetty.

Madras Export Processing Zone, Chennai

The MEPZ Special Economic Zone was established in 1984 with the objective of promoting foreign direct investment, enhancing foreign exchange earnings, and creating greater employment opportunities. The zone was converted into a special economic zone in 2003 and facilitates exports through the reduction of transaction costs. To this effect, the Ministry of Commerce and Industries has introduced special features that include offshore banking units and container freight stations to be set up within the zone, as well as liberalized customs procedures. Garments, software and engineering products contributed more than 50% of export value. Recent growth has been in the engineering sector with special reference to automobile ancillaries.

Cochin Export Processing Zone, Kerala

The Cochin Export Processing Zone is situated in southwest India in the state of Kerala and set up for export oriented production. It is a designated foreign territory within India for the purposes of trade and customs duties, with special rules for facilitating foreign direct investment. It is run directly by the Government of India.

Noida Export Processing Zone, New Delhi

The Noida Export Processing Zone was established in 1985 and is located on the outskirts of New Delhi, in the Gautam Buddha Nagar district of Uttar Pradesh. It is just 30 km away from the international airport of Delhi, just 18 km from the Inland Container Depot. The zone has a strong industrial base with more than 3,000 industries. It is located on 310 acres of land.

Vishakhapatnam SEZ, Andhra Pradesh

VSEZ, formerly known as VEPZ, was established in the year 1989. Set up in a sprawling 360 acres of prime land in one of the fastest growing cities of India, Visakhapatnam Special Economic Zone offers state of the art infrastructure coupled with a liberal package of incentives, concessions and support services. The export-friendly administrative zone ensures the expedience of all approvals and clearances. Visakhapatnam Special Economic Zone is headed by the Development Commissioner. Besides being the administrative head of VSEZ, he is also the nodal officer for licensing and monitoring the performance of VSEZ, SEZs set up in Public/Private sector and units set up under the 100% EOU Scheme. The jurisdiction of Development Commissioner, Visakhapatnam Special Economic Zone covers the states of Andhra Pradesh, Chhattisgarh and the Union Territory of Yanam.

Tax Incentives to SEZ Developers

Income tax

Deduction from Profits and Gains from export of goods/services as follows (Section 10AA)

- 100% income tax exemption for first five years
- 50% income tax exemption for next five years
- Income tax exemption for next five years to the extent of profits
- Reinvested (Maximum 50%)
- Capital Gains tax exemption on relocation to SEZ (Section 54GA):- This is a controversial issue as to be eligible for income tax exemption; the unit should be a new unit. Further, a press statement from Hon. Minister for Commerce and Industry, Mr. Kamal Nath, mentions that SEZs are basically for fresh investments
- No TDS by Overseas banking Units (OBUs) on interest on deposits/borrowings from non-residents

- No MAT (Minimum Alternate Tax)
- Transferee Developer enjoys 100% income tax exemption for the balance period of 10 assessment years.

Indirect tax

- SEZ units may import or procure from domestic sources. Duty free, all requirements of capital goods, raw materials, consumables, spares, packaging materials, office equipment, DG sets are provided for the implementation of their project in the Zone without any license or specific approval
- No import duty on these goods
- No excise duty on these goods procured from DTA (Domestic Tariff Area)
- No service tax on services availed from DTA
- No Value Added Tax (VAT) and Central Sales Tax (CST) on goods procured from DTA
- On goods procured from DTA, drawback under section 75 allowed to SEZ unit
- Goods imported/procured locally duty free could be utilized over the approval period of five years.

A Special Economic Zone can be established by a private company (e.g., individual, NRI, domestic company, or foreign company), state government, or a combination. For SEZ developers or units of SEZ's to acquire any foreign direct investment (FDI), they must be in compliance with related policies and procedures. The following are common SEZ policies and procedures with or without the addition of FDI:

- Where the developer has leasehold rights, leases should be for a minimum of 20 years.
- The types of units specified for an SEZ (e.g., manufacturing, service, trade, or warehouse) must comply with approved minimum area coverage requirements.
- Minimum land areas for adjacent or vacant space bordering an SEZ is determined by the types of units in the SEZ. The adjacent area should not include any public access roads.

Foreign direct investment (FDI) is progressively being acknowledged as an imperative aspect of economic growth in developing countries. Besides financial capital, FDI facilitates the transfer of technology, organizational and managerial practices and skills, as well as entrance to international markets. More and more countries are pushing for policies to generate constructive and enabling environments to attract FDI. In addition to lowering the barriers to FDI, India is aggressively liberalizing FDI regimes.

Regional Advantage

A business entity established in an underdeveloped state or union territory, or in a specified technologically underdeveloped district, that began manufacturing or production operations before March 31, 1995, qualifies for a 30% tax exemption on earnings for 10 years beginning with the first year of production. Parallel remuneration is presented to small-scale industrial activities that began manufacturing or production on cold storage plants before March 30, 2000.

A manufacturing entity established before March 2000 in a particular class of an underdeveloped state specified in the Eighth Schedule of the Constitution is entitled to tax exemptions. Underdeveloped areas set by the central Government as Category A give 100% tax exemption on income for the first five years of operations and 30% for the next five years. Related remuneration is offered for an industrial activity set up in an industrially underdeveloped district stipulated by the Central Government as Category B. The exemption for such activities is 100% on earnings for the first five years and 30% for the next three years.

A manufacturing enterprise established before March 31, 2003, in any part of India for the generation of power or its allocation is entitled to 100% tax exemption on its earnings for the first five years and 30% for the next five years.

All the income of a profit-making entity in oil production in any part of India established after October 1, 1998, is exempt from tax for the first seven years.

A particular activity that develops, maintains, and operates new infrastructure services established on or after April 1, 1995, is entitled to tax exemption of 100% on profits for the first five years of operation and 30% for the following five years. Such services include roads, highways, bridges, airports, ports, rail systems, irrigation, sanitation and water supply, and any other similar public facility notified in the Official Gazette. The exemption is available for any 10 successive years of the first 12 years of development, maintenance, and operation of such infrastructures. The limit for claiming the exemption increases in the case of highway projects from 10–20 consecutive years.

A venture established before March 31, 2000, and engaged in providing basic or cellular telecommunications services including radio paging, domestic satellite or network services and electronic data interchange services is allowed 100% tax exemption on profits for the first five years and 30% for the subsequent five years. A similar exemption is available for operating industrial parks established and running before March 31, 2002.

An approved company established before April 1, 1999, in scientific and industrial R&D is qualified for 100% tax exemption on its profits for five years. An accepted activity engaged in developing and building housing projects that began on or after October 1, 1998, and completed before 31 March 2001, is entitled to 100% tax exemption on profits.

A venture that begins operating a hotel before March 31, 2001, in a hilly or rural area, place of pilgrimage or other location earmarked by the Central Government for the development of tourism is allowed up to a 50% exemption on profits for the first ten years of operation. For a hotel established prior to March 31, 2001, in any place other than urban cities, the exemption is 30% on profits for the first 10 years. In addition, a 30% tax break is available on the first 10 years of income for an enterprise that begins working before March 31, 1995.

Incentives

Export Incentives and Free Trade Zones

An absolute tax benefit is provided to companies that are established in free trade zones (FTZs) for the first 10 years of operations. These FTZs include Kandla Free Trade Zone (KAFTZ), Gujarat; Santa Cruz Electronics Export Processing Zone (SEEPZ), Mumbai; Madras Export Processing Zone (MEPZ), Tamil Nadu; Cochin Export Processing Zone (CEPZ), Kerala; Noida Export Processing Zone (NEPZ), Uttar Pradesh; and Falta Export Processing Zone (FEPZ), West Bengal. Official, newly established 100% export-oriented industrial activities and units in electronic hardware and software technology parks are permitted to a similar tax break.

An Indian company or a non-corporate resident engaged in the hotel or travel agency trade can enjoy a 50% tax break on income resulting from services provided to foreign tourists, plus any portion of the left over income that is transferred to a reserve account from the profit and loss account. Profit must be expected in convertible foreign exchange.

A 50% tax freedom is available on profits from ventures such as the construction of buildings, roads, dams, bridges, assemblage or installation of machinery or plants, and construction executed outside of India. The supposed freedom should be recognized to a Foreign Project Reserve Account and utilized for the purpose of business within the next five years, and not to be used for distribution by way of dividends or profits. A similar tax exception advantage is accessible on profits from housing projects supported by a global currency and aided by the World Bank. The total tax immunity should be transferred to a Housing Projects Reserve Account and utilized for the purpose of business within five years. An occupant tax payer occupied in the export of manufactured goods or computer software can claim deduction from profits on the basis of the fraction of export turnover to total income. The profits must be received in convertible foreign exchange.

Other Incentives

A foreign institutional investor in shares and securities in India would be accountable to a 10% tax on long-term capital gains and 30% on short-term capital gains. Long-term is defined as at least one year for equity shares and three years for other securities. Dividends, interest or long-term capital gains of an infrastructure capital fund or infrastructure capital company earned from investments made on or after June 1, 1998, in any venture engaged in developing, maintaining and constructing any infrastructure facility, and which has been permitted by the central Government, is not liable of tax.

Dividends paid by domestic entities to their shareholders are excused from tax. However, the domestic corporation would have to pay a "tax on circulated profits" computed at 10% of total dividends distributed by the company.

Statutory tax rate

The nationwide corporate tax rate is 35% for domestic companies and 48% for foreign companies. The 1999/2000 budget announced a surcharge of 10% which makes the effective rate for domestic companies 38.5%.

Dividends acknowledged, dispersed or paid after June 1, 1997, are not subject to maintenance tax. However, companies making distributions are accountable for a 10% tax on the dividend amount paid. Dividends paid to an overseas company are subject to a withholding tax of 20%.

Under Indian law, the maintenance rates on interest paid to companies vary with the type of loan or security involved. The rates most likely to apply to overseas investors in the absence of a free rupee market is same to that applied to foreign currency loans:

• Rate of withholding tax on foreign currency loans, foreign currency non-resident accounts and foreign currency deposits with public limited companies	20%
• Bonds of an Indian company purchased with foreign currency	10%
• General rate	48%

The maintenance tax on royalties is 20%. This rate applies to royalty agreements entered into after May 31, 1997, as clear under domestic law and accepted by the central government, or when it is in accordance with enforced industry policies. A 30% rate applies to agreements completed on or after April 1, 1976, as accepted by the central government or when it is in agreement with the enforced industry policies. For standard agreements set before April 1, 1976, the rate is 50% of net royalties after expenses. If an agreement has not been approved by the Indian Government, the tax rate is 55% for agreements set on or after April 1, 1994, and 48% for agreements set on or after April 1, 1997.

Tax incentives to SEZ developers

Income Tax

- Deductions from profits and gains of export of goods and services as follows (Section 10AA):
- 100% income tax exemption for first five years
- 50% income tax exemption for next five years
- Income tax exemption for next five years on profits
- Maximum 50% reinvestment
- Capital gains tax exemption on relocation to SEZ (Section 54GA) for new units
- No TDS by overseas banking units (OBUs) on interest on deposits and loans from non-residents or aliens
- No MAT (Minimum Alternate Tax)
- Transferee developer enjoys 100% income tax exemption for the balance period of 10 assessment years.

Indirect tax

- SEZ units may import or procure from domestic sources, duty-free, to satisfy requirements of capital goods, raw materials, consumables, spares, packaging materials, office equipment, DG sets, and so on for implementation of projects in SEZs without any specific license or approval
- No import duty on these goods imported
- No excise duty on these goods procured from DTA (Domestic Tariff Area)
- No service tax on services availed from DTA (Domestic Tariff Area)
- No Value Added Tax (VAT) and Central Sales Tax (CST) on goods procured from DTA (Domestic Tariff Area)
- On goods procured from DTA, drawback to SEZ unit allowed under Section 75
- Goods imported and procured locally duty-free can be utilized over the approved period of five years.

Labor Laws and Labor Costs

Indian Labor Laws

Indian labor laws are essentially labor-friendly and provide a minimum floor of guarantees and benefits to all employees. It is important to note that a foreign company is unable to contract out of these minimum protections. Investors should pay special attention to the Industrial Disputes Act of 1947, which provides a large number of protections for employees; the Shops and Establishments Act, which governs the hours of work, payment of wages, leave, holidays, terms of service and other conditions; the several wage and remuneration acts, which regulate the payment of wages, bonuses, and equalize pay for men and women; and the Employees Provident Fund Act of 1972, which provides for the institution of provident funds, pension funds, and deposit linked insurance funds for employees in establishments.

Restrictive labor laws can make the large scale usage of Indian employees challenging. A harsh "hire and fire" policy would quickly be struck down by the Indian judiciary. For example, companies that employ more than 100 workers need government permission to fire them. Any termination policy should be checked against the current law prior to its implementation.

Regional Labor Cost Comparison

These figures shown in various categories of labor have taken New York as a weighted benchmark and compared with 13 regional cities in Asia. This gives some indication of Indian labor costs. The results demonstrate that India exhibits exceptional value for labor—on almost all charts, the Indian cities of Mumbai and Delhi rank near the bottom in terms of wage levels. That, combined with India's labor-friendly labor laws, means that unlike China, significant savings can still be had on hiring costs in India.

Car mechanics were defined as having completed an apprenticeship, with five years of experience and to be about 25 years old. While it's no real surprise to see that Asia's economic powerhouses have the highest salaries, it is interesting that Indian mechanics work the longest hours and earn some of the lowest salaries. Compared to New York mechanics, Indians earn nearly 23 times less and work an additional 20% longer a week. The latter figure may have to do with the general quality of vehicles on Indian roads.

Gross annual income of car mechanics (US $)

	Income	Weekly hours worked
New York	40,700	40
Hong Kong	19,200	48
Taipei	14,900	45
Singapore	12,800	44
Seoul	11,500	48
Kuala Lumpur	9,800	48
Shanghai	7,500	40
Bangkok	5,000	48
Beijing	3,300	43
Manila	2,900	46
Jakarta	2,700	49
Delhi	2,100	48
Hanoi	2,050	44
Mumbai	1,600	48

Building laborers were defined as unskilled or semi-skilled laborers, aged 25 and single. Again we find that the cost of labor in India is well below other countries in Asia. Laborers in India are not only the lowest paid in the region, they earn a quarter of a Shanghai laborer's salary. What this shows is that labor costs in India are now significantly less than those in China.

Product managers were defined as employees in the pharmaceutical, chemical or food industry currently at middle management with a university or technical college degree and at least five years of experience. Typically, a product manager is 35 years old and married with no children. Indian product managers earn about two and a half times less than their Chinese counterparts. A sizeable difference

Gross annual income of building laborers (US $)

New York	51,400
Taipei	16,000
Hong Kong	15,400
Seoul	11,100
Singapore	11,000
Shanghai	5,400
Kuala Lumpur	3,900

exists again between Delhi and Mumbai, mainly because there is a current preference to work in Mumbai. The high salary differences between Asia's economic centers such as Singapore and Hong Kong and the emerging markets of China and Southeast Asia would indicate that product managers tend to be based in regional headquarters rather than out in the field. This may change as these markets develop and require more hands-on attention from an executive level.

Skilled workers were defined as those possessing vocational training with

Gross annual income of product managers (US $)

New York	105,800
Singapore	59,100
Seoul	42,400
Hong Kong	42,200
Taipei	33,700
Bangkok	31,200
Beijing	28,500
Kuala Lumpur	24,200
Shanghai	22,100
Delhi	17,000
Jakarta	10,900
Hanoi	10,400
Manila	9,400
Mumbai	8,500

10 years of experience with a large company in the metal-working industry. They were an average of 35 years old, married with two children. The previous disparity of skilled workers between China and India starts to disappear at this level, although Shanghai still remains 20% more expensive than Mumbai. Interestingly, Mumbai ranks below Delhi, albeit by a very small amount. This may be due to Delhi's role as the political center of the country and the number of public sector jobs.

Gross annual income of skilled workers (US $)

New York	74,400
Seoul	33,300
Hong Kong	19,400
Taipei	17,800
Singapore	15,300
Kuala Lumpur	9,500
Jakarta	8,600
Shanghai	7,600
Bangkok	7,500
Beijing	5,600
Delhi	5,500
Mumbai	5,400
Manila	3,500
Hanoi	2,800

List of items and activities with sectoral cap on foreign investment

Sector	Investment cap	Description of activity/items/conditions
1. Private sector banking	74%	Subject to guidelines issued by the reserve bank of India.
2. Non-banking financial companies	100%	FDI/NRI/investments allowed 19 NBFC activities shall be subject to specific condition.
3. Insurance	26%	FDI up to 26% in the insurance sector is allowed on the automatic route subject to obtaining license from the insurance regulatory and development authority (IRDA).
4. Telecommunications	49%	• Basic and cellular, unified access services, national/international long distance, v-sat, public mobile radio trunked services, global mobile personal communications services and other value added telecom services: FDI is permitted up to 49% under automatic route while FDI beyond 49% but up to 74% is allowed under FIPB route; these limits are subject to guidelines notified in the Press Note 5 (2005 series) • ISP with gateways, radio paging and end-to-end bandwidth: FDI is permitted up to 49% under automatic route and FDI beyond 49% but up to 74% is allowed under FIPB route; these services would be subject to licensing and security requirements • No equity cap is applicable to manufacturing activities • FDI up to 100% is allowed for the following activities in the telecommunications sector: a. ISPs not providing gateways (both for satellite and submarine cables) b. Infrastructure providers providing dark fiber (IP Category 1) c. Electronic mail d. Voice mail • FDI is permitted up to 49% under automatic route and FDI beyond 49% but up to 100% is allowed under FIPB route. The above would be subject to certain conditions.
5. (i) Petroleum refining (private sector)	100%	FDI permitted up to 100% in case of private Indian companies.
(ii) Petroleum product marketing	100%	Subject to the existing sectoral policy and regulatory framework in the oil marketing sector
(iii) Oil exploration in both small and medium sized fields	100%	Subject to and under the policy of government on private participation in: a. Exploration of oil b. The discovered fields of national oil companies
(iv) Petroleum product pipelines	100%	Subject to and under the government policy and regulations thereof.
6. Housing and real estate	100%	Only NRIs are allowed to invest in certain specific areas.

(continued)

(continued)

Sector	Investment cap	Description of activity/items/conditions
7. Coal and lignite		• Private Indian companies setting up or operating power projects as well as coal and lignite mines for captive consumption are allowed FDI up to 100% • 100% FDI is allowed for setting up coal processing plants subject to certain condition • FDI up to 100% is allowed for exploration or mining of coal or lignite for captive consumption • In all the above cases, FDI is allowed up to 50% under the automatic route subject to the condition that such investment shall not exceed 49% of the equity of a PSU
8. Venture capital funds (VCFs) and Venture capital companies (VCCs)		Offshore venture capital funds/companies are allowed to invest in domestic venture capital undertaking as well as other companies through the automatic route, subject only to SEBI regulations and sector specific caps on FDI.
9. Trading		Trading is permitted under automatic route with FDI up to 51% provided it is primarily export activities, and the undertaking is an export house/trading house/ super trading house/star trading house. However, under the FIPB route: • 100% FDI is permitted in the case of trading companies for the following activities: a. Exports b. Bulk imports with export/ex-bonded warehouse sales c. Cash and carry wholesale trading; d. Other import of goods or services provided at least 75% is for procurement and sale of the same group and not for third party use or onward transfer/distribution/sales • The following kinds of trading are also permitted, subject to provisions of EXIM policy: a. Companies for providing after sales services (that is not trading per se) b. Domestic trading of products of JVs is permitted at the wholesale level for such trading companies who wish to market manufactured products on behalf of their joint ventures in which they have equity participation in India c. Trading of hi-tech items and items requiring specialized after sales service d. Trading of items for the social sector e. Trading of hi-tech, medical and diagnostic items f. Trading of items sourced from the small scale sector under which, based on technology provided and laid down quality specifications, a company can market that item under its brand name g. Domestic sourcing of products for exports

(continued)

(continued)

Sector	Investment cap	Description of activity/items/conditions
		h. Test marketing of such items for which a company has approval for manufacture provided such test marketing facility will be for a period of two years, and investment in setting up manufacturing facilities commences simultaneously with test marketing
		FDI up to 100% permitted for e-commerce activities subject to the condition that such companies would divest 26% of their equity in favor of the Indian public in five years, if these companies are listed in other parts of the world. Such companies would engage only in business to business (B2B) e-commerce and not in retail trading.
10. Power	100%	FDI allowed up to 100% in respect of projects relating to electricity generation, transmission and distribution, other than atomic reactor power plants. There is no limit on the project cost and quantum of foreign direct investment.
11. Drugs and pharmaceuticals	100%	FDI permitted up to 100% for the manufacture of drugs and pharmaceuticals provided the activity does not attract compulsory licensing or involve the use of recombinant DNA technology and specific cell/tissue targeted formulations.
		FDI proposals for the manufacture of licensable drugs and pharmaceuticals and bulk drugs produced by recombinant DNA technology and specific cells/ tissue targeted formulations require prior government approval.
12. Road and highways, ports and harbors	100%	In projects for construction and maintenance of roads, highways, vehicular bridges, toll roads, vehicular tunnels, ports and harbors.
13. Hotel and tourism	100%	The term hotels include:
		Restaurants, beach resorts and other tourist complexes providing accommodation and/or catering and food facilities to tourists. Tourism related industries include travel agencies, tour operating agencies and tourist transport operating agencies, units providing facilities for cultural, adventure and wild life experiences, surface, air and water transport facilities, leisure, entertainment, amusement, sports and health units for tourists and convention/seminar units and organizations.
		For foreign technology agreements, automatic approval is granted if:
		• Up to 3% of the capital cost of the project is proposed to be paid for technical and consultancy services
		• Up to 3% of the net turnover is payable for franchising and marketing/publicity support fees
		• Up to 10% of gross operating profit is payable for management fee, including incentive fees

(continued)

(continued)

Sector	Investment cap	Description of activity/items/conditions
14. Mining	100%	For exploration and mining of diamonds and precious stones, FDI is allowed up to 100% under automatic route For exploration and mining of gold and silver and minerals other than diamonds and precious stones, metallurgy and processing, FDI is allowed up to 100% under automatic route Press Note 18 (1998 series) dated Dec. 14, 1998 would not be applicable for setting up 100% owned subsidiaries in so far as the mining sector is concerned, subject to a declaration from the applicant that he has no existing joint venture for the same area and/or the particular mineral
15. Advertising	100%	FDI up to 100% allowed on the automatic route.
16. Films	100%	Film production, exhibition and distribution including related services/products, FDI up to 100% allowed on the automatic route with no entry-level condition.
17. Airports	74%	Government approval required beyond 74%.
Development of new airports	100%	Available only for greenfield projects.
18. Mass rapid transport systems	100%	FDI up to 100% is permitted on the automatic route in the mass rapid transport system in all metros including associated real estate development.
19. Pollution control and management	100%	In both the manufacture of pollution control equipment and consultancy for the integration of pollution control systems is permitted on the automatic route.
20. Special economic zones	100%	All manufacturing activities except: • Arms and ammunition, explosives and allied items of defense equipment, defense aircraft and warships • Atomic substances, narcotics and psychotropic substances and hazardous chemicals • Distillation and brewing of alcoholic drinks • Cigarette/cigars and manufactured tobacco substitutes
21. Any other sector/ activity	100%	If not included in Annexure A.
22. Air transport services (domestic airlines)	100% for NRIs 49% for others	No direct or indirect equity participation by foreign airlines is allowed.

(continued)

(continued)

Sector	Investment cap	Description of activity/items/conditions
23. Townships, housing, built- up infrastructure and construction development projects. This sector would include, but not be restricted to, housing, commercial premises, hotels, resorts, hospitals, educational institutions, recreational facilities, city and regional level infrastructure.	100%	The investment shall be subjects to specific guidelines.

Chapter 6
Demographic and Geographic Overview of India

Demographics

India is the world's second most populous country (after China). The following provides an overview of key demographics from India based on 2011 estimates:

- Population: 1,210,193,422
- Population growth rate: 1.344%
- Birth rate: 20.97 births/1,000 population
- Fertility rate: 2.62 children born/woman
- Death rate: 7.48 deaths/1,000 population
- Life expectancy: 66.8 years
  Male: 65.77 years
  Female: 67.95 years
- Literacy rate: 74.04%
  Male: 82.14%
  Female: 65.46%
  State of Kerala: 93.91% literacy (highest in India)
  State of Bihar: 63.82% literacy (lowest in India)
- Unemployment rate: 10.8% (2010)
- Age Structure:
  0–14 years: 29.7%
  15–64 years: 64.9%
  65-over years: 5.5%

Source CIA World Factbook, 2011

Dezan Shira & Associates and C. Devonshire-Ellis (eds.), *Doing Business in India*,
India Briefing, DOI: 10.1007/978-3-642-27618-7_6,

Religions

- Hindus 80.50%
- Muslims 13.4%
- Christians 2.3%
- Sikhs 1.9%
- Buddhists 0.8%
- Jains 0.4%
- Other Religions & Persuasions 0.6%
- Religion not stated 0.1%

Source: 2001 census and analyst estimates

Geography

India is the seventh largest country based on geographical area, occupying 3,287,263 km^2 (with 2,973,193 km^2 land, and 314,070 km^2 water). It is bordered by Bangladesh, Bhutan, Burma, China, Nepal and Pakistan.

India's climate is generally tropical monsoon in the south and temperate in the north. Possessing the most arable land area after the United States (48.83% of the country) and excellent water access, Indian life naturally revolves mostly around agriculture and activities in small villages, where the majority of Indians live.

The country is a republic consisting of 28 states and seven union territories—each described in detail in the following pages.

Language

In total, 1,652 languages and dialects are spoken in India. Hindi and English are the official languages. While the majority of Hindus speak Hindi and many Muslims speak Urdu, there are several other regional or state languages spoken, as detailed below:

Rank	Language	Speakers	Percentage (%)
1	Hindi dialects	422,048,642	41.03
2	Bengali	83,369,769	8.11
3	Telugu	74,002,856	7.37
4	Marathi	71,936,894	6.99
5	Tamil	60,793,814	5.91
6	Urdu	51,536,111	5.01
7	Gujarati	46,091,617	4.48
8	Kannada	37,924,011	3.69
9	Malayalam	33,066,392	3.21
10	Oriya	33,017,446	3.21

ANDAMAN AND NICOBAR ISLANDS

Area	8,249 sq km
Population	379,944
Capital	Port Blair
NSDP at current prices	US$441.7 million (2007-08); 9.26% Y/Y growth
Per capita NSDP at current prices	US$1000 (2007-08); 5.58% Y/Y growth
Literacy rate	86.27 percent
Principal religions	Hinduism, Islam and Christianity
Principal languages	Hindi, Nicobarese, Bengali, Tamil, Malayalam, Telugu and English

- Andaman and Nicobar Islands have 27 ports that are strategically located near three major shipping routes
- The Islands consist largely of small and medium-sized enterprises engaged in timber and agricultural industries
- There are many investment opportunities in paint, flour mills, soft drinks, textiles, steel craftsmanship, and fisheries

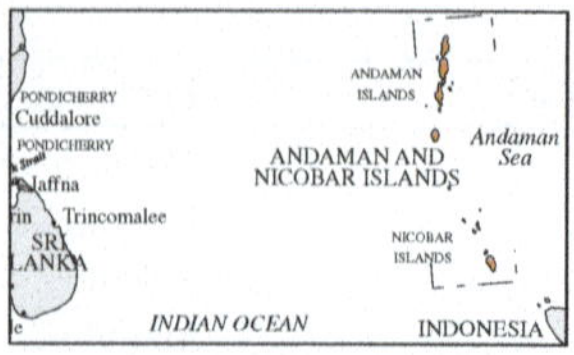

Overview

Andaman and Nicobar Islands (ANI) are two groups of islands (totaling 572 islands of various sizes, of which 37 are inhabited) located in the Bay of Bengal, in the eastern part of India. The northernmost point, Landfall Island, is 901 km away from the mouth of the Hoogly River and only about 190 km from Burma. The southernmost point is Indira Point, just 150 km away from Indonesia. ANI has a moderate climate all year around and as much as 90% of its hilly islands are covered with evergreen forests.

The original inhabitants of the islands were aborigines who lived in the forests, hunting and fishing. The aboriginal tribes living in ANI are the Andamanese, Onges, Jarawas and Sentinalese, all of Negrito origin, while the tribes of the Nicobars are the Nicobarese and Shompens, both of Mongoloid origin.

The ANI government has provided an investment-friendly environment through several policy measures and incentives to encourage inflow of investment into the various sectors of its economy.

Business Opportunities

The government of the Andaman and Nicobar Islands has put special emphasis on the balanced growth of industries without disturbing the ecology of the islands. Most industries in ANI are small and medium-sized enterprises, mainly timber and agricultural-based. Trade and investment opportunities abound in the industries of paint, flour mills, soft drinks, textiles, and steel craftsmanship.

Agriculture

Andaman Islands are known mainly for rice production, while Nicobar Islands are known for coconut and areca nuts. The islands are also well known for various spices including clove, pepper, and cinnamon. Sugarcane, red oil palm, fruit and vegetables are also among the crops cultivated in ANI.

All these could be profitably utilized for the development of agriculture-based and food processing industries. Small vegetable and fruit processing industries based on banana, mango, pineapple and papaya can be set up.

Fisheries

The islands have a long coast line of 1,912 km, having rich potential for fisheries development. It has an exclusive economic zone of 600,000 km^2, which is 30% of the total exclusive economic zone of India. The estimated marine potential of the islands is 244,000 tons. The government especially promotes the industries of fish culture, fish processing and other allied industries like fish pickling, canning, and fish oil.

The area for fresh water fish culture in ANI is estimated to be 91 ha, but there is a possibility for creation of small check dams in the slopes of the hills. Reef fish are important industry in ANI. In the waters of the island, over 1,100 species of fish are identified, of which about 30 species are commercially exploited at present. Currently "private traders" are engaged in processing, packing, and exporting high value marine life (reef fish, lobsters, shrimps, shark flesh and fins, etc.) in frozen form. A very small number of entrepreneurs have a letter of permission to capture and export live groupers.

Tourism

The Andaman and Nicobar Islands are known as an eco-friendly tourist destination, an image that the government would like to maintain, focusing on high-end tourists. ANI received approximately 130,000 tourists in 2009.

Infrastructure

Infrastructure development is an area of focus for the government of the Andaman and Nicobar Islands.

Roadways

The state transport department and private operators run regular city and suburban bus services from Port Blair to Rangat, Mayabunder and Diglipur. The transportation department has extended its services to 10 islands (from Diglipur in the north to Campbell Bay in the south) in addition to Port Blair.

Aviation

Port Blair is connected with Chennai, Delhi, and Kolkata by air. Presently flights are operated by Air India, Indian Airlines, Jet Airways, King Fisher, and Jet Lite. Air India operates between Kolkata and Port Blair as well as between Chennai and Port Blair. Jet Airways operates between Delhi, Chennai and Port Blair. King Fisher operates between Chennai and Port Blair. Jet Lite operates between Delhi, Kolkata, and Port Blair. Foreign charter flights may land in Port Blair following the guidelines of the Director General of Civil Aviation. To reduce the cost of travel from and to the islands, the government has placed the renovation of the Port Blair airport into an international airport high on the agenda.

Helicopters also operate to and from Port Blair passing through various routes: Carnic, Campbell Bay, Kamorta, Teressa, Chowra, Neil Island, Mayabunder, Diglipur, Hut Bay, Katachal, Rangat, and Havelock.

Ports and Waterways

Ports are strategically located and are in the vicinity of three major international shipping routes. These are 27 notified ports which are spread over the entire island.

The Directorate of Shipping Services runs routes connecting Port Blair with Kolkata, Visakhapatnam and Chennai. Passenger ship services run from Kolkata and Chennai to Port Blair and back three to four times per month, while service is available to Visakhapatnam once each month.

There are also regular inter-island ferry services from Port Blair connecting to all tourist locations. Vehicle ferries are available at important locations and some harbor ferries and private tourist boats are also available.

Power

Due to the distinct, geographically scattered characteristic of the ANI, diesel generators on each island (supplying 68 MW of power in total) take the place of a single power grid. The government is planning to devise an alternative source of power as a solution. Although the current reliance on renewable energy power is still very minimal, South Andaman is planning to increase their total power supply by 33 MW using fuels such as bio mass, coconut waste, and coal dust.

Resources

ANI Official Site
www.and.nic.in/

ANDHRA PRADESH

Area	276,754 sq km
Population	84.67 million
Capital	Hyderabad
NSDP at current prices	US$83.2 billion (2009-10); 8.80% Y/Y growth
Per capita NSDP at current prices	US$994 (2009-10); 7.77% Y/Y growth
Literacy rate	67.66 percent
Principal religions	Hinduism, Islam, Christianity and Buddhism
Principal languages	Telugu, Hindi, Tamil and English

- Andhra Pradesh has recently witnessed growing investments in its IT and ITeS, automotive, engineering and electronics sectors
- The state is the largest exporter of bulk drugs and pharmaceuticals in India
- Andhra Pradesh was ranked as one of the top three states in India to attract corporate investors in 2009

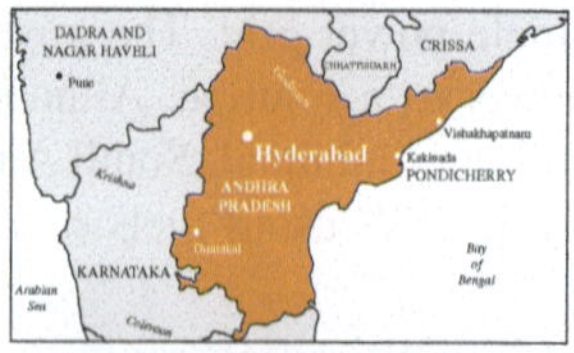

Overview

Andhra Pradesh is the fifth largest state in India, covering an area of 276,754 km^2 (approximately the size of Italy). The state is bounded by Tamil Nadu to the south, Orissa and Chhattisgarh to the north, Maharashtra and Karnataka to the west and the Bay of Bengal to the east. It has the longest coastline of all the states in India—972 km—and a variety of geographic features ranging from high hills, undulating plains to a coastal deltaic environment.

Andhra Pradesh is a resource-rich land of minerals which include coal, oil and natural gas, bauxite, limestone, gold, and diamonds. It is an agriculturally-prosperous state, with fertile land, water and productive agro-climatic conditions. The state is among the largest producers of food grains, fruit, vegetables, cotton, maize, dairy and poultry products in the country as well. It is also the largest exporter of bulk drugs and pharmaceuticals, contributing about 33.3% of the total exports from the country. In addition, leather and textile industries have shown promising growth over the last several years. Andhra Pradesh is home to many large public and private sector companies such as General Electric, HSBC, and IBM and is considered the hub of industrial activity in South India. Hyderabad and Visakhapatnam, the two main cities of Andhra Pradesh, have become the centers for manufacturing, information technology, tourism and services.

High-Tech City, a state IT park, is the largest IT facility in the country. As the name suggests, Hi-Tech City features some great technological revolutions in the form of IT parks located in the Hyderabad area. In the middle of the High-Tech City stands a 10 story cylindrical building that houses technology giants Microsoft, IBM, Metamor, Toshiba, Oracle, and Wipro. Specialty parks for the biotech sector have been proposed and are under construction as well. In addition to the industrial parks set up by the government, the state has two special economic zones and growth centers. With a high-tech telecommunications infrastructure, the state ensures good connectivity to other parts of the world.

Andhra Pradesh is one of the leading exporters of software products in the country. It is a major player in information technology given its skilled manpower, good technical and social infrastructure, and proactive business development policies. The government has established several world-class academic institutions and dedicated research organizations in different sectors, such as polytechnic colleges and industrial training institutes offering high quality technical education.

Business Opportunities

Key industries in Andhra Pradesh include automobiles and auto components, biotechnology, drugs and pharmaceuticals, food, IT, mines and minerals, textiles and leather and tourism. The state was ranked as one of the top three states to attract corporate investors in 2009 and at time of writing 71 out of the top 500 global companies have a presence there. A number of local companies such as Satyam Computers, GVK, Nagarjuna and Dr. Reddy's Laboratories and based in Hyderabad and have emerged as major players both domestically and internationally.

Infrastructure

Roadways

As Andhra Pradesh is predominantly an agriculture-oriented economy, roads are an essential means of transporting agricultural productions and raw and finished goods. The state is maintaining 70,394 km of roads, comprising 4,730 km of national highways; 10,470 km of state highways; 32,205 km of major district roads; and 22,989 km of rural roads. Andhra Pradesh will also be a part of the National Highways Development Project, the largest highway project ever undertaken by the country, and the state will have 1,834 km of four-lane roads after the construction is completed, with an additional 519.5 km proposed.

Railways

Andhra Pradesh has rail connectivity to all the major cities of the country, for the transportation of goods traffic such as coal, iron ore, cement, food grains, fertilizers, minerals, petroleum products and general merchandise. The Hyderabad Metro Rail Project is also being developed to meet the needs of commuters in Great Hyderabad.

Aviation

The state is well linked internally by air, with three major airports located at Hyderabad, Visakhapatnam and Tirupathi. The Hyderabad International Airport at Begumpet (which no longer provides civil aviation services) was replaced by the Rajiv Gandhi International Airport at Hyderabad, which is the first greenfield airport in the country. Flying time is two hours or less to the major cities in India and four hours from important cities of the Middle East and South East Asia. Tirupathi Airport is being upgraded to the status of international airport.

Ports

Andhra Pradesh has a 974 km-long coastline, which provides numerous opportunities for the state to develop a number of ports along the coast. It has one major port at Visakhapatnam controlled by the central government and 14 non-major ports controlled by the state government. Among the latter, to improve infrastructure the state government is privatizing Gangavaram, Krishnapatnam, and Kakinda ports.

Power

A key player in the country's power sector, the state has the second largest power generating utility in the country with an installed capacity of around 13,409 MW. The two cheapest sources of thermal power generation, coal and natural gas, are in abundance in Andhra Pradesh.

The power consumption in the state is continuously on the rise with the per capita consumption amounting to 929 kWh in 2009–2010. To meet the increasing demand, the government is implementing projects at state level and promoting projects in the private sector as well as planning to add additional power capacity of 5,484.79 MW during its 11th five year plan from 2007 to 2012.

Telecommunications

The Andhra Pradesh Telecom Circle serves the entire state of Andhra Pradesh including the twin cities of Hyderabad and Secunderabad. Companies such as BSNL, Reliance, Bharat and TATA have extensive optical fiber cable networks in the state that provide a wide range of communication networks.

Resources

Official Portal of Government of Andhra Pradesh
http://www.aponline.gov.in/apportal/index.asp

ARUNACHAL PRADESH

Area	83,743 sq km
Population	1.38 million
Capital	Itanagar
NSDP at current prices	US$906 million (2008-09); 16.41% Y/Y growth
Per capita NSDP at current prices	US$751 (2008-09); 15.05% Y/Y growth
Literacy rate	66.95 percent
Principal religions	Buddhism, Hinduism and Christianity
Principal languages	Assamese, Bengali, Hindi and English

- Arunachal Pradesh is the largest state in the northeast area-wise
- Arunachal Pradesh is a predominantly agriculture-based society with good potential for investment in agricultural activities, including the cultivation of orchids and a variety of medicinal plants
- The state is famous worldwide for its handloom and handicraft industry

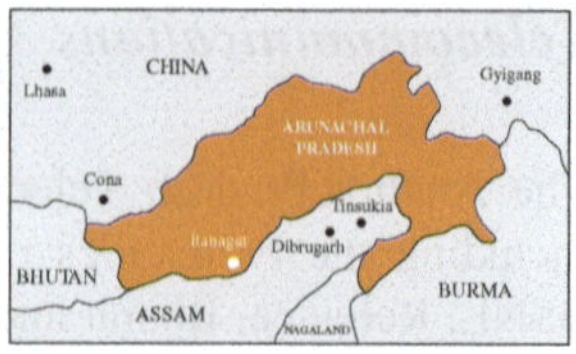

Overview

Arunachal Pradesh has a total land area of 83,743 km. It shares its western border with Bhutan, north-eastern border with Tibet and China and eastern border with Myanmar and the national boundaries with the states of Assam and Nagaland. Itanagar is the capital of Arunachal Pradesh, which is located at an altitude of 530 m above minimum sea level. The state largely consists of submontane and mountainous ranges, sloping down to the plains of Assam. These divide the state into five river valleys, namely, the Kameng, the Subansiri, the Siang, the Lohit and the Tirap.

The state is situated in the Eastern Himalayan province, the richest bio-geographical province of the Himalayan zone. It is known for its rich forest resources and mineral deposits. It is a land of deep river valleys and beautiful plateaus. Due to rich biodiversity of flora and fauna, Arunachal Pradesh has a vast market potential for the cultivation of orchids and a variety of medicinal plants. The industries of the state are based on locally available raw materials and forest produces.

Business Opportunities

In spite of its hilly terrain, Arunachal Pradesh provides a wealth of business opportunities. It has abundant forest cover, minerals and hydroelectric power resources, which can be utilized for setting up industrial units in the state. Major mineral deposits in the state are limestone, dolomite, quartzite, graphite, coal, marble, oil, natural gas, kyanite, mica, iron and copper. Most of the industries in the state are based on forest products such as timber, veneer and plywood. A wide variety of crafts such as weaving, painting, pottery, basketry and woodcarving are found among the people of Arunachal Pradesh.

To promote investments in Arunachal Pradesh, the government has set various incentives for entrepreneurs seeking to establish industrial units in the state. These include schemes for central capital investment; transport subsidies; central interest subsidies; comprehensive insurance; price preference, and quality control.

Agriculture and Horticulture

Agriculture is the mainstay of the economy of Arunachal Pradesh—nearly 75% of the state's total workforce is engaged in agriculture and allied activities. It is mainly dependent on "shifting" or "jhum" cultivation. The principal crops are rice, maize, millet and wheat. In particular, the state government is encouraging the cultivation of cash crops like potatoes, sugarcane, etc.

Horticulture is the backbone of the rural economy in Arunachal Pradesh. It has vast potential, owing to its good climate and topography, for the development of varied varieties of tropical, sub-tropical and temperate fruit like apples, oranges and pineapples; vegetables (including off-season vegetables); spices; aromatic and medicinal plants; and mushrooms. Most of the state is covered by dense and rich forest.

The agriculture and horticulture based industries are being developed on the following product lines:

- Fruit-based alcoholic beverages
- Ginger processing and dehydration
- Apple cultivation and processing
- Processing of citrus fruit
- Tapioca production units for production of sago and starch
- Cold storages
- Multipurpose fruit and vegetables processing

Cane and Bamboo

The cane and bamboo industry of Arunachal Pradesh is of a very high standard. Hats of different sizes and shapes; various kinds of baskets; cane vessels; a wide variety of cane belts; elaborately woven brassiers of cane and fiber; bamboo mugs with carvings; a variety of ornaments and necklaces are some of the products of the industry. Of all these, the largest production is in baskets, which are beautiful not only because of the fine texture but also because of the unusual shapes.

Carpet Making

Carpet making is one of the most important industries in the state, especially in the districts of Tawang, West Kameng, Changlang and Upper Siang. Arunachal Pradesh's carpets have been acclaimed nationally and internationally on the basis of quality of carpet weaving in the state. Carpets are woven with varied colors, designs (geometric, dragon, floral) and shapes. The other main products of the industry are wall hangings, cushion pads, telephone pads and floor coverings. With the increase in demand, carpets have become a major item of trade as well as a major occupation for women of the state.

Tourism

Arunachal Pradesh is emerging as a major tourist destination in the north-eastern region. It is endowed with a rich biodiversity of flora and fauna. The state is also home to wide varieties of orchids.

Arunachal Pradesh has tremendous scope for development of various types of tourism activities, such as cultural tourism, adventure tourism, historical tourism, wildlife tourism, nature based tourism and eco-tourism. The government of Arunachal Pradesh has been undertaking several developmental schemes in order to explore more places of tourist interest, as well as to provide infrastructure facilities such as the construction of tourist lodges and huts, wayside amenities, development of lakes, and provisions for adventure sports at various places of tourist interest in the near future.

Infrastructure

Arunachal Pradesh, being a hilly terrain, requires adequate and efficient provision of well-connected roadways, railways and airways networks. Such infrastructure services are indispensable for integrating the state with the rest of the nation; facilitating trade and commerce; as well as improving the quality of life of the people.

Roadways

Itanagar, the capital of Arunachal Pradesh, is connected by a network of roads with the first and second-tier cities and towns in the neighboring states as well as with other cities in India. The state transport buses operate on a daily basis or on alternate days from Itanagar to some of the district headquarters.

Railways

There is no main railway head in the state. The nearest railway station is at Harmoti in Assam, 23 km from Naharlagun and 33 km from Itanagar.

Aviation

The nearest airport is Tezpur in Assam, 216 km from Naharlagun and 226 km from Itanagar. Naharlagun is also connected by Helicopter service from Mohanbari (Dibrugarh) and Guwahati (Assam).

Power

The total installed power generation capacity of the state is around 201.9 MW, with the state's share in central sector stations as 118.6 MW and state sector stations as 83.3 MW. Arunachal Pradesh also uses 15.88 MW of thermal energy and 8.5 MW of Hydro-electric energy.

Telecommunications

Itanagar and all the district headquarters are connected with the rest of the country and the world through telephone, STD, ISD, Telex and fax facilities.

Resources

Official Website of Government of Arunachal Pradesh
www.arunachalpradesh.nic.in/

ASSAM

Area	78,523 sq km
Population	31.17 million
Capital	Guwahati
NSDP at current prices	US$17.8 billion (2009-10); 10.76% Y/Y growth
Per capita NSDP at current prices	US$592 (2009-10); 9.37% Y/Y growth
Literacy rate	73.18 percent
Principal religions	Hinduism, Islam, Buddhism, Sikhism and Christianity
Principal languages	Assamese, Bengali, Hindi, Bodo, Karbi, Mishing, Rabha and English

- Assam is the largest tea-producing state in India
- The state is also a leading producer of crude oil and natural gas, with major companies including Oil India Limited, Oil and Natural Gas Corporation Limited, Assam Industrial Development Corporation, and Assam Gas Company

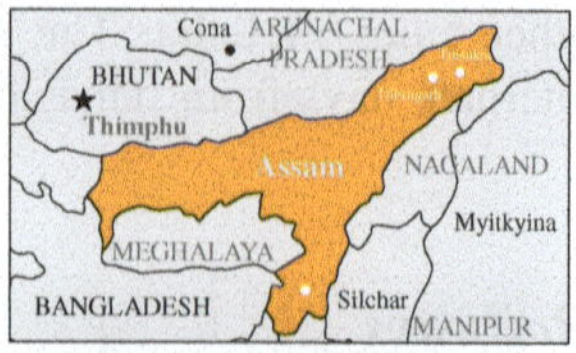

Overview

Known as the land of the red river and blue hills, Assam is a northeastern state of India, sharing international borders with Bhutan to the north and Bangladesh to the west. Assam is predominantly an agricultural state, with 74% of its population engaged in agriculture. The state produces significant quantities of agricultural products such as tea, rice, maize and jute.

Apart from its agricultural identity, Assam possesses many other growing sectors, including oil and natural gas production and IT. Assam is a leading producer of crude oil, cement and fertilizers, accounting for 15% of India's crude output and about 50% of India's total onshore production of natural gas. Assam has shown significant progress in the field of information technology and IT exports. The state has witnessed the establishment of software technology parks in different places in the state. SoftDTA, HCL Comnet Systems & Services Ltd., Eastern Star Software and Datamation Consultants Pvt. Ltd are examples of some major companies which have set up operations in software technology parks.

In addition, Assam is well-known for its silk industry, with many Assamese women still wearing dresses made of silk, and the Central Silk Board, the State Government, as well as the North Eastern Council making efforts to preserve this tradition by improving the host plants, building see organizations, setting up cooperatives and providing marketing facilities.

Business Opportunities

Assam has abundant river waters, hydrocarbon potential, low ash coal resources, limestone and dolomite deposits. The natural climate of Assam is ideal for plantation crops such as tea and rubber. Assam also possesses vast potential for forest-based industries, including bamboo, medicinal herbs and wood, which are utilized for setting up forest-based industries.

Both the central and state governments have provided exclusive incentives to investors such as enormous subsidies to support power, transportation, land, and infrastructure development for setting up business in the state. The sector has attracted major international funding institutions in the development of roads, railways, airports, power stations and other essential urban infrastructure. Companies including Oil India Limited, Oil and Natural Gas Corporation Limited, Assam Industrial Development Corporation, Assam Gas Company and the Assam Electronics Development Corporation have made significant contributions to the modernization and development of the state.

To further the progress of industrialization in the state, several export promotion industrial parks, industrial infrastructure development centers, export processing zones and dedicated industrial growth centers have been developed in commercially viable locations in the state. There have been several food processing parks, an agriculture export zone for ginger, and industrial growth centers created as well.

Infrastructure

The state's capital city of Guwahati is one of the communication and transportation hubs for the north-eastern region.

Roadways

The total length of roads in the state is around 69,000 km, covering both metalled and non-metalled surfaces. They account for approximately 60% of the total road length in the north-east. Currently, two road-cum-rail bridges and one road bridge crosses over the Brahmaputra River. The fourth bridge is being erected over the river near Dibrugarh and the construction of the fifth bridge in Guwahati is expected to begin soon. Three more bridges are expected to be built thereafter. Reopening Stilwell Road and corridor through Myanmar to connect onto the Trans Asian Highway is now under consideration; this will speed up the trade with Bangkok and Singapore by reducing the travel time. All the towns of the state are well connected by the Assam State Transport Corporation and other tourist bus services, run by private operators.

Railways

Assam is well connected with the rest of the country by railway network and the length of railways in Assam is about 3,950 km. Within the state, all the major towns like Dibrugarh, Tinsukia, Jorhat, Nagaon, Guwahati, Tezpur, Barpeta and Bongaigaon are linked by railways. Assam is undertaking projects to expand its rail connectivity by adding alternative rail routes as well as upgrading the current facilities with faster trains.

Aviation

The Lokapriva Gopinath Bordoloi International Airport in Guwahati is located 18 km away from the city center and has direct flights connecting to prominent cities such as New Delhi, Kolkata, Mumbai, and Chennai. Regular air services connecting six civil airports are available in Assam: these airports are Guwahati, Tezpur, Jorhat, Dibrugarh, Silchar and North Lakhimpur. Indian Airlines, Air Sahara, Jet Airways and Air Deccan, Kingfisher Airlines, Spice Jet and Indigo fly operate regular flights into and out of Guwahati. Indian Airlines connects Guwahati to the capitals of most of the other north eastern states. Druk Air also operates an international weekly flight between Bangkok and Guwahati. Some of the tea gardens in the state have their own air-strips and aircraft. Major investments planned for upgrading the current air infrastructure is expected to bring over 15% compound annual growth rate within the next 5 years.

Ports and Waterways

In Assam, waterways are the only means of transportation to many inland areas in the remote parts of the state. Assam's internal waterway network connects with the port of Chittagong in Bangladesh as well as to Kolkata and Haldia in West Bengal. There are seven ports through which imports and exports to Kolkata and Haldia port are transferred. The two most important navigable rivers of Assam are Brahmaputra and the Barak. The Brahmaputra has been declared National Waterway No. 2. Two public sector organizations, Central Inland Waterways Corporation and Directorate of Inland Waterways, Assam are operating water transport services on the river Brahmaputra and Barak on a commercial basis. These services are used for the transportation of both passengers and goods. The types of cargo handled are mainly jute, coal, fertilizers, forest, agricultural products, cement and machinery.

Power

Assam has a huge potential for development of infrastructure for generation, transmission and distribution of electricity. It has abundant reserves of natural gas and has the potential to generate cheap and eco-friendly power from small hydro electric stations. With the work of major energy stations like NEEPCO and NHPC in power generation, Assam will be able to boost its power supply and become a self sufficient state and possibly generate a surplus of power in several years. The Assam Gas Cracker Project to be finished in 2012 will also provide vast opportunities for polymer based industries and engineering industries in petro chemical sector.

Telecommunications

The telecommunication network in the state is expanding faster than the rest of India with 269 telephone exchanges, with approximately 120,000 working connections. Mobile services are also available.

Resources

The Official Website of the Government of Assam
http://assamgovt.nic.in/

BIHAR

Area	94,163 sq km
Population	103.8 million
Capital	Patna
NSDP at current prices	US$31.7 billion (2009-10); 8.81% Y/Y growth
Per capita NSDP at current prices	US$331 (2009-10); 7.25% Y/Y growth
Literacy rate	63.82 percent
Principal religions	Hinduism
Principal languages	Hindi and English

- Bihar is the largest producer of vegetables and second largest producer of fruit in India, with sugar as the state's largest agriculture-based industry in Bihar
- The state has advantages in the areas of mining and extraction, cement, steels and automobiles
- Bihar has surplus of water resources, with vast potential to be used as a renewable energy source

Overview

Bihar is located in the eastern part of India, with a total land area of 94,163 km^2. It is bounded on the north by Nepal, on the east by West Bengal, on the west by Uttar Pradesh and on the south by Jharkhand. It has a number of rivers, the most important of which is the Ganges. Since Bihar has a tropical to subtropical climate, rainfall is the most significant factor in determining the nature of vegetation. The topography of Bihar can be described as a fertile alluvial plain occupying the Gangetic valley. The plain extends from the foothills of the Himalayas in the north to a few miles south of the river Ganges. Rich farmland and lush orchards stretch out throughout the state.

Bihar has an abundant mineral resources base, including steatite, pyrites, quartzite, crude mica and limestone. Its beneficial climate and gains in green technology have enabled the state to become a leading producer of commodities, such as rice, wheat, sugarcane and jute. Bihar is also one of the largest producers of fruit and vegetables in India.

In addition, there are large vital industrial units in the state in the sectors of textiles, leather, information technology, engineering goods and tourism.

Business Opportunities

Large and small business houses exists in the areas of mining and extraction, textiles, sugar mills, rice mills, oil refineries, cement, steel, fertilizers, automobiles and engineering products.

Agriculture

The people of Bihar are largely dependent on agriculture and related activities for living. With good water supplies and irrigation, the land is fertile. Principal food crops are rice, wheat, maize and pulses. The main cash crops are sugarcane, potato, tobacco, oilseeds, onion, chillies, jute and roselle. Industries based on agricultural products like sugar mills, edible oil mills, spices and other agriculture-based industries have a good demand and export potential. Bihar is the largest producer of vegetables and second largest producer of fruit in India, with sugar as the state's largest agriculture-based industry in Bihar.

Private sector participation is being encouraged in packaging and food processing to ensure better quality. Also, the state welcomes private investment for comprehensive development of the tea industry and the capital subsidy is available for setting up tea processing units.

Sugar Industry

The sugar industry is the largest agriculture-based industry in Bihar. Currently, the production of sugarcane is 13 million MT annually and Bihar is planning to raise that number to 46.72 million MT by 2015. Investment opportunities in sugar and allied industries in Bihar include:

- Green field sugar mills and capacity expansion of existing sugar mills
- Ethanol manufacturing
- The manufacturing of molasses-based alcohol and commercial spirits
- The manufacturing of bagasse-based paper
- Engineering units related to the sugar industry
- Manufacturing of sugar-based confectionery

Textiles

Bihar has strong weaving traditions, with over 90,000 weavers in the state. The major locations for the textile industry are Bhagalpur, Gaya, Nalanda, Darbhanga, Madhubani, Siwan and Patna. Bihar is India's second state after West Bengal in jute production and jute textiles. Due to the availability of raw jute, cheap labor, sufficient power, water and transportation in the northern part of Bihar, some jute mills are located in this region, including in Karbisganj in Purnia district, Katibar and Muktapur in Samstipur district.

Tourism

Tourism is becoming an increasingly important industry in Bihar. Rich farmlands and lush orchards are spread throughout the state. Important places of tourist interest are: Rajgir, Nalanda, Vaishali, Bodh Gaya, Patna (ancient city of Patliputra), Sasaram (tomb of Shershah Suri) and Madhubani (known for famous Madhubani paintings).

Infrastructure

Infrastructure in the state includes reliable transportation network (railways, roadways, airways and waterways); excellent power and an telecommunications system.

Roadways

Bihar has an efficient and reliable road network. It has around 14,575 km of roads in total. Bihar's portion of the Golden Quadrilateral passes through Mohania, Sasaram, Aurangabad, Sherghati and Bhaluachatti. A total budget of 17,900 crores is set for constructing 4-laning roads, state highways, and major district roads in the next 3 years. An additional 3,400 km of link routes will be constructed and 4,460 km of roads will be upgraded in rural areas.

Railways

Bihar has an extensive and well-developed railway system. The main rail junctions are at Patna, Gaya, Muzaffarpur, Katihar and Samastipur, etc. A few railway routes connecting important places like Muzaffarpur-Samastipur-Barauni-Katihar and Muzaffarpur-Chapra-Siwan have been converted into broad gauge.

Aviation

There is an international airport at Patna. There are landing grounds in all major districts of the state and Gaya, Muzaffarpur, Raxoul and Jogbani have domestic airports.

Ports and Waterways

Bihar is an entirely land-locked state, but the port of Kolkata is accessible. There are a large number of rivers in Bihar which provide links to many important cities in India and also link to Haldia Port. Rivers with the total navigable length of over 1,300 km connect various parts of the state.

Power

A new power policy is being implemented to augment power generation and distribution through private investment. Bihar's vast water resources also allow the state to utilize hydro-thermal energy.

Telecommunications

Bihar has achieved a significant improvement in telecommunication services and facilities. All the district headquarters, cities and important industrial locations in the state are now connected with STD/ISD facilities.

Resources

Bihar Government Website
http://gov.bih.nic.in/

CHANDIGARH

Area	114 sq km
Population	1.05 million
Capital	Chandigarh
NSDP at current prices	US$4 billion (2009-10); 16.14% Y/Y growth
Per capita NSDP at current prices	US$2904 (2009-10); 7.97% Y/Y growth
Literacy rate	86.43 percent
Principal religions	Sikhism and Hinduism
Principal languages	Hindi, Punjabi and English

- Chandigarh is the first planned city in India and is known for its architecture and landscaping
- It is a gateway to many neighboring states, opening it up to investment opportunities in the tourism industry
- Major industries include food, repair service, basic metals and alloys, but analysts suggest future development into a "knowledge city"

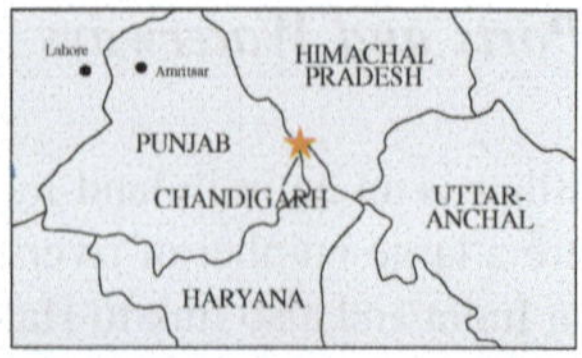

Overview

Chandigarh is a unique union territory of India. It is the only city which is the capital of two states (Punjab and Haryana) simultaneously. The city lies at an altitude varying from 304.8 to 365.76 m above sea level, located in the foothills of the Shivalik Hill ranges. It is bordered by Kandi (Bhabhar) in the north east and Sirowal (Tarai) and alluvial plains in the remaining part.

Business Opportunities

Chandigarh is becoming one of the preferred investment hot spots in India. It is a gateway to the hilly state of Himachal Pradesh and is easily accessible from all the neighboring cities like Punjab, Haryana, and Delhi. As a result, it has many investment opportunities in the tourism sector. Chandigarh's economy is dominated by various industrial units relating to food products, repair services, basic metals and alloys. Also, due to its competent human resource base, it is a preferable destination for the global information technology companies and has the potential to become a knowledge city in the years to come.

Information Technology

Chandigarh provides an ideal stage for the growth of the information technology culture and for optimum utilization of the benefits of IT revolution.

The Chandigarh government has the goal of creating a knowledge-based society through the extensive use of IT. The ultimate goal is to use IT as a channel for effective interaction between the administration and the public.

Tourism

Chandigarh is one of the cleanest and greenest cities in India, with a rich human resource base and cultural heritage. It is famous for its landscaping and some of its great architectural creations. Chandigarh also acts as a gateway to many pilgrimage centers in the neighboring states of Punjab, Haryana and Himachal Pradesh. It offers places of varying interest to tourists, including the Rock Garden; the Rose Garden; Sukhna Lake; Pinjore Garden; the Museum and Art Gallery; the City Museum; the Tower of Shadows; the Geometric Hill Museum of Evolution; Kala Gram; Log Huts; Nepli Forests; Fitness Trails (in Leisure Valley); the National Gallery of Portraits; the Central Plaza; the International Doll Museum and Smriti Upvan.

Infrastructure

In order to attract investment into the territory, the government of Chandigarh has undertaken various infrastructure projects to provide sound physical connectivity with other parts of the country. Chandigarh's efficient transportation system and power generating system made the territory a popular investment spot for investors.

Roadways

The union territory of Chandigarh is well served by an excellent road network. Its asphalt roads are being changed into RCC roads as a part of its long term project. The Chandigarh Government is paying for the road construction by purchasing plastic waste from rag pickers. Another unique feature of Chandigarh's roads is its classified 7Vs road systems: V-1) fast roads connecting Chandigarh to other towns, V-2) arterial roads, V-3) fast vehicular sector dividing roads, V-4) meandering shopping streets, V-5) sector circulation roads, V-6) access roads to houses, V-7) foot paths and cycle tracks. Buses can only run through V-1 to V-4 roads and walls are installed on V-3 roads to separate the sectors. This road system is not only helpful for the traffic circulation, but also effective in controlling the noise level and pollution in residential areas. Chadigarh's road system connects it to a number of popular towns and pilgrimage centers in just short distance. The newly introduced grid transport system in local bus services shortened the traveling time for the passengers.

Railways

Chandigarh railway station is about 8 km from the city centre. Shatabdi Express and Himalayan Queen provide two train services on a daily basis between Chandigarh and Delhi. Paschim Express connects the city to Mumbai; Sadbhavna to Lucknow; Kerala Sampark Kranti to Kerala and Chennai Express to Chennai.

Aviation

Chandigarh's airport is 12 km from the city center. Indian Airlines and Jet Airways connect Chandigarh with Delhi, Leh and Amritsar. There is a well maintained tourist information center at the airport. The Chandigarh government is also working on upgrades of Chandigarh Airport to international level to enhance its connectivity to the other parts of the world and to improve its export potential.

Power

Chandigarh has one of the better power supply and electricity distribution systems in India. It gets power from neighboring states and central generation projects. All the villages around the city stand electrified and have been extended the facility of public lighting. The government has undertaken a project to provide an uninterrupted power supply with a reliability of 99.99%. Also, a new grid transport system has been introduced for a quick and efficient public transportation system in the city.

Resources

Official Website of Chandigarh Administration
www.chandigarh.nic.in/

CHHATTISGARH

Area	135,194 sq km
Population	25.54 million
Capital	Raipur
NSDP at current prices	US$21.3 billion (2009-10); 13.60% Y/Y growth
Per capita NSDP at current prices	US$869 (2009-10); 11.75% Y/Y growth
Literacy rate	71.04 percent
Principal religions	Hinduism
Principal languages	Chhattisgarhi, Hindi and English

- Chhattisgarh's Bailadila mines have one of the best quality iron ore deposits in the world
- The state's large coal deposits have the potential of developing the state into a power hub of India
- Chhattisgarh produces around 20 percent of India's steel and cement

Overview

Chhattisgarh was carved out of the state of Madhya Pradesh and is the ninth largest state in India. It is bounded by southern Jharkhand and Orissa in the east; Madhya Pradesh and Maharashtra in the west; Uttar Pradesh and western Jharkhand in the north and Andhra Pradesh in the south. The principal river of the state is the Mahanadi. The great Vindhyachal mountain range dominates its landscape. The state's rich cultural heritage includes ancient monuments, carved temples, Buddhist sites, palaces, caves and rock paintings.

The state has various natural resources like forests, rare wildlife, surface water and waterfalls. It is the richest state in terms of mineral resources, with an abundance of all major minerals, including diamonds. The state's Bailadila mines have one of the best quality iron ore deposits in the world. Also, rich deposits of bauxite, limestone, dolomite and corundum are found in the state, in addition to sufficient enough coal deposits to transform the region into a power hub.

The state government has undertaken various initiatives to curtail unproductive administrative overheads and encourage public–private partnerships. The government has been focusing on the critical areas of law, education, health, environment, social safety nets, fiscal reforms and e-governance and aims to privatize in these areas. Realizing that its large human resource base is key to Chhattisgarh's prosperity, the state has been making significant efforts to tap the creative energies of its citizens.

Business Opportunities

Within three years of its formation, Chhattisgarh embarked on social and economic development through policy reforms, with a focus on infrastructure development and improving the investment climate in the state. The state has rich natural resources and has large untapped potential for development. In addition to its present areas of strength (including those in cement, mining, iron and steel), a number of sectors are emerging with substantial potential for private investment and business in Chhattisgarh; the most prominent among these are electricity generation and infrastructure development.

Agriculture

Agriculture and related activities account for over 80% of the workforce in the state. Out of the geographical area of 13,789 thousand ha, gross cropped area is about 43%. The predominant crop of the state is rice and as a result, the state is known as the "rice bowl" of Madhya Pradesh. Other important crops grown in the state are paddy, maize, wheat, soybeans, sunflowers and ground nuts.

Mineral Resources

Chhattisgarh is the richest state in terms of mineral wealth. It hosts a wide variety of minerals found in igneous, sedimentary and metamorphic terrains. These mineral resources have immense potential for large investment in mining, setting up mineral based industries and generating employment in the state. The large deposits of coal, iron ore, limestone, bauxite, dolomite and tin ore are located in several parts of the state.

Chhattisgarh produces around 20% of the country's steel and cement and is the only tin-ore producing state in the country. It is nestling atop the world's largest Kimberlite area. Eight blocks have been demarcated for diamond exploration and analysts predict that Raipur district is likely to yield substantial quantity of diamonds in the future. Apart from diamonds, four blocks of gold exploration and five blocks for base metal investigation have been demarcated. The state is also encouraging the establishment of a gems and jewelry park.

Information Technology

The state of Chhattisgarh has prepared its IT policy with a vision of establishing an information society consisting of informed, active and responsible citizens. It seeks to provide all citizens with widespread and easy access to government services in the local language, effectively addressing the existing digital divide and promoting entrepreneurs within the state. In addition, the Chhattisgarh Infotech and Biotech Promotion Society have been set up to give impetus to IT growth in the state. The society ensures top-of-the-board institutionalized coordination and implementation of the state's plans for enabling benefits of IT for the entire state.

Mining

Mining has evolved as an emerging sector adding remarkable state revenue. Chhattisgarh has rich mineral resources and is a major resource base for mineral-related industries. The state holds a major share of coal deposits in India. Chhattisgarh has the largest reserve of tin in the country and possesses the best quality of iron ores. Over one-fifth of the iron ore in India is found in the state. Limestone is also abundant in the state. Other prominent ore reserves include: coal, dolomite, quartzite, bauxite, rare, alkali and base-metals (including nickel, chromium, and platinum group elements—PGE), gold and diamonds. Having large deposits for such valuable resources at proximity, Chhattisgarh is an ideal location for low cost power, steel and cement production.

Aluminum

Chhattisgarh is looking to develop an aluminum park at Bhanpuri, near Raipur, for the promotion of downstream products. Those that are looking into investing in downstream industries will be given priority in the approval of Prospecting License and Mining Lease. The aluminum park will be home to more than 100 industrial units manufacturing various aluminum and metal products. The products manufactured are required by different industries, such as civil aviation, automobile and construction.

Exports

Chhattisgarh has a large focus on the export industry. The city of Bhilai accounts for 75% of state exports, while other export cities include Urla, Bhanpuri and Sirgitti. Important exportable products of the state include: steel, handicrafts, handlooms, blended yarn, food and agriculture products, iron, aluminum, cement, minerals and engineering products.

Infrastructure

The government of Chhattisgarh has identified the importance of adequate and efficient infrastructure in order to facilitate socioeconomic development of the state. The state also offers significant opportunities for infrastructure development through private sector participation.

Roadways

Chhattisgarh is well connected by road networks. There are three national highways passing through the state (2,184 km), along with many state highways and district roads connecting all district headquarters of the state (8,031 km).

Railways

Railways are a dominant factor in the industrialization of the state. The total length of railroads in Chhattisgarh is 1,108 km. Raipur, Bilaspur, Durg, Rajnandgaon, Raigarh and Korba are important railway stations. The state capital is linked to most of the Indian states and to a major seaport by rail line network. Raipur is conveniently located at the center of the rail routes between Mumbai and Kolkata and is also well-connected to Delhi and Chennai by fast train Rajdhani Express. There are direct trains also to many cities, such as Ahmedabad, Aliahabad, Varansi, Banglore, Cochin, Pune and Hyderabad. A new railway zone "South East Central Railway" began operating to service the heavy traffic in mining and metal industry with its headquarters located in Bilasper district. In fact, the railway division in Bilasper district became India's most lucrative railway, accounting for 17% of entire Indian railways revenue.

Aviation

The state has two domestic airports at Raipur and Bilaspur. Only Raipur airport is in service. The state also has air strips at Bhilai, Korba, Raigarh, Jagdalpur, Ambikapur, Jashpur Nagar and Sarangarh.

Power

Chhattisgarh's central location is advantageous in transferring power supply to all parts of India and the state is on its way onto becoming the power-hub of India. News reports suggest a continuous inflow of power industries relocating to Chhattisgarh. There are huge coal reserves in the vicinity, offering cheap power generation opportunities and there is enough water from the state's largest reservoir of Hasdeo Bango. Chhattisgarh is in the western grid and is linked to the southern and northern grids, due to its surplus of power can be easily transmitted to any of India's four grids. Among the states receiving power supply from Chhattisgarh are Delhi, Gujarat, and Karnataka.

The government is initiating investor-friendly policies to attract investors, such as welcoming investments in greenfield power projects with the lowest cost of production in India. Private sectors are also permitted to install captive power plants for generation and transmission of power supplies directly within the estate without any restrictions.

Telecom

Chhattisgarh is in the process of acquiring State Wireless Area Network (SWAN), which is a combination of wireless and line network. The number of telephone connections in the state is 1,210,503 and the number of telephone exchanges is 608.

Resources

Official Government website of Chhattisgarh
http://chhattisgarh.nic.in

DADRA AND NAGAR HAVELI

Area	491 sq km
Population	342,853
Capital	Silvassa
Literacy rate	77.65 percent
Principal religions	Hinduism
Principal languages	Hindi, Gujarati and Marathi

- Dadra and Nagar Haveli is strategically located between Gujarat and Maharashtra, the two most economically developed states
- The major industries of Dadra and Nagar Haveli include textiles, papers, plastics, engineering products, chemicals, pharmaceuticals and dyeing

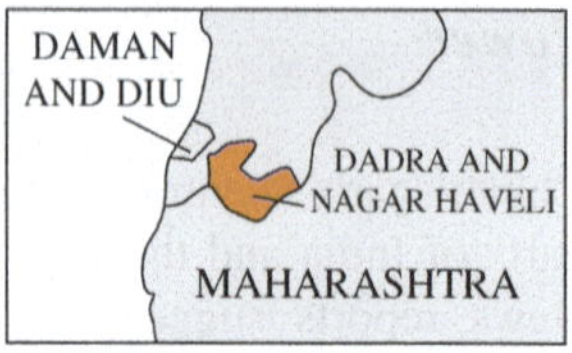

Overview

The Union Territory of Dadra and Nagar Haveli, with a total land area of 491 km^2, is located on the western side of the foothills of the Western Ghats. It is surrounded by the states of Gujarat and Maharashtra and is located at almost equal distance from Mumbai (Maharashtra) and Surat (Gujarat).

Land under forest cover in the territory constitutes about 40% of the geographical area. The terrain is mainly hilly, while the central plain is rich with fertile soil. The state is very diverse with many types of flora and fauna and is fast developing as a major weekend getaway for city dwellers and tourists.

Due to its advantageous location, a large number of industrial units have been established in the territory, mainly in the fields of textiles, papers, plastics, engineering products, chemicals, pharmaceuticals and dyeing. Since the territory is in South Gujarat's heavy agro-climatic zone, a wide variety of agricultural crops are also grown.

Business Opportunities

Dadra and Nagar Haveli have a good labor climate; adequate infrastructure facilities as well as varied agricultural production. The Omnibus Industrial Development Corporation of Dadra and Nagar Haveli is the main authority to assist and promote the economic development of the territory's industrial sectors. Some of the government policy measures include tax holiday and sales tax exemptions for the newly established units to Dadra and Nagar Haveli. The government is also investing significant amounts of capital to promote local tribal handicrafts.

Agriculture

Dadra and Nagar Haveli is predominantly a rural area with a 79% tribal population. Agriculture is the main occupation of the people of the territory. Rice is the staple crop of the region, with approximately 10,000 ha of land allocated for rice cultivation, and other crops like nagli, tur, urad, jawar and niger are also grown here under rain-fed conditions. Wheat, sugarcane, oilseed, banana, mustard and vegetables are grown under irrigated condition. Fruit like mango, sapota, guava and coconut are also grown by the tribal farmers. The government supplying the irrigation and improved agriculture facilities to the tribal planters has reduced their burden of having to rely on nature and increased production.

Small-Scale Industry

Industrial development started with the establishment of an industrial estate under the cooperative sector by Dan Udyog Sahakari Sangh Ltd. Thereafter, three government industrial estates have been developed at Silvassa, Masat and Khadoli. In the textile sector, the industrial units are engaged in spinning (mainly cotton and micro yarn spinning) and processing (mainly text rising, twisting, weaving and knitting activities). While, the main activity of the plastics sector is injection and blow molded articles, which includes industrial as well as domestic household products and furniture. The paper industry manufactures corrugated paper boxes, sheets, rolls and paper tubes.

Tourism

Tourism has been assigned high priority, keeping in view the dense forest area and favorable climate of the territory. Prominent places of tourist interest include: Tadekeshwar Shiva Mandir, Bindrabin, Deer Park at Khanvel, Vanganga Lake and Island Garden, Dadra, Vanvihar Udhyan Mini Zoo, Bal Udhyan, Tribal Museum, and Hirvavan Garden at Silvassa. The territory also acts as a convenient base to explore the hill resort and the tribal land of Saputara in Gujarat (route via Dharampur), the Parsi temple at Udwada, the pilgrimage sites of Trambakeshwar, Nasik and Shirdi.

To further encourage tourism activities, some traditional and modern cultural activities like the celebration of Tarpa Festival, Kite Festival and World Tourism Day are organized every year. The development of water sports at Dudhani has been completed. The construction of an amphitheater close to Yatri Niwas, Silvassa is in progress.

Infrastructure

The government of Dadra and Nagar Haveli has undertaken several infrastructure projects to provide sound physical connectivity of the union territory with other parts of the country.

Roadways

The union territory depends heavily on Maharashtra and Gujarat's road network as the territory can only be accessed after crossing these two states from Mumbai. At present, the total length of roads in the territory is 580 km of which 545.45 km are surfaced road. Almost all villages are connected by all-weather roads. The union territory of Dadra and Nagar Haveli is close to Mumbai-Baroda-Delhi National Highway No. 8 (Western Express Highway). Currently, four lane roads connecting Silvassa to Athal, Piparia and Masat are under construction.

Railways

The nearest railway stations are Bhilad (12 km) and Vapi (14 km) on the Western Railway. All major Mail/Express trains are available at Vapi including August Kranti Rajdhani, Shatabdi, Ahinsa and Karnavati. The other rail head, Bhilad (20 km) is on the Mumbai-Ahmedabad route.

Aviation

There is no main airport in the union territory. The nearest airport is Mumbai, 180 km away, connecting to all the major states and cities within the country and internationally.

Power

The territory has established an excellent network of electricity with all villages electrically connected. It is a main source of energy for industry. The power requirement of the union territory is being met from central sector power generating stations located in the western region, which allows the price of power supply to stay low. Having power supply cover a small area of land makes it easier to prevent power disconnection, lowering power tariffs, and further attracting investment.

Telecommunications

Dadra and Nagar Haveli has an efficient telecommunications network. Facilities like email and internet are available at Silvassa, whereas STD, ISD and postal facilities are available even in remote areas of the territory.

Resources

Official Government Website
www.dnh.nic.in/

DAMAN AND DIU

Area	112 sq km
Population	242,911
Capital	Daman
Literacy rate	87.07 percent
Principal religions	Hinduism
Principal languages	Gujarati

- Daman and Diu has the geographic advantage of being quite close to Mumbai, which is situated approximately 193 kilometers away.
- Due to its strategic location and its scenic beauty, Daman and Diu is witnessing rapid growth in its tourism industry

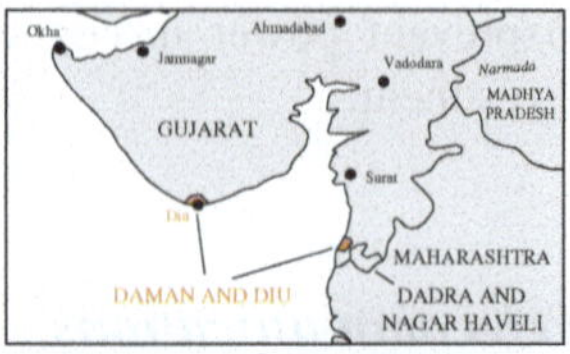

Overview

Daman and Diu covers a total area of 112 km^2, with Daman spanning 72 km^2 and Diu spanning 40 km^2. Daman, the capital, is bounded by Gujarat on the east; by the Arabian Sea on the west; by the Kolak River on the north; and by the Kalai River to the south. Diu is a tiny island with a coastal length of 21 km situated slightly off the coast of Kathiawar near the Port of Veraval in Gujarat, about 768 km from Daman and bounded by the Junagadh and Amreli Districts of Gujarat in the north and by the Arabian Sea from three sides. Diu is connected by two bridges with the mainland and is 4.6 km long by 13.8 km wide. The topography is generally plain and the altitude is about 6 m above sea level.

Due to its advantageous location and scenic beauty, it is considered to be one of the more preferred tourism destinations, with tourist traffic rising year on year. It enjoys much greenery and provides an atmosphere conducive to the growth of various agricultural crops.

Business Opportunities

The union territory of Daman and Diu is becoming a preferred destination for investors due to its fast development of industrial and tourism sectors. The Omnibus Industrial Development Corporation of Daman and Diu is the main authority to assist and promote the region's economic development in various areas covering industries, tourism and agriculture-related activities.

Agriculture

Important field and garden crops are rice, ragi, bajra, jowar, groundnut, pulses, beans, wheat, banana, mango, sapota, coconut and sugarcane. The total area under irrigation is 393.93 ha and non-irrigated area is 3,304.73 ha. There are no major forests in the union territory.

Small-Scale Industry

There are 2,930 small-scale and medium-scale industries in Daman and Diu. The Omnibus Industrial Development Corporation undertook projects with two industrial estates, while other industrial estates are Dabhel, Bhimpore, Kachigam and Kadaiya.

Tourism

The union territory of Daman and Diu has been declared as a special tourism destination due to its strategic location and scenic beauty. It has beautiful beaches, churches, forts and rich cultural heritage. Important tourist places in Daman are: Bom Jesus Chruch, Our Lady of the Sea Church; Our Lady of Remedios Church; Fort of Moti Daman; Fort of Nani Daman; Jampore Beach; Mirasol Garden and Mirasal Water Park.

Infrastructure

The government of Daman and Diu has undertaken several infrastructure projects to provide sound physical connectivity of the territory with the other parts of the country. Its transport links by road, rail and air to the business centers of Mumbai, Surat, Baroda and Ahmedabad are vital.

Roadways

The total length of roads in Daman and Diu are 191 and 78 km respectively. Daman is situated on the southern border of Gujarat state. It is about 193 km from Mumbai and 367 km from Ahmedabad. Mumbai-Ahmedabad National Highway No. 8 connects Daman and Vapi.

Railways

There is no rail link with Daman and Diu. The nearest railway station from Daman is Vapi (about 12 km), on the Western Railway's Mumbai-Delhi route. All major express/mail and local train stations are accessible at Vapi. A taxi service is also available between Daman and Vapi charged on a per head basis. The other nearby railway head is Valsad Junction, about 35 km away. Similarly, Diu does not have a railway facility. Its nearest railway station is Delwada 9 km away. Veraval, which is directly connected to Rajkot, Ahmedabad and other major cities is located 90 km in distance from Diu.

Aviation

Diu is well-connected by air. It has one airport at Nagoa which provides Diu-Mumbai daily flights by Jet Airways. Daman's nearest airport is Mumbai, where both domestic and international flights are easily available.

Power

Daman and Diu receive adequate power allocation from central sector power stations in the western region. All villages in the territory have electricity.

Telecommunications

Efficient telephone services exist in the union territory through STD and ISD facilities to every important place, both national and international. Telex and fax facilities are also easily available.

Resources

Official Website of Daman
http://www.daman.nic.in/
Official Website of the District Administration of Diu
http://diu.gov.in/

DELHI

Area	1,483 sq km
Population	16.7 million
Capital	Delhi
NSDP at current prices	US$34.4 billion (2008-09); 15.41% Y/Y growth
Per capita NSDP at current prices	US$1995 (2008-09); 12.22% Y/Y growth
Literacy rate	86.34 percent
Principal religions	Hinduism, Islam, Sikhism and Christianity
Principal languages	Hindi, Punjabi, Urdu and English

- Delhi is the nation's capital city and the largest commercial center in northern India
- Major sectors of FDI growth include real estate, business process outsourcing, information technology and telecom
- Delhi is the largest center for small-scale industries, including manufacturing of televisions, automobile parts, textiles and software

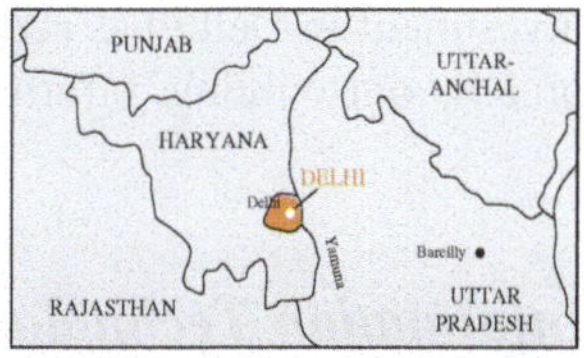

Overview

Delhi, the capital of India, is its third largest city covering an area of 1,483 km^2. It lies in the northern part of the country and is surrounded by Haryana on all its sides except the east, where it borders with Uttar Pradesh. It is comprised of two contrasting yet complimentary parts, Old Delhi and New Delhi, and is the travel hub of Northern India.

Standing along the west end of the Gangetic Plain, the city is rich with culture, architecture and human diversity. It is one of the fastest growing Indian cities and home to a fair amount of business and commercial activity in addition to its main role as the political center of the nation. It has an economy supported by agriculture, tourism, commerce and a well-established industrial set up. The city has also become the most vibrant creative arts center in India. Delhi also plays host to a number of national and international events including sports related events, conferences and seminars.

Delhi is becoming one of the nation's most preferred investment destinations, providing opportunities in almost all sectors, particularly information technology, tourism and small scale industry.

Business Opportunities

Delhi is considered to be one of the most preferred investment hot spots in India. It has efficient infrastructure and a relatively high standard of civic amenities. It has a rich cultural heritage and many places of tourist interest, including historical monuments, museums, art galleries, gardens and markets. Foreign direct investment in Delhi has seen major growth in sectors such as real estate, business process outsourcing, information technology and telecom.

Information Technology

The government of Delhi, recognizing the enormous potential of IT and IT enabled services, has embarked upon an ambitious journey to spread its benefit all over the city. This includes several measures, like setting up the first Information Technology Park of Delhi at Shastri Park with the most modern state-of-the-art infrastructure. The government has also engineered an IT policy with the aim of creating a conducive environment for investment in the sector and consequent growth of the IT industry and IT infrastructure.

Small Scale Industry

Delhi is the largest center for small industries and the small scale sector has played an important role in the industrial development of the city. These industries manufacture a wide variety of items like televisions, tape recorders, light engineering machines, automobile parts, sports goods, bicycles, footwear, textiles, fertilizers, medicine, leather goods and software. In order to assist, finance and promote the interest of these industries, the Delhi government has set up Delhi State Industrial Development Corporation. The corporation established many industrial estates in Delhi, including Kirtinagar Industrial Area, Mangolpuri Industrial Area, Naraina Industrial Area and Okhla Industrial Area.

Tourism

The union territory of Delhi is a fusion of ancient and modern cultures. It has a large number of beautiful places in the form of forts, monuments, palaces, gardens, museums and bazaars constructed by different rulers during its long history. These include Lal Quila (Red Fort), Jama Masjid, Qutub Minar, India Gate, Laxmi Narain Mandir (Birla Mandir), Humayun's Tomb; Lotus Temple and Dilli Haat.

In order to promote tourism, the government set up the Delhi Tourism and Transportation Development Corporation Limited. The corporation distributes tour-related materials through tourist information centers throughout the city, conducts city sight-seeing and excursion tours, offers adventurous outdoor activities and has also undertaken in restoration of monuments.

Infrastructure

Delhi has one of the best developed infrastructure facilities in the form of a well-connected transportation network and an efficient power supply system.

Roadways

Delhi has a well-connected road network. The total length of its road network is roughly 28,508 km. Delhi has the second most dense road network. It has five national highways passing through its territory, namely, NH-1, NH-2, NH-8, NH-10 and NH-24. They connect the national capital with the rest of the country. It consists of three inter-state bus terminals at Kashmeri Gate, Sarai Kalen Khan and Anand Vihar.

Delhi Transport Corporation (DTC) buses are the most popular means of transportation in Delhi. They not only operate within the cities but also operate to neighbouring states. All buses run on compressed natural gas to limit pollution, making DTC the world's largest compressed natural gas bus service. Other bus services by private companies are also available.

Railways

Delhi's railway network consists of four important railway stations: Old Delhi, New Delhi, Hazrat Nizamuddin and Sarai Rohila railway station. To divert the heavy traffic at New Delhi and Old Delhi railway stations, a new railway station is under construction. Over 350 passenger trains and 40 cargo trains travel to Delhi's railways daily.

To relieve traffic congestion, the Delhi Metro Rail Corporation aims to establish a complete metro rail network covering the entire city by the year 2021. The first two phases of the project created a total of 142 stations expanding over 189.63 km by late 2010. Currently, parts of North Delhi, East Delhi, Central Delhi and West Delhi are reachable through the metro system. The third phase of the project, which was approved by the Delhi Government in 2011, will cover 108 km. New routes will cover South Delhi, Gurgaon and Noida.

Aviation

Delhi has a well-developed aviation sector and has an extensive network of international and domestic flights. It has three airports, Indira Gandhi International

Airport for international flights; Palam Airport for national air services; and Safdarjung Airport for training purposes. The Indira Gandhi International Airport, rated as India's busiest and largest airport, is conveniently located 24 km south of New Delhi. There are 56 airlines in operation connecting to 55 scheduled international destinations. The airport is directly accessible by metro railway or through the national highway system.

Resources

Government of National Capital Territory of Delhi
http://www.delhigovt.nic.in/index.asp

GOA

Area	3,702 sq km
Population	1.45 million
Capital	Panaji
NSDP at current prices	US$3.7 billion (2007-08); 24.72% Y/Y growth
Per capita NSDP at current prices	US$2382 (2007-08); 20.66% Y/Y growth
Literacy rate	87.40 percent
Principal religions	Hinduism and Catholicism
Principal languages	Konkani, Marathi and English

- Goa's main industries are electronics, pharmaceuticals, agro-chemicals and tourism
- A new international airport is being established and roads widened to facilitate access to metropolitan cities and centers of trade and commerce
- Goa Industrial Development Corporation established over 7,000 small-scale industrial units and 20 industrial estates

Overview

Goa, a tiny emerald land on the west coast of India, is situated between the borders of Maharashtra and Karnataka. It covers a total area of 3,702 km^2 and comprises two Revenue districts, North Goa and South Goa. To its north runs the Terekhol River, which separates Goa from Maharashtra, and to the south lies the North Canara district of Karnataka. To the east are the Western Ghats and on the west is the Arabian Sea. Panaji, Margao, Vasco, Mapusa and Ponda are Goa's main towns. A striking feature of the state is the harmonious relationship among its various religious communities.

Goa has emerged as one of the most developed states in India and is recognized as being one of the best states with regard to investment environment and infra-structure. It is well connected to metropolitan cities and centers of trade and commerce through road, rail, and sea-routes as well as by air and the connections will improve further with the establishment of a new international airport and widening of national highways. Goa has a natural port in Mormugao, as well as minor ports, which have tremendous potential to improve trade facilities. It has full-fledged internet connectivity and a large network of telephone exchanges, helping it to become a front runner in the development of the economy.

There are rich forests and mineral resources in Goa and a variety of agricultural and horticultural crops are grown here. The state has shown remarkable progress in areas such as tourism, electronics, pharmaceuticals and agro-chemicals. It makes a substantial contribution of foreign exchange through mining and tourism to the national exchequer.

Business Opportunities

Goa is considered a global business destination attracting investment from both local and foreign entrepreneurs, multinational companies and international agencies, including non-resident Indians. A wide range of forests, navigable rivers, a long coastline rich in marine wealth and a natural harbor as well as beautiful and clean beaches attract a large number of tourists, both domestic and international. There is tremendous scope for promoting the state's tourism sector.

Industries

The state has 7,322 small-scale industrial units, 209 large scale industries and 20 industrial estates. The Small Industries Service Institute, Margao is involved in extending techno-managerial and economic consultancy services for the development of small scale industries. Because of large mineral products like ferro-manganese, bauxite, manganese and iron ore, there is immense potential for developing mineral-based industries in the state. Such mineral resources make a substantial contribution to the economy of the state through exports.

The State Government has been providing incentives to set up new environmentally friendly and viable industrial units in the less developed areas. Efforts are also being made to create high value-added industries with high employment potential.

The information technology industry is very well suited to Goa owing to the industry's non-polluting nature and the fact that it makes conservative demands on precious resources such as land, electricity and water. Goa is well placed to move towards being a knowledge economy. The government has recognized that information technology is the key to enhancing the welfare of its citizens as it can create employment opportunities for an increasing proportion of the population in a variety of diverse sectors.

Fisheries

Fishing is another traditional and important economic activity here. Goa, being located on the west coast of India, has a coastline extending over 100 km and inland waterways of another 250 km, rich in marine wealth. Prawns, mackerel and sardines are readily available. Many small scale units are based on these resources like salt curing of mackerel, fish meat, fish oils and dried fish.

Fishing has also given a big boost to canning, freezing and other fish processing units in the state, which expanded the state's export opportunities. Fish oil extraction and fish meal manufacturing plants can also be set up by utilizing these rich fisheries resources. To combat the decline in fish catch due to overexploitation and excessive mechanization, the government has issued policy bans on fishing during breeding season and on issuing licenses to new vessels.

Tourism

Goa has emerged as an important tourism destination in India, both for domestic and foreign tourists. It has natural scenic beauty, golden and silvery, beaches, springs, lakes and waterfalls. It is also famous for its man-made monuments, forts, churches, temples and wild life sanctuaries. A blend of the eastern and western culture, as well as very friendly and hospitable people, makes Goa a veritable tourist paradise. Since tourism is a major economic activity of Goa, it has made a substantial contribution to the economic development of the state in terms of employment generation and valuable foreign exchange earnings to the nation.

Infrastructure

Goa has an excellent road and rail network, centrally located airport and well-developed seaports. It has one of the country's highest tele-densities. Fiber optic connectivity has also spread its network across the state, bringing state of the art telecommunication to the people. There is sufficient power reserve in the state. Accordingly, the government of Goa has undertaken several infrastructure projects to encourage private sector participation and investment.

Roadways

Goa is connected by road to all the major towns and states in India. It is easily accessible by roads from Mumbai, Pune, Bangalore, Mangalore, Kolhapur and Hyderabad. Of the motorable roads in the state, national highways constitute 224 km; state highways 232 km; and district roads 815 km. NH-17 connects Goa to Bombay, Mangalore, Mormugao Harbour, Cortalim and Verna. NH-4A connects Panaji to Belgaum and to cities in the Deccan. Additions to the National Highway, comprising 135 km of expressway, 6 major bridges, 6 tunnels, 10 fly-overs, toll plazas and other road structures, are being installed linking Patradevi to Pollem.

Railways

Goa is linked with Maharashatra and Karnataka States through the Konkan Railway, which is a railway of 760 km connecting Mumbai and Mangalore. The

Konkan Railway traverses the entire length of the state, contributing to the growth of trade and industry. Vasco da Gama is connected with Bangalore and Belgaum on the South Central Railway, at present for goods traffic only.

Ports and Waterways

Goa has a well-developed internal water transport network formed by a grid of navigable rivers. This offers industries a most economical mode of transport for their goods and raw materials throughout the state. Mormugao is the major port in the state and can accommodate over 50 ships in outer anchorage. This is a modern port exporting the largest amount of iron ore in India.

Aviation

Goa's Dabolim International Airport is just 25 km away from the state capital, Panaji. It is one of the few destinations in India, where international chartered flights are allowed to land from different countries like Great Britain, Germany, Russia, Finland, Sweden and Norway. Some international flights to Gulf countries have also been introduced. Once the new greenfield international airport project in Mopa is completed, the air traffic in Goa will improve in its efficiency.

Telecommunications

Goa is well connected to a national and international telecommunications network hub. In addition to Bharat Sanchar Nigam Limited (BSNL), the backbone provider owned by the government of India, private players like Reliance, Tata Teleservices, Airtel etc., offer various telecommunications services, wireless voice and mobile internet. A number of broadband and dial-up connectivity options are available, including satellite link, infrastructure for setting up VPN's, video conferencing and voice telecommunications.

Goa has achieved an almost 100% automatic telephone system, with a very good network of telephone exchanges. All towns are well connected to the STD and ISD network. Goa has a fiber optical cable network spread throughout the state, which provides high speed access to a wide range of internet related services.

Power

Except for one 48 MW Haptha-based power plant and two cogeneration power plants, Goa does not have its own power generation plants. Most of its power is distributed from central generating stations from the neighboring state grids and amounts up to 398 MW. However, sub-stations and additional power transformer are being installed across Goa.

Resources

Official Portal of the Government of Goa
https://www.goa.gov.in
Goa Industrial Development Corporation
http://www.goaidc.com/home.html
Goa Chamber of Commerce and Industry
http://www.goachamber.org/cms/index.php

GUJARAT

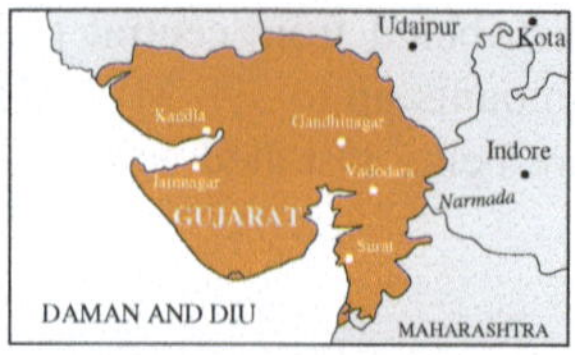

Area	196,024 sq km
Population	60.38 million
Capital	Gandhinagar
NSDP at current prices	US$63.5 billion (2008-09); 9.96% Y/Y growth
Per capita NSDP at current prices	US$1111 (2008-09); 8.40% Y/Y growth
Literacy rate	79.31 percent
Principal religions	Hinduism, Jainism, Islam and Buddhism
Principal languages	Gujarati, Hindi and English

- Gujarat's coastline is a third of the nation's waterfront
- Eight out of every ten diamonds in the world is polished in Surat, the "Diamond Capital of the World"
- Gujarat is the second leading producer of gold in the world
- Gujarat has the largest number of oil and gas fields of any Indian state

Overview

Gujarat is situated on the west coast of India, covering an area of nearly 200,000 km (5.96% of India's total area). It is bound by Arabian Sea on the west, by Rajasthan on the northeast, by Madhya Pradesh on the southeast, and by Maharashtra on the south. It shares a common international border with Pakistan at its northwestern fringe. It has a coastline of approximately 1,600 km, the longest among all the states in India.

Gujarat is India's leading industrial state. It houses a number of multinational corporations, private sector companies, public sector enterprises and a large number of medium and small scale companies, such as ABB, GM and Pfizer. It is a manufacturing powerhouse with world-class production capabilities in textiles, petrochemicals, pharmaceuticals and agricultural products. The state is also known for its robust social and physical infrastructure.

One of Gujarat's most prospering sectors is gems and jewelry. Gujarat is the second leading producer of gold in the world and also contributes a remarkable 85% to the country's total jewelry production. Eight out of every ten diamonds in the world is polished in Surat, one of Gujarat's major cities, the "Diamond Capital of the World." Gujarat is also the hub of the oil and gas industry, possessing the largest number of the oil and gas fields in India. It is the largest producer of crude oil, accounting for 53% of the national production and the second largest producer of onshore natural gas in India, accounting for 30% of national production. India's largest liquefied natural gas terminals are in the process of being set up at Dahej port.

Gujarat is rich in bioresources and has a forest cover of 1.88 billion ha. It has 10.7 million ha of highly diversified cropping area and is a leading producer of horticultural crops. Moreover, the state is rich in mineral resources such as limestone, lignite and bauxite, as well as natural gas. It is also a leading producer of cement and soda ash. In terms of agriculture, the state is a leading producer of cotton, castor seeds and phylum husk.

Business Opportunities

The state is keen to leverage its natural resource base and entrepreneurial spirit to sustain its leadership position in the Indian economy. To attract investment, Gujarat has set up single window facilities at the district level.

Infrastructure

Gujarat has actively sought private participation to improve existing infrastructure facilities and was the first in the country to develop port facilities, estates and roads in conjunction with the private sector.

Roadways

The total length of roads in Gujarat is approximately 137,617 km, out of which state highways take up 19,163 km. NH-8A operates Ahmedabad-Limbdi-Morbi-Kandla route, NH-8B connects Bamanbor-Rajkot-Gondal-Jetpur and Porbandar. NH-8C connects Chiloda-Gandhinagar and Sarkhej. The first Express Highway No.1 also runs between Ahmedabad and Vadodara.

Railways

The rail traffic in Gujarat mainly falls under the following divisions of the Western Railway, namely—Vadodara, Rajkot, Bhavnagar, Mumbai and Ahmedabad. The total length of railway lines in the state is 5,188 km. Gujarat is connected to the rest of India by railways at six points—three towards Rajasthan, one towards Madhya Pradesh and two towards Maharashtra. Northern Saurashtra, central and eastern Gujarat are well connected through broad gauge lines, while southern Saurashtra and Kutch do not have direct connectivity to the rest of the country by broad gauge lines.

Aviation

Gujarat has the highest number (14) of airports of any Indian state. Of these, Ahmedabad is an international airport conveniently located 8 km from

Ahmedabad Railway Station and 17.1 km from Gandhinagar. International flights are operated by Air India, Jet Airways, Malaysia Airlines and Singapore Airlines. There are also thirteen domestic airports in Gujarat. Domestic airlines are run by Indian, Jet Lite, Air Deccan, Kingfisher Airlines, Spice Jet, Go Air and IndiGo. Air India, Jet Airways and Air Sahara operate both domestically and internationally.

Ports

Gujarat has a 1,600 km long coastline, representing a third of the nation's water front. The State has one major port located in Kandla, which handles the most traffic among all major ports in India (13%). It also has 11 intermediate ports and 29 minor ports, geographically dispersed across southern Gujarat (13 ports), Saurashtra (23 ports) and Kutch (4 ports). Ports in Gujarat handle 35% of the total cargo in India and this number is predicted to grow to 39% by 2015. Many of Gujarat's ports are privatized and the cargo handled by them account for 80% of cargo handled by all private ports in India. Gujarat is the only state so far in the country where ports are being built on the build-own-operate-transfer scheme.

Power

Gujarat has an uninterrupted supply of power. It is ranked third place in terms of total installed capacity of power generation in India with one of the highest per capita power consumption rates. It has rich gas reserves and is the only Indian state with 2,200 km-long integrated state-wide gas grid.

Telecommunications

Gujarat has one of the highest tele-density among Indian states. The telephone connectivity in Gujarat accounts for around 7% of telephone connections in India for both telephone line and mobile services.

Resources

Official Gujarat State Portal
http://www.gujaratindia.com/
Vibrant Gujarat
http://www.vibrantgujarat.com/

HARYANA

Area	44,212 sq km
Population	25.35 million
Capital	Chandigarh
NSDP at current prices	US$43.7 billion (2009-10); 14.97% Y/Y growth
Per capita NSDP at current prices	US$1757 (2009-10); 13.01% Y/Y growth
Literacy rate	76.64 percent
Principal religions	Islam, Sikhism and Hinduism
Principal languages	Hindi

- Haryana has one of the highest per capita incomes in India
- Its prominent industries include agro-based food processing, electronics and IT, automobiles, textile sectors, and software-Haryana is India's third largest software exporter
- Haryana is also the leading producer of automobiles and automotive components

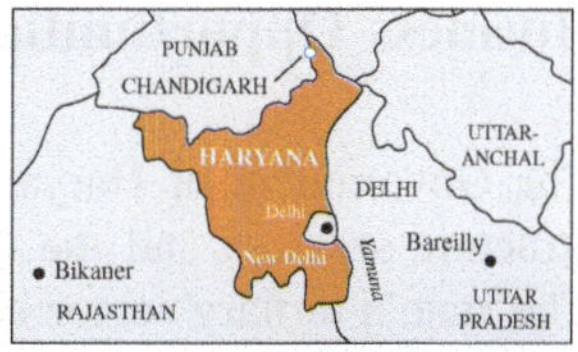

Overview

Haryana, with a total land area of 44,212 km, lies in the northern part of India. It is bounded by Uttar Pradesh on the east; Punjab on the west; Himachal Pradesh on the north; and Rajasthan on the south. It borders the National Capital Territory of Delhi from three sides, and has become a preferred destination for investors worldwide. About 40% of the National Capital Region falls in Haryana state and 30% of the state is notified NCR.

Chandigarh, the capital of Haryana, was the first planned city in the country with a high standard of civic amenities. It is also a home to a fair amount of business and commercial activity. Haryana's close proximity to Delhi, northern India's largest commercial hub, provides numerous investment opportunities.

Agriculture is the foundation of more than 65% of Haryana's population and contributes to 26.4% of Haryana's GDP. Main crops are rice, wheat, jowar, bajra, maize, barley and pulses, sugarcane, cotton, oilseeds and potato. The government is promoting sustainable agriculture by encouraging resource conserving technologies and organic farming.

Haryana has a sound industrial and infrastructure base, offering excellent locations to entrepreneurs to set up their industrial units. It offers a rich reservoir of skilled, motivated and relatively low-cost manpower. It ranks as one of the highest per capita income states. As a result, it has been able to attract sizable investment from multinational companies such as IBM India, Nestle India and Tata Consultancy Services, large business houses, foreign investors, non-residents Indians and small scale entrepreneurs.

Major export items are software, handloom products, scientific instruments, garments, automobiles and automotive components, electrical appliances and rice.

Business Opportunities

The Government of Haryana is emphasizing the planned development of infrastructure services and the diversification of the agricultural and industrial base. The state's tertiary sector is the fastest growing sector, driven by growth in subsectors like IT. The state government has clearly identified additional opportunities in property development and retailing, and petrochemicals.

Infrastructure

Haryana has impressive infrastructure facilities in terms of well-developed roadways, railways and airways networks; reliable telecommunication services; and an efficient power supply system. All such services have made the state an investor-friendly destination. Accordingly, the Government of Haryana has undertaken several infrastructure projects, with a view to encourage capital flow into the state as well as increase the productivity level of the various economic sectors.

Roadways

Haryana has an excellent network of road transport. All villages are well connected with metalled roads. The total length of roads in the state is more than 34,772 km. There are 11 national highways in the state, some of which are:

- National Highway No.1, which passes through Haryana from Delhi to Ambala, linking Punjab, Himachal Pradesh and Jammu and Kashmir
- National Highway No.2 (Delhi-Mathura Road), which passes through Faridabad, linking vast areas to Uttar Pradesh and Madhya Pradesh
- National Highway No.8 (Delhi-Jaipur Highway), which passes through Guraon's prestigious industrial estate, Industrial Model Township Manesar, and Growth Center Bawal, linking vast areas right up to Ahemdabad and Mumbai
- National Highway No.10, which passes through Haryana from Delhi to Dabwali

Railways

Haryana is well connected on the rail network. Ambala, Panipat, Kalka, Kurukshetra, Rohtak, Jind, Hissar and Jakhal are important railway stations. There is also a railway workshop at Jagadhari. A proposal is underway to provide a rail corridor connecting towns around Delhi, linking the major towns of Haryana like Faridabad, Gurgaon, Bahadurgarh and Kundli. A rapid mass transportation system linking Haryana's main towns with Delhi is being planned.

Aviation

Haryana is well-linked to rest of the country through air services. There are civil aerodromes at Pinjore, Karnal, Hisar, Bhiwani and Narnaul. The nearest airports are located in Punjab, Delhi and Chandigarh.

Power

Haryana became the first state in India to achieve 100% rural electrification in 1970. Presently, it has a total installed contracted generation capacity of 5,665 MW. Seventeen new sub-stations and 6,500 new transformers are installed to enhance the power distribution system. The State is also planning to generate 1,400 MW of electricity through the use of renewable energy.

Telecommunications

Bharat Sanchar Nigam Limited (BSNL) and most of the leading private sector players such as Reliance Infocom, Tata Teleservices, Bharti Telecom, Idea and Hutchison Essar have operations in the state.

Resources

Official Web Portal of Haryana Government
http://www.haryana.gov.in/

HIMACHAL PRADESH

Area	55,673 sq km
Population	6.85 million
Capital	Shimla
NSDP at current prices	US$7.8 billion (2009-10); 12.47% Y/Y growth
Per capita NSDP at current prices	US$1110 (2009-10); 10.49% Y/Y growth
Literacy rate	83.78 percent
Principal religions	Buddhism
Principal languages	Hindi and Pahari

- Some of the prominent industries of Himachal Pradesh include agriculture, IT, biotechnology and tourism
- The government has given the tourism industry high priority and is committed to improving infrastructures in the state for this purpose; encouraging private sectors to participate
- Himachal Pradesh's large water resources provides immense hydroelectric potential

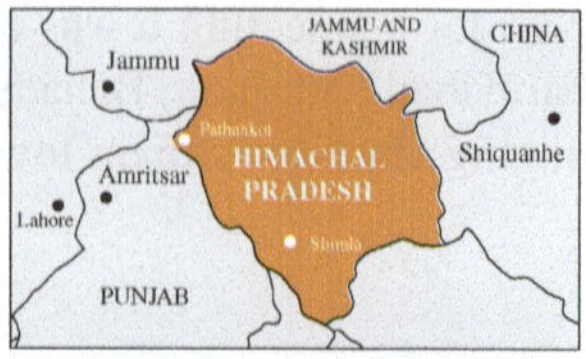

Overview

Himachal Pradesh is situated in the heart of the Western Himalayas. It covers an area of 55,673 km^2 and is bordered by Jammu and Kashmir to the north; Punjab to the west and southwest; Haryana in the south; Uttar Pradesh in the southeast; and Tibet and China on the east. Its topography is varied as is its climate. The region is home to shadowy valleys, rugged hills, glaciers, gigantic pines, and roaring rivers. The northeastern part of the state is decorated with snow-covered, silver-headed mountains, lakes and green prairies. The state is identified as "Dev Bhumi" and is believed to be the abode of gods and goddesses and is populated with stone and wood temples.

The forests of Himachal Pradesh constitute two-thirds of the state's geographic area and are crucial to the region's environmental and economic well-being. They are a storehouse of rich biodiversity and vital to preserving the fragile Himalayan ecosystem. They also act as the primary source of livelihood for the rural population. The favorable climate facilitates the production of a wide variety of crops, including vegetables, fruit, flowers, rice, and commercial crops.

Business Opportunities

Opportunities remain in agriculture-based, forest-based, food processing, beverages, information technology, electronic and high-tech industries. The government of Himachal Pradesh offers attractive tax and fiscal benefits to prospective entrepreneurs and investors.

Agriculture

Being a predominantly agricultural state, it produces a large variety of food including maize, rice, wheat and other cereal crops. The large climate range also gives farmers the ability to cultivate a large variety of fruit ranging from temperate to subtropical.

Agriculture, the main occupation in Himachal Pradesh, has an important role in the economy of the state. It provides direct employment to about 71% of the working population. Income from the agriculture and allied sectors accounts for nearly 21.7% of the total state domestic product. Total food grain production during 2010–2011 was 1,579 thousand tons.

Rice and wheat are also important cereal crops; soybean, sunflower and rapeseed are important oilseed crops; and urid, bean, moong, kidney bean and gram are important pulse crops in the state.

Maize is the most important crop of Himachal Pradesh, where surplus is available for processing. Under the state industrial policy, a number of incentives are available to the investors in the food processing industry. Processors of ginger, potato and vegetables offer great potential for investment. Because the temperate climate of the state is quite suitable for production of disease-free seed, the government is encouraging private sector participation in the exploitation of vast seed production potential.

The state has also made significant progress in the development of horticulture. The topographical variations and differences in altitude coupled with fertile, deep and well-drained soil favor the cultivation of temperate to subtropical fruit. The main fruit under cultivation are apple, pear, peach, plum, apricot, mango, litchi, guava and strawberry. The region is also suitable for the cultivation of ancillary horticultural products like flowers, mushrooms, honey, hops, tea, and medicinal and aromatic plants.

Information Technology

The government has developed an IT Vision-2010 in collaboration with NASSCOM to make Himachal Pradesh an IT destination. Under the IT policy, the status of industry has been accorded to all IT projects, including IT-related services and educational institutions. As such, all the incentives available to the industry under the presently applicable industrial policy are also being made available to the IT units in the state.

Biotechnology

Himachal has the potential to develop various types of industries using its raw material base of fruit, vegetables, high value cash crops and other naturally growing herbal plants. These industries can be in the following: biopharmaceuticals, bioprospecting, fermentation, post-harvest processing, bioprocessing, pharmaceuticals, biochemical, genetically engineered micro-organisms, enzyme production, environment protection and animal husbandry.

Tourism

Tourism has been recognized as one of the most significant sectors of the economy in Himachal Pradesh and as a major engine for future growth. The state has some natural advantages to help develop tourism as an industry. It has a rich treasure of pilgrimage sites, it is endowed with geographical and cultural diversity and the environment is clean. It is also home to Rishies like Vyas, Prashar, Vashist, Markandey and Lamas. Hot water springs, historic forts, forests, mountains, rivers, and natural and man-made lakes are all potential tourist destinations. The tribal areas are known for their natural beauty and have recently been opened up to foreign tourists.

The tourism industry has been given a very high priority and the government has developed appropriate infrastructure for its development, including the provision of public utility services, roads, communication networks, airports, transport facilities, water supply and civic amenities. The private sector is being encouraged to invest in tourism related projects on a build-operate-transfer basis.

For the promotion and development of the state from a tourism point of view, the government is focusing on the following areas: history related tourism; identification of new areas/tourist destinations; promotion of village tourism; improvement of infrastructure; pilgrimage tourism; tribal tourism, eco-tourism; adventure tourism; wildlife tourism; and cultural tourism.

Infrastructure

Himachal Pradesh's infrastructure is the lifeline and major means of communication in the predominantly mountainous state. This includes an efficient transportation system (roadways, railways, airways and waterways) and suitable power network, mainly hydroelectric.

Roadways

The state's 16,807 inhabited villages are scattered over slopes of numerous mountain ranges and valleys. Currently, the total length of the road is about 30,913 km. Eleven National Highways, covering 1,471 km, connect to the state.

Approximately 450 km of additional roadway and 32 bridges will be added in 2012. Realizing the importance of constructing roads for connecting production areas with market centers, the Himachal Pradesh Government has proposed to connect every town and village with roads in the coming years.

Railways

The state of Himachal Pradesh is well connected through an efficient rail network. The rail heads in the state are located at Kalka, Pathankot and Una. Kalka, located 90 km away from Shimla, is connected by a broad-gauge. Chandigarh (120 km) and Delhi (380 km) can also be reached by train.

Aviation

Himachal Pradesh is well-linked with other states and cities of India through reliable air services. There are three airports in the state, Shimla at Jubbar Hatti, Kangra at Gaggal and Kullu at Bhuntar. Jubbarhatti airport is located 23 km from its capital city and has connecting flights to the nation's capital, Delhi.

There are also three airports under private sector: Banikhet in Chamba district, Paonta Sahib in Sirmaur District and Sunder Nagar in Mandi District. The government is also encouraging private sectors to consider helicopter services to enhance mobility to and within the state.

Waterways

Since there are no big water bodies in the state, water transport is mainly confined to the small artificial lakes created by hydroelectric projects. Currently, there are four major bodies of water where ferry transport activities are being carried out. These are Govind Sagar Lake in Bilaspur district, Pandoh Lake in Mandi district, Pong Lake in Kangra district and Chamera Lake in Chamba district.

Power

Himachal Pradesh has immense hydroelectric potential thanks to its five river basins. The Chenab, Rabi, Beas, Satluj and Yamuna, all of which originate in the Western Himalayas, pass through the state. The total identified potential in the state stands at 21,000 MW, which is a quarter of India's total hydroelectric power potential. An additional 2,106 MW of power capacity is expected to be installed during 2011–2012.

Resources

Himachal Pradesh Government, India—Official Web portal Home Page
http://himachal.nic.in/

JAMMU AND KASHMIR

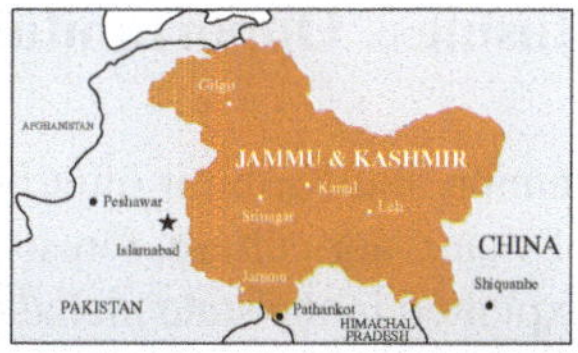

Area	222,236 sq km
Population	12.54 million
Capital	Srinagar (summer), Jammu (winter)
NSDP at current prices	US$6.1 billion (2007-08); 9.51% Y/Y growth
Per capita NSDP at current prices	US$546 (2007-08); 7.97% Y/Y growth
Literacy rate	68.74 percent
Principal religions	Islam and Hinduism
Principal languages	Urdu, Dogri and Kashmiri

- The Jammu and Kashmir area is largely agricultural, with about 80 percent of population depending on agriculture
- The main industries of the state include handicrafts, gems and jewelry, agriculture, horticulture and sericulture
- The state's rich reserves of water, agriculture, forests, herbal and mineral resources provide investment opportunities and certain mineral-based projects are open to private investment

Overview

Jammu and Kashmir, with a total land area of 222,236 km^2, constitutes the northern most extremity of India. It shares a border with Himachal Pradesh to the south, Pakistan to the west, the People's Republic of China to the north and east, and Afghanistan to the northwest. It consists of three district regions, namely, Jammu, Kashmir and Ladakh. Srinagar is its summer capital, and Jammu its winter capital. Geographically, the state has been divided into four zones, namely, the mountainous and semi-mountainous plain commonly known as the Kandi belt; hills including Shivalik ranges; mountains of Kashmir Valley and Pir Panchal range; and the Tibetan tract of Ladakh and Kargil.

The state is rich in art, culture and history as well as in archaeological and historical sites. The local population is adept at weaving and designing textile products. The handicraft and handloom sector act as the source of foreign exchange earnings for the economy.

The state is also rich in flora and fauna and possesses large mineral deposits. The snow clad mountains, lakes and pleasant weather conditions provides tremendous potential for investment in the tourism sector. The Kashmir Valley is famous for its mountainous landscape. Jammu is known as the "City of Temples," attracting large numbers of pilgrims every year. Ladakh, also known as "Little Tibet," is renowned for its remote mountain beauty and Buddhist culture.

Business Opportunities

Jammu and Kashmir offer boundless investment opportunities. It has rich reserves of water, agriculture, forests, herbal and mineral resources. Minerals commercially exploited in the state include coal, gypsum, bauxite, lignite, graphic and limestone. Some mineral-based projects have been opened to private investment. Main industrial units in the state which have been accorded the priority status include handlooms, handicrafts, gems and jewelry. However, the main occupation of the people in the state is agriculture and related activities like horticulture, sericulture and floriculture.

Agriculture

About 80% of the population of the state depends on agriculture. Rice, wheat and maize are the major crops. Barley, bajra and jowar are cultivated in some parts. Gram is grown in Ladakh. The horticulture industry in Kashmir has become the bulwark of the rural economy, providing jobs to thousands of people directly and indirectly. Major horticulture items are apples, pears, cherries, walnuts, almonds, peaches, saffron, apricots, strawberries and plums.

The state has a suitable climate for growing a variety of flowers. The floriculture industry offers a good source of supply to the domestic and international market. There is potential for this activity to be propagated on a commercial basis.

Tourism

Jammu and Kashmir, a bejeweled crown of India, provides varieties of cultural, religious spots, adventure and sightseeing activities. It is famous for its towering snow clad mountains, bubbling streams, transparent and sparkling lakes, flower meadows, colorful orchards and rare fauna. All such features of Jammu and Kashmir have always attracted numerous tourists from all over the world. Tourism has emerged as one of the major contributors to the state's economy.

There are various places of tourist attraction in the state which are visited by both foreign and domestic tourists. The Kashmir Valley is described as paradise on earth. Some other important tourist locations include Chashmashahi springs, Shalimar Bagh, Dal Lake, Dachigam, Gulmarg, Pahalgam, Sonamarg and Amarnath shrine in the Valley, Vaishnodevi shrine and Patnitop near Jammu and Buddhist monasteries in Ladakh. Ladakh festival in September and Sindhu Darshan in June are popular events. However, efforts are being made to support houseboat owners and develop village tourism in Jammu and Kashmir.

Infrastructure

The state has well-developed transportation system, comprising of roadways, railways and airways. It also has an efficient and reliable power and telecommunications network. In order to fully utilize the capacity of all such facilities as well as to upgrade their standards, the government has undertaken several infrastructure projects.

Roadways

The total road length maintained by PWD in the state is 15,012 km. Jammu and Kashmir is very well connected with the rest of the country through the National Highway system up to Leh through Kargil (Ladakh).

Railways

The state is well-linked to the rest of the country through a reliable rail network. Rail connectivity has been extended up to Jammu. Work on the Jammu-Udhampur railway line has been completed while work extending the railway line to Srinagar and Baramulla is ongoing.

Airways

There are major airports in Srinagar, Jammu and Ladakh connecting Jammu and Kashmir with the rest of the country. The nearest airport in Ladakh is located 6 km from the city center and Jammu airport is located 8 km from the city center. Srinagar airport, located 14 km from the city center, also has international flights to countries in the region.

Power

The state's total electricity requirement is met by purchasing power from the national grid. Top priority has been accorded to the power sector with great effort being put into tapping the state's vast hydroelectric potential estimated at 20,000 MW. The government's Power Development Department has opened up micro-hydroelectric projects for private investment.

Telecommunications

Modern telecommunication facilities including ISD, STD, Telex and Fax are widely available across the state. All districts are connected through India's computer network. The state also has access to internet facilities provided by the government agencies as well as by private agencies.

Resources

Official website of Jammu & Kashmir Government
http://jammukashmir.nic.in/—under construction
Official website of Jammu & Kashmir State Industrial Development Corporation
http://www.jksidco.org/

JHARKHAND

Area	79,714 sq km
Population	32.96 million
Capital	Ranchi
NSDP at current prices	US$14.7 billion (2008-09); 9.26% Y/Y growth
Per capita NSDP at current prices	US$484 (2008-09); 7.71% Y/Y growth
Literacy rate	67.63 percent
Principal religions	Buddhism, Jainism, Islam and Christianity
Principal languages	Santhali, Mundari, Krukh, Kortha, Nagpuria, Sadri, Khariya, Panchparagnia, Ho, Malto, Karmali, Bhojpuri, Hindi, Urdu and Bengali

- Jharkhand has the richest mineral base in India
- The state has large coal production; this allows for large capacity of thermal energy
- Many investment opportunities are available in Jharkhand's automotive industry

Overview

Jharkhand has been carved out of Bihar as the 28th state of the Indian Union. It is bounded by West Bengal in the east; Uttar Pradesh and Chhattisgarh in the west; Bihar in the north and Orissa in the south. Ranchi, the capital of Jharkhand, is located at a height of 2,100 feet above sea level in the heart of the Chotanagpur plateau.

The state has the richest mineral base in India and is widely recognized as a region of immense potential. As much as 40% of India's total mineral resources are deposited in the state. This includes large deposits of mica, bauxite, granite, gold, silver, graphite, magnetite, dolomite, fireclay, quartz, feldspar, coal, iron and copper. Jharkhand is the sole producer of coking coal and uranium. It is also blessed with forests and woodlands, water and energy reserves, as well as fertile land, all of which have helped make it one of India's most developed states.

Business Opportunities

The resource rich state of Jharkhand has an immense potential for investment due to its large mineral deposits, skilled labor force and responsive administrative set up. It has a well-established industrial base comprising of reputed business houses. The state, along with the adjoining areas of West Bengal, Orissa, Bihar and Chhattisgarh, provides a large consumer market. Its renowned technical institutions are a constant source of qualified and efficient manpower.

Automotive Parts

This sector offers several opportunities for investment due to the availability of raw materials and a large consumer market both in and around the state. These advantages include:

- Presence of large steel plants as a source of easy freight
- World class industries create an excellent vendor base to support the sector
- Several industries like Usha Martin, Timken, Cummins, Tinplate and Indal produce a wide range of engineering products
- Various industrial units involved in activities like mining and coking coal
- A good combined market for the sector is provided by Jharkhand along with Bihar, Orissa, West Bengal and Chhattisgarh
- Demand for white goods like refrigerators, washing machines and air conditioners is already high and rapidly increasing

Minerals

Because the state is a rich reserve of mineral resources, it has immense potential for the growth of mining and mineral-based industries. The important minerals available in the state are coal, iron ore, limestone, copper ore, bauxite, pyrite, china clay, fine clay, dolomite, graphite, soap stone, quartz sand and silica sand. Given this, there are numerous opportunities for investors. These include potential in the following areas:

- Iron ore (export potential)
- Steel production
- Sponge iron plant
- Cement plant
- Graphite electrodes and graphite powder
- Granite (export potential)
- Chemicals and fertilizers
- Bleaching powder, calcium carbide and lime related chemicals
- Ground mica, mica bricks and electrical appliances

The state government has been making all efforts to attract investment into this industry. These include the simplification of the procedures with respect to grant of mining leases, the provision of certain relief to make mining activities easier, and suitable steps for the adoption of state-of-the-art technology in mining.

Tourism

The Jharkhand Government has accorded “industry status” to the tourism sector and has initiated several steps to attract investment into it. It has been offering incentives for the provision of certain tourist facilities by the private investors, including hotels and motels, tourist resorts, camps and facilities for adventure tourism, and amusement parks.

Information Technology

The government considers the IT sector as an important tool to help change the state into a knowledge based-society. It has resolved to make Jharkhand an IT powerhouse and a front runner in the IT revolution. In order to fulfill these objectives, it has formulated an IT policy “to ensure overall socioeconomic development, sustained growth, transparency in government decisions, and enhanced service delivery to the people through an effective use of IT.”

Infrastructure

Jharkhand has a well-developed network of airways, railways and roadways. Its location, close to the ports of Kolkata, Haldia and Paradeep, provides an additional advantage to this connectivity. Numerous investment opportunities exist in the further expansion of the infrastructure in the state. These include:

- Construction of new roads and airports, expansion of existing roads, highways and airports
- Development of industrial parks and zones
- Development of three-tier growth centers
- Setting up IT and telecommunications infrastructure

Roadways

The total length of roads in the state is 5,668 km, which includes 1,006 km of national highways and 4,662 km of state highways. The Golden Quadrangular Super Highway also passes through the state. In order to further develop an efficient road network, the Jharkand Government aims to encourage private participation in the construction and maintenance of roads and bridges. They also hope to encourage private investment in the construction of expressways along the main high-density corridors across the state and in the management of interstate and intrastate bus terminals.

Railways

The state has an extensive and well-developed rail-network, providing vital links to the important cities and ports of India. It has efficient goods handling facilities at Ranchi, Bokaro, Dhanbad and Jamshedpur. In addition, ore loading facilities are available at Kiriburu, Lohardaga and at all the coal mines.

Aviation

The state has a good air linkage with the rest of the country. Ranchi, the state capital is connected with Delhi, Patna, Mumbai and Kolkata by regular air services. There are airstrips in Jamshedpur, Bokaro, Giridih, Deoghar, Hazaribagh, Daltonganj and Noamundi. An air cargo complex is being established in Ranchi, which is expected to bring many benefits to industries that mainly rely on exports of high value and perishable goods.

Power

There is immense potential to establish thermal, hydroelectric, geothermal atomic, methane and gas-based power plants in the state. The availability of coal in abundance makes Jharkhand an ideal state for setting up thermal power plants. The Government of Jharkhand has taken several initiatives for the development of this industry. It has signed a memorandum of understanding with the Government of India as a token of its commitment to the reforms in the power sector. Providing electricity to rural areas has been made top priority and work on renovation and modernization of existing power generating stations has already commenced. Electricity connections are present in 14,667 villages out of 32,620 villages, accounting for 45% of all villages in the state. The state is attracting private investment in the industry for its further growth.

Telecommunications

Jharkhand Telecom Circle, which is a newly created territorial unit of Bharat Sanchar Nigam Limited (BSNL), provides telecom services to all parts of the state.

The government has been upgrading the telecommunications facilities. All district headquarters are currently connected to the main network through reliable media.

Resources

Official Website of Government of Jharkhand
http://jharkhand.gov.in/

KARNATAKA

Area	191,791 sq km
Population	61.13 million
Capital	Bangalore
NSDP at current prices	US$59.7 billion (2009-10); 10.05% Y/Y growth
Per capita NSDP at current prices	US$1020 (2009-10); 8.88% Y/Y growth
Literacy rate	75.60 percent
Principal religions	Hinduism, Jainism, Islam and Christianity
Principal languages	Kannada, Telugu, Tamil, Malayalam, Hindi and English

- FDI inflows rank third nationally: 6.5 percent
- Karnataka's capital, Bangalore, is known as "The Silicon Valley of India"
- The state has the highest amount of investment in biotechnology in India
- Karnataka's software export accounts for more than 35 percent of India's software exports

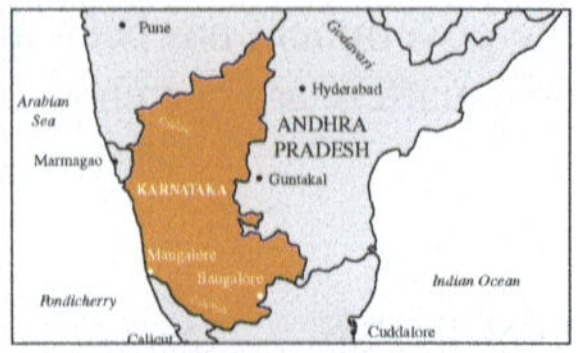

Overview

Located at the heart of southern India, Karnataka occupies a total area of 191,791 km^2 and is the eighth largest state in India. Its coastline is 320 km long.

Karnataka has become the information technology powerhouse of India. Much of the activity is focused on the state's capital, Bangalore. There are large numbers of software companies, employing hundreds of IT professionals every year. Bangalore is a melting pot of various races and cultures. This garden city has well-laid out parks, avenues of blossoming trees and a pleasant climate. It is also home to top-of-the-line companies in other sectors like engineering, pharmaceuticals, biotechnology, food processing, apparel, electronics and automobiles.

Well located on the agricultural and horticultural map of India, Karnataka produces a variety of food and cash crops. While it is an attractive hot spot for tourists due to its scenic beauty, the state has also become an industrial metropolis.

Business Opportunities

Karnataka has always been at the forefront of industrial growth in India. With its inherent capabilities coupled with its enterprising citizens, Karnataka provides an ideal choice for investment in India. Endowed with a favorable climate, it is involved in the production of several food and non-food crops. The main industrial units in the state are in the areas of information technology, biotechnology, textiles, steel, cement, handloom weaving and tourism. Karnataka is also known as the capital of Agarbathi (incense sticks), silk, coffee and sandalwood. There is an abundant availability of educated and trained technical manpower, particularly in engineering, management and basic sciences fields.

Industries

The state has the distinction of building a strong and vibrant industrial base, which combines the strengths of a large public sector, privately owned large and medium industries as well as a very wide and dispersed small-scale sector. Good labor relations have helped the state achieve preeminence on the industrial map. The government has been consistently pursuing progressive industrial policies to meet the changing needs of the state's economy and industry. Karnataka is among the most preferred destinations for foreign investment in India and over 66 of world's Fortune 500 companies have a presence here.

Being a major producer of cotton and silk, Karnataka has become a major center for textiles and garments with high export potential. The Karnataka Government actively encourages this by setting up apparel parks that offer modern facilities. In the handicrafts industry, Karnataka produces a wide range of objects like exquisite sandalwood carvings, intricate inlay work on rosewood, splendid bronzes, colorful toys, stone studded jewelry and incense sticks.

Karnataka is also home to other industries like electronics, telecommunications, aerospace, processed foods, automobiles, banking and finance, mining, steel, and cement production, all of which provide employment to a large number of people in the state.

Agriculture and Allied Activities

About 70% of the total population resides in rural areas, where their main occupation is agriculture and related activities, sustaining approximately 63% of the population. Major food and non-food crops are rice, raji, maize, wheat, oilseeds, pulses, groundnut, sunflower, cotton, silk, sandalwood, sugarcane and tobacco. The state's coffee production accounts for 70% of the nation's coffee production.

Karnataka enjoys a prominent position on the horticultural map of India. The state has natural resources, a favorable climate and an enterprising farming community, which offer ample opportunities for the all-round development of horticulture. The horticultural policy focuses on area expansion, dissemination of new technology and production and supply of planting materials. In addition, Karnataka ranks second among all states for floriculture production.

Minerals

Karnataka is rich in mineral resources. Its two major mines produce about 84% of India's gold production and the state has the second-largest iron ore reserves in India. Other minerals found in Karnataka include silver, copper, limestone, dolomite, chromite, magnesite and granite.

Biotechnology

Karnataka leads the Indian biotechnology revolution with its excellent infrastructure and a highly integrated environment for research. It is host to over 187 leading biotechnology companies and start-ups, as well as R&D facilities such as the Indian Institute of Science, the National Center for Biological Sciences, the Jawaharlal Nehru Center for Advanced Scientific Research, the University of Agricultural Sciences, the Central Food Technological Research Institute, and the Institute of Bio-Informatics and Biotechnology. The Karnataka Government is also planning to establish ten Biotechnology Finishing Schools to foster more qualified, industry-ready manpower.

Karnataka is the first state to establish a large scale biotechnology center to cater to the needs of farmers, with the objective to produce quality-plant materials and conserve the genetic diversity of horticulture plants. The state also formed a biotechnology policy to encourage investment, develop infrastructure and enhance human resources.

Information Technology

Karnataka, the silicon state of India, is a favored destination for information technology and other knowledge-based industries. The state has undertaken major initiatives in the e-governance area and has computerized all treasuries. It is programmed to implement the delivery of income certificates, birth and death certificates, old age pensions and domicile certificates under the Rural Digital Services Project.

Besides computerizing government offices, the latest information for farmers regarding crop production techniques, horticulture, animal husbandry, fishery, sericulture and dairy farming has also been computerized. The majority of Bangalore's software exports are in the high technology areas, IT access networks, optical networks, video broadcasting, Bluetooth, WAP, 3G Wireless Applications, VOIP, ATM switches and SDH.

The Karnataka Government's IT policy outlines its dedication to utilize the development of IT to improve the state's infrastructure. The policy aims to reduce poverty, empower women, create job opportunities in the IT industry, ensure effective communication between citizens and government through e-governance, promote business with non-English speaking countries and maintain Karnataka's position as a leading IT state.

The Karnataka government is planning on establishing Information Technology Investment Regions (ITIR) near Bangalore International Airport where investment amounting up to US$20 billion is expected by the year 2030. Approximately 255,000 direct and 857,000 indirect employment opportunities will be generated through this project and the government is inviting private companies engaged in the IT sector to participate.

Infrastructure

The Government of Karnataka has recognized the importance of sound and efficient infrastructure facilities in the overall socioeconomic development of the state. Accordingly, it has undertaken several infrastructure projects to attract significant investments into the economy. The state has a wide network of roads, railways, seaports and airways as well as an efficient power and telecommunications system. All such infrastructure services help to facilitate the movement of goods and services as well as connect the state with the rest of the nation. The government is also seeking the private sector's investment into the state's infrastructure development. It is planning to double the amount of investment from the present value of 4.5%. There were 88 projects worth Rs. 87,000 in various stages of development as of May 2010.

Roadways

The total length of roadways in Karnataka extends over 150,000 km. There are 96 road work projects underway and the length of road network is expected to increase by another 10,000 km.

Aviation

Karnataka has two international airports at Bangalore and Mangalore. Bangalore International Airport is the first private airport in India. Mysore airport has been upgraded and Hubli, Belgaum and Mangalore airports are currently undergoing upgradation. Karwar and Bidar defense airports will be opened for civil operation. New airport projects are proposed at Hassan, Shimoga, Bellary, Bijapur and Gulbarga. The government is also undertaking a project to set up 20 helipads to allow better accessibility within the state.

Railways

The total rail network in Karnataka connecting to major locations within the state is around 3,300 km. Mangalore is connected to Mumbai and other northern states through the Konkan Railway. Two monorail projects are underway in Bangalore, which is expected to alleviate traffic congestion in the capital city.

Ports

Karnataka has a major port in New Mangalore and 10 minor ports in Karwar, Belekeri, Tadri, Honnavar, Bhatkal, Kundapur, Hangarkatta, Malpe, Padubidri and Old Mangalore. The ports in Tadadi and Haldipur are undergoing expansion.

Power

Karnataka has 1,205 power stations. One third of the state's power capacity is generated from hydro sources. The state has the goal of reaching power-surplus status by the year 2014.

Telecommunication

Karnataka has 27.7 million subscribers using its wireless services and continues to receive more than a million new subscribers each year. It is ranked fourth in India in terms of number of internet subscribers.

Resources

Official Website of Government of Karnataka
http://www.karnataka.gov.in/Pages/Default.aspx
Karnataka Online
http://www.karnatakaonline.in/
Karnataka Udyog Mitra
http://www.kumbangalore.com/default.aspx?MenuID=45

KERALA

Area	38,863 sq km
Population	33.39 million
Capital	Thiruvananthapuram
NSDP at current prices	US$37.8 billion (2008-09); 15.31% Y/Y growth
Per capita NSDP at current prices	US$1113 (2008-09); 14.41% Y/Y growth
Literacy rate	93.91 percent
Principal religions	Hinduism, Islam and Christianity
Principal languages	Malayalam

- Kerala has the highest literacy rate among all states in India and one of the highest Human Development Index rankings
- The state is a major producer of coconut, rubber, pepper, cardamon, ginger, banana, cocoa, cashew, coffee and tea and has the highest-producing marine fish industry nationally
- Kerala is known for excellence in e-governance

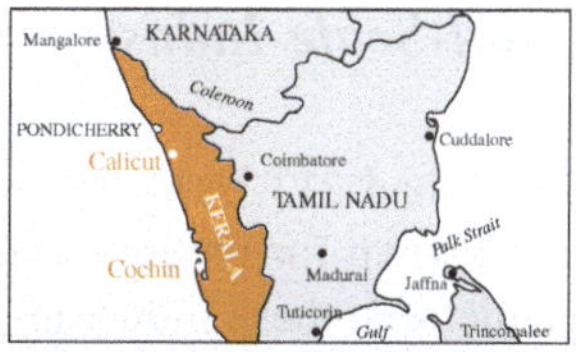

Overview

Kerala, situated on the southernmost tip of India, stretches along the coast of the Arabian Sea and is separated from the rest of the subcontinent by the steep Western Ghats. It is comprised of hills, valleys, midland plains, a coastal belt and backwaters. Numerous large and small rivers cut across the state with their tributaries and branches making the land quite fertile.

The state of Kerala constitutes one of the most advanced societies in India. Its literacy rate is the highest among all Indian states and is well above the national average. It has achieved good health standards, with low infant and maternal mortality rates.

Business Opportunities

Kerala's abundant natural resources provide immense opportunities for investors. The variety of cash crops and large forest reserves all help to create an investment friendly climate. Additionally, Kerala has important mineral deposits of limonite, monazite, zircon, clay and quartz sand. The state has the most literate workforce and the highest human development index in India, which have helped to create a conducive environment to establish business in the state. In addition, information technology and tourism also attract significant investments into the state's economy.

Small-Scale Industry

Kerala had 213,740 small-scale industries registered as of March 2010. Kerala is well known for its traditional industries such as handloom weaving, cashews and handicrafts; these industries employ more than 1 million people in the state. Other important industries include rubber and tea production, ceramics, electric and electronic appliances, telephone cables, transformers, bricks and tiles, drugs and chemicals, general engineering, plywood splints and veneers, soaps, oils, fertilizers as well as khadi and village industry products. There are a number of manufacturing units for production of precision instruments, machine tools, petroleum products, paints, pulp paper, newsprint, glass and non-ferrous metals. The principal export products in the state are pepper, cashew, coir and coir products, tea, cardamom, ginger, spices oil and marine products. Tea accounts for 3.2% of total exports at Cochin port, cashew kernels 1.51%, marine products 3.84%, coir products 4.9%, spices 2.27%, coffee 0.86%. Recently food processing has also been recognized as an important industry in Kerala for its potential for future growth and the possibility of generating numerous employment opportunities.

Agriculture

About 56% of Kerala's total geographical area is net sown area. About 50% of the population depends on agriculture. A unique feature of Kerala is the predominance of cash crops and the state has the highest gross income per net cropped area. The state is a major producer of coconut, rubber, pepper, cardamom, ginger, banana, cocoa, cashew, coffee and tea. Spices like nutmeg, cinnamon and cloves are also cultivated. For instance, coconut occupies 36% of net cropped area. While, the four plantation crops of rubber, coffee, tea and cardamom accounts for 31.58% of the net cropped area in the state and 43% of the area in India. Kerala accounted for 91% of India's rubber production, 75% of cardamom production, 22% of coffee production and 5% of tea production during 2008–2009.

Fishery

As Kerala has large water resources, with a 585 km coastline and a continental shelf area of 39,139 km^2, fishery is one of the major industries, contributing 3% to the state's economy. The state is a habitat to about 40 commercially viable marine species including seerfish, prawn, ribbon fish and mackerel. Kerala's fish reserves account for about 20–25% of India's total fish production and was ranked as the highest contributor of marine fish in India in 2009. Kerala's marine exports accounted for 15.81% of the nation's export during 2009–2010. Main export products were frozen fish (27%), frozen shrimp (24%), frozen cuttle fish (22%) and frozen squid (17%).

Information Technology

As the use of IT is increasingly being considered critical to the economic development of the state, the Government of Kerala has undertaken many IT related initiates. Kerala State IT Mission (KSITM) handles all IT-related activities including e-governance, information distribution between citizens and government, interfacing between industry and government, and assuring speedy and transparent governance. Kerala is especially known for its excellence in implementation of e-governance and was ranked as the second best in India. The state has many core IT infrastructures including a state data center, new data center and Kerala State Wide Area Network connectivity. Common IT infrastructures equipped with functions such as citizens' call centers, email servers, video conferencing and e-district allow effective interaction between the citizens and the government. Various capacity building and enhancement initiatives are also underway to improve IT infrastructure in Kerala.

Tourism

Tourism in Kerala is growing as a major source of income, job opportunities and foreign exchange revenue as the state is emerging as one of the most acclaimed tourist hot spots in India. Often called "God's own country," Kerala offers scenic splendor, a moderate climate, a clean environment and cultural diversity. Some of the important places of interest include Thiruvananthapuram; Kollam; Pathanamthitta; Alappuzha; Kottayam; Idukki; Ernakulam; Thrissur; Palakkad; Mal appuram; Kozhikode; Wayanad; Kannur and Kasaragod. Kerala is seeking private sector actors to invest in its tourism industry.

Infrastructure

Kerala has the most developed infrastructure facilities in terms of transportation (roadways, railways, airways and waterways) and power generation. They not only facilitate the movement of passenger and goods traffic, but also integrate the state with the rest of the country. Accordingly, the Government of Kerala has undertaken several infrastructure projects, from time to time, in order to attract significant investments into the state. All such services make the state an ideal destination for investors and form an important role in the prosperity of an economy.

Roadways

There are 9 National Highways running through Kerala totaling 1,535 km in length as well as 4,341.651 km of state highways and 18,900.058 km of major district roads. The roads are continuously being repaired in Kerala and four-laning construction and land acquisition for NH-17 and NH-47 are in progress.

Railways

Kerala's railways stretch 1,198.9 km and cover 13 railway routes. The Thiruvananthapuram, Palakkad and Madurai divisions of the Southern Railway control various railway operations in the state. The majority of railway operations are handled by railway division at Thiruvananthapuram.

Airways

Kerala has three airports at Thriuvananthapuram, Kochi and Kozhicode. All three airports cater to domestic and international destinations. The airport coming up at Moorkhanparmaba was approved by the Environment Ministry and Aviation Ministry. The construction of Kannur Airport is expected to begin soon, which is expected to bring a major boost to business, tourism sector and its textile industry in North Kerala.

Waterways

Transportation through waterways is becoming increasingly important as the roadways in Kerala are becoming heavily congested. Kerala has a coastline of 585 km, with one major port at Cochin where most trade activities take place, and 17 minor intermediate ports. Currently only three ports in Vizhinjam, Azhikkal and Beypore are in operation, handling 1,000, 5,000 and 50,000 tons of cargo respectively. New cargo port facilities at Thangassery (Kollam) have just begun operation. The continuous development of the existing ports and upgradation of minor intermediate ports are part of the Eleventh Plan. Kerala State Government is encouraging private sector actors to participate in developing its port sector.

Power

As the power sector is important for Kerala's infrastructure development, an increase in the production of power is necessary to meet its growing demand.

Kerala's energy is generated by hydro, thermal and wind sources. Of its total installed capacity of 2,746.19 MW, as much as 1,933 MW is generated by its 24 hydro stations. Thermal energy and wind energy generate 783.11 and 30.08 MW respectively. Though the power development has been based mainly on the exploitation of the state's abundant hydroelectric potential, Kerala is on its way to achieving self-sufficiency with recent efforts to exploit thermal power to its full potential. A major policy initiative of the State Government has been to involve private sector participation in augmenting the state's power supply. Energy capacity generated by the private sector was 256.98 MW, which accounted for 9.36% of total capacity. Kerala State Electricity Board set a goal to provide reliable power to all households at an affordable cost by 2011. The Board is planning to add 610.50 MW of power capacity through hydro and non-conventional sources during the Eleventh plan. It also has 1,000 MW coal-based projects planned for its Twelfth Plan period.

Resources

Official Web Portal of Government of Kerala
http://www.kerala.gov.in/
Kerala State Planning Board—Government of Kerala
http://www.spb.kerala.gov.in/index.php?option=com_content&view=article&id=30&Itemid=60

LAKSHADWEEP

Area	32 sq km
Population	64,429
Capital	Kavaratti
Literacy rate	92.28 percent
Principal religions	Islam
Principal languages	Malayalam and Mahal

- Lakshadweep is the only coral reef island in India and is an important asset in terms of biodiversity of marine life
- Coconut is the only major crop, with a production of 65 million nuts per year
- Because diesel, the main mode of electricity generation, is expensive and environmentally harmful, the government has begun to shift their energy source to renewable energy, setting up wind farms and turbines

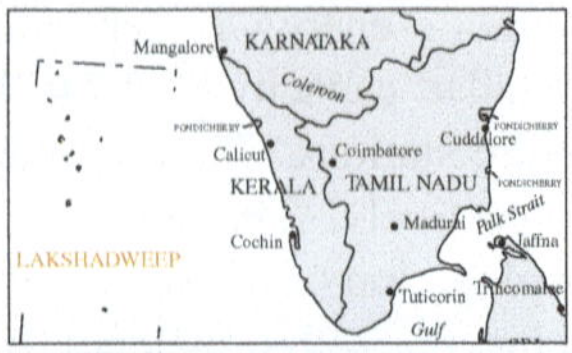

Overview

Lakshadweep is the smallest union territory in India, with a total land area of 32 km^2. About 43.6% of the population lives in rural areas, while 56.3% of the population lives in urban areas. Lakshadweep is a group of about 27 islands, of which only 11 are inhabited. These coral islands consist of 12 atolls, 3 reefs and 6 submerged sand banks. They are irregularly scattered in the Arabian Sea and lie about 220–440 km from the coastal city of Kochi in Kerala. These islands are linked with Kochi by ferry, helicopter and plane services.

Lakshadweep is the only coral reef island in India and is rich in flora and fauna. Due to its beautiful beaches and pollution-free environment, it has become a top tourist destination for water sports and fishing.

The people of this union territory are mainly dependent on agriculture for their livelihood. Coconut is the only major crop here while fishing is another mainstay. Lakshadweep is not an industrially developed territory but there are a few small enterprises such as boat building, tuna canning, coir yarn spinning, a fiber factory, bakeries, a hosiery factory, vinegar and unrefined sugar production. Some industries like oil and flour milling and furniture making are managed as cooperatives. The administration of Lakshadweep has been trying to attract investors into the economy. It has undertaken several policy measures and incentives for the overall improvement of the territory, which it believes has great potential.

Business Opportunities

The Lakshadweep islands are considered an important ecological asset in terms of the biodiversity of marine life. The government is carefully taking steps to promote ecotourism to preserve the natural environment while giving a boost to the industry, which it believes has great potential.

Agriculture

More than 90% of the territory's population depends upon agriculture. Coconut is the only major crop with a production of 65 million nuts per year. The Lakshadweep coconut is branded as an organic product and its productivity is highest in India amounting to 22,310 coconuts per ha. Many crops like pulses, solanaceous, cucurbitacious, and tuber crops can be grown successfully in the coconut gardens as inter crops without irrigation during the southwest monsoon period. However, there is no major irrigation system as there are no rivers or canals.

Fisheries

Fishing is another major activity. Outside of coconut cultivation, it has become the main source of income for the people of Lakshadweep. Lakshadweep has a coast line of 132 km. The sea around the island is highly productive. The islands stand first in India in per capita availability of fish, mainly skipjack tuna. The estimated potential resources of the sea around Lakshadweep are about 100,000 tons of tuna and shark respectively.

Small-Scale Industries

Coconut fiber extraction and conversion of its fiber products is the main industry in the islands. Under government ownership, there are seven coir fiber factories, five coir production-cum-demonstration centers, and seven fiber curling units, functioning under the coir sector. These units produce coir fiber and coir yarn in addition to other coir products like curled fiber and corridor matting. A few coir twisting units also function in the private sector.

Tourism

Tourism in Lakshadweep plays a vital role in generating income and employment as well as promoting the overall development of the islands. Important tourist places are Agatti, Bangaram, Kalpeni, Kadmat, Kavaratti and Minicoy. The vast expanses of the shallow lagoons provide an ideal setting for water sports enthusiasts. Private investors are encouraged to take part in the tourism industry.

Infrastructure

Roadway

The Lakshadweep Public Works Department is in charge of construction and maintenance of roads on the islands, although both road and rail networks are highly limited in the territory. Approximately 167 km of roadway has been constructed and 70 link roads crossing various islands are undergoing construction.

Aviation

Agatti is the only airport in Lakshadweep. Helicopter transfer is available from Agatti to Bangaram Island Resort during monsoon season and to Kavaratti throughout the year. The Government of India has recently approved provision of the second helicopter for transporting patients, an inter-island passenger service, and for other emergency purposes. For trips to other cities in India or to foreign destinations, Cochin International Airport in Kerala can be used. The flight from Cochin to Agatti takes approximately one and a half hours. It operates six days a week.

Waterways

Water is the main mode of transportation between the islands and mainland. Three all-weather ships and three fair weather ships with limited cargo capacity, two inter-island mainland and eight inter-island speed boats, four cargo barges and one oil carrier were available in 2009. Four passenger ships, MV Tippu Sultan, MV Bharat Seema, MV Amindivi and MV Minicoy operate between Cochin and Lakshadweep. They handle passenger traffic between the mainland and the islands as well as the inter-island transportation. Where there is an absence of adequate berthing facilities for ships, small crafts are being installed to transport passengers and cargo from ships.

Power

Every home in the islands has been electrified. Because diesel, the main mode of electricity generation, is expensive and environmentally harmful, the government has begun to shift their energy sources to renewable energy, setting up wind farms and turbines. The islands of Lakshadweep receive abundant sunlight throughout the year, except during monsoon, providing an ideal opportunity for the use of solar power. During monsoon season, when there is a lot of wind, transporting diesel will become even more difficult which makes wind energy a much better alternative.

Telecommunication

Information and communication technology has played an important role in enhancing connectivity between geographically dispersed islands.

Resources

Official Website
http://lakshadweep.nic.in/

MADHYA PRADESH

Area	308,000 sq km
Population	72.60 million
Capital	Bhopal
NSDP at current prices	US$38.4 billion (2009-10); 13.39% Y/Y growth
Per capita NSDP at current prices	US$545 (2009-10); 11.54% Y/Y growth
Literacy rate	70.63 percent
Principal religions	Hinduism, Jainism, Islam and Buddhism
Principal languages	Hindi

- Alsoknown as the "Heart of India" for its central location, Madhya Pradesh has easy access to surrounding states
- Madhya Pradesh's agricultural industry sustains about 74 percent of the population
- The state is the third largest cement producer in India

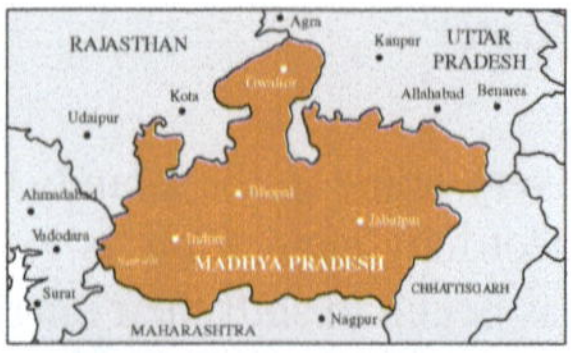

Overview

Madhya Pradesh, located in the center of India, is the country's second largest state covering an area of 308,000 km. It is bounded by Uttar Pradesh in the north; by Chhattisgarh in the east; by Gujarat and Rajasthan in the west; and by Maharashtra in the south. Filled with all types of geographical features ranging from hills to plains and plateaus to rivers and lush green forests, it has vast deposits of natural resources like copper ore, limestone, bauxite and granite. A wide range of wood and forestry products and large number of prominent herbs are also available in abundance. The state has been home to many religions including Hinduism, Buddhism, Jainism and Islam.

Madhya Pradesh occupies a pivotal position and is known as the "Heart of India." There are many renowned public and private companies functional in the state, covering diverse areas ranging from the cement industry to pharmaceuticals. A continuous supply of skilled workers, a congenial work environment and a proactive government make the state an attractive industrial option. The state also allows industrial units to have captive power plants to produce power as per their requirements. Located in the center of the country, it is conveniently located between India's coastal metropolises. It is developing into an important logistic hub for the country.

Business Opportunities

Madhya Pradesh is one of the favored destinations for foreign investors. Its excellent location, bordering onto seven Indian states, allows easy access to the booming national markets of the country. It is the leading producer of quality wheat, rice, pulses and several other agricultural products and ample opportunities exist to set up and develop agricultural industries. The state is endowed with rich mineral resources, an educated and skilled workforce as well as many high technology industries. These include the automobile industry, electronics manufacturing, and cement production. The tourism and information technology sectors also provide immense opportunities for attracting investments into the state.

Agriculture

Agriculture is the mainstay of the state economy, with about 74% of the population depending on it for their livelihood. The major crops grown in the state are rice, wheat, maize, gram, soybean, groundnut and mustard seeds. Commercial crops like cotton and sugarcane are also grown in considerable quantities in a few districts. The state is ranked fourth for wheat production and eighth for rice production in India. This production capacity combined with the favorable climate provide agro-based industries with great potential for development.

The State Government is also developing horticulture. Madhya Pradesh is known as a large producer of ginger, garlic, turmeric, chili, coriander, banana, guava, tomato, oranges, and papaya. Some medicinal crops and narcotic crops are also grown in the state.

Information Technology

Madhya Pradesh is making remarkable achievements in promoting IT in government as well as the private sector, including e-governance, computerization in government departments and various IT related activities in rural areas. In order to help sustain its technological edge, the state has invested in IT education and provided institutions for future IT professionals. It has also opened up private participation for computer education in schools and colleges.

An IT policy has been formulated to attract private investment in the IT sector. It focuses on setting up kiosks to provide e-mail, internet and other value-added services in rural areas. The existing public grievance system is being upgraded so as to facilitate access to citizens through kiosks.

To encourage private sector participation in e-governance and citizen services initiatives, the State Government has formulated the following guidelines

- Proposals for participation and investment shall be without any burden of financial expenditure on the State Government;
- Projects of e-governance for citizen services shall be allowed on non-exclusive basis to any investor

- Every investor shall be required to set up a minimum of fifteen such kiosks in every block
- All the transactions taking place at the kiosks shall function on a use and pay basis

As a result, several companies have shown interest in setting up kiosks in the state. The government has set up the software technology parks at Bhopal, Indore and Gwalior so as to provide the necessary infrastructure for IT companies.

Minerals

The state of Madhya Pradesh is richly endowed with mineral wealth. It is the sole producer of diamonds in India. Coal, limestone, manganese ore, bauxite, copper ore, dolomite, fire clay and slate are the main minerals occurring in the state. In terms of the mineral production, the state ranks third in India and is fast emerging as a dimensional stone producer.

Cement

Madhya Pradesh is the third largest producer of cement in India. It is rich in cement producing minerals and has access to the appropriate expertise to run cement plants. At present, several major groups like the Birla Corporation, Vikram cement, Prism cement, Diamond cements, Maihar cement and ACC Cement are developing manufacturing plants in Madhya Pradesh.

Infrastructure

The Government of Madhya Pradesh has made infrastructure development an area of key focus. Accordingly, it has undertaken several infrastructure projects to attract large investments into the state. It is also trying to develop the state into a logistics hub with excellent road-rail-air connectivity, with strong power resources and a modern telecommunication network. Such infrastructure facilities are essential for efficient and cost effective movement of people and materials, fully utilizing the existing resources.

Roadways

Madhya Pradesh has a well-developed road network, connecting key urban and tourist centers within the country. The total length of roads in the state is

72,416 km. Out of this, the length of the national and state highways are 4,676 km and 8,333 km, respectively.

Railways

Madhya Pradesh has a well-connected rail network. Major railway junctions in the state are Bhopal, Bina, Gwalior, Indore, Itarsi, Jabalpur, Katani, Ratlam and Ujjain. The main rail route linking northern India with southern India passes through the state. Also, there are divisional railways headquarters located at Bhopal, Ratlam and Jabalpur.

Aviation

The state has convenient air linkages to all the major cities of India as well as international cities. Major airports in the state are located in Bhopal, Indore, Khajuraho, Jabalpur and Gwalior. There are regular flights to Delhi, Mumbai, Kolkata, Hyderabad, Bangalore, Chennai, Varanasi and Nagpur.

Telecommunications

Madhya Pradesh has made rapid strides in the field of basic telephony. It has internet connectivity in all 45 districts.

Power

The total installed power generation capacity in the state is 7,405 MW. Madhya Pradesh is rich in low-grade coal suitable for power generation and has immense potential for hydroelectric power.

MAHARASHTRA

Area	308,000 sq km
Population	112.37 million
Capital	Mumbai
NSDP at current prices	US$161.9 billion (2009-10); 20.10% Y/Y growth
Per capita NSDP at current prices	US$1465 (2009-10); 18.38% Y/Y growth
Literacy rate	82.91 percent
Principal religions	Hinduism
Principal languages	Marathi

- Maharashtra is a leader in biotechnology, companies including Glaxo Wellcome, Novartis, Pfizer and Johnson & Johnson all have presence in the state
- Maharashtra is among the top three IT export states and has the highest FDI growth rate in IT field
- Maharshtra is home to over 20 percent of the total number of broadband subscribers in India

Overview

Maharashtra, located in the northern center of India, is the third largest state covering an area of 308,000 km. It is bounded by Gujarat and Madhya Pradesh to the north, the Arabian Sea to the west, Chhattisgarh to the east, and by Karnataka and Andhra Pradesh to the south. It is situated on the west coast of India, with a 720 km coastline along the Konkan region. Maharashtra is dominated by a plateau, its western upturned rims rising to form the Sahyadri Range parallel to the sea. This is the physical backbone of the state while the Satpuda Range covers the northern part of the state and serves as its natural boundary. The Ajanta and Satmala Ranges run through the central part of the state.

Maharashtra's industrial sector occupies a prominent position in the state's economy. Food products, tobacco and related products, cotton textiles, other textile products, paper and paper products, printing and publishing, rubber, plastic, chemical and chemical products, machinery, electronic apparatus and appliances, and transport equipment contribute substantially to the industrial production in the state.

Maharashtra has the highest level of urbanization amongst all the Indian states. It has been identified as India's powerhouse with Mumbai as the center point of India's financial and commercial markets. As the commercial and financial hub of India, Mumbai attracts a large number of foreign investors. Pune, the second largest city in Maharashtra, is the state's cultural capital and is rapidly maturing into a prime industrial town in its own right.

Business Opportunities

Maharashtra has always been at the forefront of the country's industrial development and continues to attract the largest amount of investment, both domestic and foreign. The state has established strengths in every sector including engineering, automobiles and auto components, chemicals, drugs and pharmaceuticals, textiles, information technology and biotechnology. It offers good infrastructure, excellent educational facilities, quality trained manpower, a professional work ethic and a conducive business environment. A wide variety of horticultural crops are also grown in the state, making it a major producer of oilseeds, rice, cotton and sugarcane. In addition, the rich heritage, trade, culture, history and growing economy of the state make it a major tourist attraction.

Biotechnology

Maharashtra is a leader in biotechnology thanks to its excellent private and public institutions, superb infrastructure and proactive government policies. Some of the leading institutions in Mumbai and Pune include the Bhabha Atomic Research Center, the Indian Institute of Technology, the Tata Institute of Fundamental Research, the National Chemical Laboratory, the National Center for Cell Science, the National Institute of Virology, the National AIDS Research Institute, the Agharkar Research Institute, and the National Environmental Engineering Research Institute. These are all doing pioneering research work in the field of biotechnology. There are also some defense research institutions in the state conducting advanced research in biomedical, bioinformatics and biotechnology. Some major companies in the industry have a presence in Maharashtra and they include Glaxo Wellcome, Novartis, Pfizer and Johnson & Johnson.

Information Technology

Maharashtra is one of the largest software exporting states and is known as the largest market for IT hardware and internet in India. The Government of Maharashtra has recognized the IT industry as an important developing sector and is focusing on providing IT related infrastructure and fiscal incentives to IT units, IT in governance and institutional framework for the sector. The government is promoting IT initiatives in Nagpur, Nashik and Aurangabad, which are cities with highest IT growth potential as well as the most backward regions with low HDI. The government is focusing specifically on development of Maharashtra's strength in AVGC (Animation, Visual effects, Gaming and Comics) fields. They are also committed to sustainability by promoting Green IT. These initiatives have enabled the IT industry to establish a firm foundation for itself in India.

The whole state has been connected through a fiber optic cable network and a statewide network of training institutions have been established to build a pool of world-class IT professionals, in order to provide strength and support to the state's IT industry. The State Government has framed an IT policy in order to make Maharashtra a favored destination for investments in the IT and ITES industries. Consequently, Maharashtra has become one of the top three states for IT exports and the FDI growth rate of its IT sector is the highest in India.

In order to provide further impetus to the IT industry, the Government of Maharashtra has set up several state-of-the-art IT parks within the state. These provide a base of operations for international IT houses.

Agriculture and Horticulture

Maharashtra is a leading state in agriculture. Principal crops grown here are rice, wheat, jowar, bajra and other pulses. The state is also a major producer of oilseeds. Groundnut, sunflower and soybean are the major oil seed crops. Important cash crops include cotton, sugarcane, turmeric and vegetables. The state is one of India's pioneers in onion production as well as being a leader in horticulture. Grapes produced in the state are now exported abroad. Mangoes, particularly the alphonso variety grown in Konkan, have already established a name on the international market.

Food Processing

The food processing industry in Maharashtra is very basic. The main processing industries in the state are in the sectors of sugar, milk, poultry, rice milling, flour milling, and milk processing. Immense opportunities exist for modernizing food processing units. Rice, wheat, soybean, jawar, grapes, pomegranates and mangoes are the main crops that are available in the state for primary and secondary processing. Similarly, there is a vast potential to develop and set up processing units for tomatoes, onion, cabbage, okra and cauliflower. In particular, fruit juice pulping and concentrating units, wineries, distilleries, pickling, rice milling, flour milling and refining units can be set up in the state's industrial areas.

Automobiles

The automobile sector has played a key role in the industrialization of the state. Every segment of the sector including two and three wheelers, passenger cars and commercial vehicles is represented. The major automobile centers in the state include Pune, Nashik, Aurangabad and Nagpur. Pune is home to large players such as Bajaj Auto Ltd, Mercedes Benz and TELCO and Nashik is home to India's largest multi-utility vehicle manufacturer, Mahindra & Mahindra. The state's key competitive advantage in the automobiles and auto components industries is the presence of established manufacturers. The strong presence of the engineering sector is an additional advantage, along with its large skilled labor base. The solid transportation infrastructure also contributes to the logistics-intensive auto industry.

Infrastructure

Maharashtra has excellent infrastructure which has played a key role in the growth of its industry and helped promote the overall development of the economy. Due to the government's emphasis on the importance of infrastructure development, Maharashtra's transportation system is very well established. The power supply is one of the most stable and reliable in India. The state also has an excellent telecommunications network.

Roadways

The total length of Maharashtra's roadway is 240,040 km out of which 218,123 km are paved. Sixteen national highways connect the state with Delhi, Calcutta, Allahabad, Hyderabad, and Bangalore. The state has an extensive road network, including a six-lane expressway linking Mumbai and Pune.

Railways

Maharashtra has 5,983 km of railway routes. The Western, Central and Harbor Railway lines connect Mumbai to distant suburbs and destinations across India. A monorail project is currently being implemented under the Mumbai Metropolitan Region Development Authority.

Aviation

Maharashtra has three international airports and five domestic airports. At present, Chhatrapati Shivaji International Airport in Mumbai is the largest and busiest airport in India, offering daily flights to most major international destinations as well as to domestic destinations. To alleviate the traffic at the Chhatrapati Shivaji International Airport, an additional airport at Navi Mumbai has been proposed.

Ports

There are two major and 53 notified minor ports in the state. Mumbai Port and Jawaharlal Nehru Port are the two major ports, which together provide the largest port facilities in India. They handle a major proportion of the country's incoming and outgoing cargo traffic.

Power

Maharashtra has a large number of hydroelectric and thermal power plants across the state. Of the total installed power generation capacity of 21,378, 9 MW, approximately 70% is generated by thermal energy and more than 15% is generated by hydropower. The state has potential capacity of 7,852 MW through renewable energy. The tax rate on non-conventional sources of energy is zero or low as 5% to promote the use of non-conventional energy in the state.

Telecommunications

Maharashtra Telecom Circle (MHTC) provides service to an area expanding over 310,762 km^2. It provides telecom services to 30 million residing in urban area and 60 million residing in rural area. The state has over 20% of broadband subscribers in India.

Resources

Government of Maharashtra Official Website
http://www.maharashtra.gov.in/

MANIPUR

Area	22,327 sq km
Population	2.72 million
Capital	Imphal
NSDP at current prices	US$1.3 billion (2008-09); 8.53% Y/Y growth
Per capita NSDP at current prices	US$475 (2008-09); 6.48% Y/Y growth
Literacy rate	79.85 percent
Principal religions	Hinduism, Sanamahi, Islam and Christianity
Principal languages	Manipuri

- In Manipur, there is vast potential in the agricultural and horticultural sectors, especially in the food processing industry
- Described as the "Switzerland of the East," Manipur's tourism industry has large potential
- The Jiribam-Tupul Railway Line is key to connecting Manipur to the rest of India

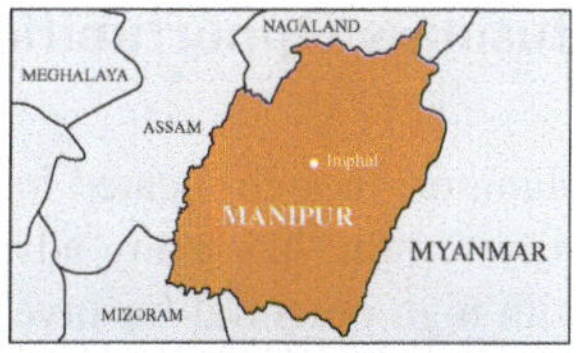

Overview

Manipur has a rich reserve of natural resources combined with scenic beauty; refreshing waterfalls; exotic orchids; rare species of flora and fauna; virgin forests; cascading rivers; hilly green landscape; and meandering streams. Loktak Lake is one of its important geographic features. Physically, the state is broken into two parts, the hills and the valley. The valley is at the center surrounded by hills on all sides.

There are three major ethnic groups in Manipur, the Meiteis in the valley, the Nagas and the Kuki-Chin tribes in the hills. Each ethnic group has its own distinct culture and tradition deeply embedded in its dances, music and customary practices. Manipuris are artistic and creative by nature and this has found expression in their handloom and handicraft products, which are world-famous for their designs, ingenuity and usefulness.

It is situated on the eastern frontier of India and is bounded by Myanmar (Burma) on the east; Nagaland on the north; Assam on the west; and Mizoram on the south.

The geographical location of Manipur is encouraging industrialization. Agriculture and allied activities form the backbone of the economy. There are numerous investment opportunities in the economy, particularly in agriculture and food processing; handloom; handicrafts; tourism and information technology. The state government has taken several policy measures and incentives to attract investors to these sectors.

Business Opportunities

Manipur, though located in a far flung northeastern corner in India with a largely hilly terrain, has many advantages and opportunities for investment. The sectors with high potential for investments are agriculture and food processing, handloom weaving, handicrafts, tourism and information technology.

Agriculture and Food Processing

The state's climate makes it suitable for growing almost any kind of agricultural and horticultural crops, making food processing industries very productive. The state produces a sizeable quantity of rice, wheat, maize, pulses, oilseeds (mustard, groundnut, soybeans and sunflowers), fruit (pineapples, limes and lemons, bananas and oranges), and vegetables (cauliflower, cabbage, tomatoes and peas).

The food processing sector plays a significant role in the diversification and commercialization of agriculture, horticulture, fisheries, poultry, animal husbandry and forestation. Due to the importance of the industry, the State Government has established a food processing training center at Imphal. A food park has also been set up in Nilakuthi.

Handloom Weaving

Handlooming is the largest cottage industry in the state, providing a large amount of employment in the state, particularly to women. The main handloom products of Manipur are saris, bed sheets, curtains, fashion garments, scarves and pillow covers. Most of the weavers who are famous for their skill and intricate designs are from Wangkhei, Bamon Kampu, Kongba, Khongman and Utlou. Fabrics and shawls of Manipur are in great demand in the national and international market.

Handicrafts

The handicraft industry has a unique place among the various crafts in India and consists of products made of cane and bamboo as well as its pottery culture. Pottery culture is very old in Manipur and flourishes in Andro, Sekmai, Chairen, Thongjao, Nungbi and parts of the Senapati District. Since cane and bamboo are abundantly available, basketry is also a common occupation of the people. Fishing equipment is also made of cane and bamboo and all products are in demand both domestically as well as internationally.

Tourism

Manipur, due to its wealth of flora and fauna, has been described as the "Switzerland of the East." Its scenic beauty makes it a top tourist destination. Its landscape includes rare species of flora and fauna, and virgin forests. Some of the major tourist spots in Manipur include Shri Shri Govindajee temple, Khwairamband Bazar (Ima Keithel), war cemeteries, Saheed Minar, Nupi Lan (Women's War) Memorial Complex, Khonghampat Orchidarium, INA Memorial (Moirang) and the Khongjom War Memorial Complex.

Information Technology

Recognizing the vast potential of the IT industry in the state, the Government of Manipur accords high priority to the electronics and information technology sector. The Manipur Industrial Development Corporation Ltd has been established to enhance the development of the electronics and information technology-based industries in the state. Many opportunities for investment exist in IT sectors such as establishing IT Parks, IT enabled service centers and information kiosks. The government is also implementing IT literacy programs in schools and colleges to foster trained and skilled manpower. They are also aiming to improve the general infrastructure of the state to promote distance learning through IT.

Infrastructure

Infrastructure in Manipur must overcome the state's hilly terrain and adequate and efficient road, rail, and aviation networks are viewed as an important pre-condition for the social and economic development of the state. Imphal, the state capital, has the second largest airport in the region and is well connected by air with Delhi, Kolkata and Guwahati. The national highway system links the state with the rest of the country.

Roadways

There are three national highways in Manipur: National Highway 39, National Highway 53 and National Highway 150. Its road connectivity will be extended to Manipur's border town Moreh at the completion of the Saurashtra-Silchar Super Highway project. Many private buses are available on a daily basis connecting Imphal to other major cities.

Railways

There is no direct rail service to Imphal. The nearest railheads are in Guwuhati or Dimapur, which have bus and air connections to Imphal. The foundation stone for a new railway line called the "Jiribam-Tupul Railway Line" was laid down in 2004. Once the Tupul railway project is completed, Manipur will have better access to the rest of India.

Aviation

Imphal Airport, located 8 km from the city center, is the only one in the state linked with other cities in the region through Air India, IndiGo, King Fisher, Jet Airways, Jet Lite, Spice Jet, Air Deccan, etc. It operates daily flights connecting to major cities including Guwahati, Kolkata, Bangalore and Delhi.

Telecommunication

Various telecommunication corporations including BSNL, Tata Indicom and Airtel, which provide wireless internet across the State.

Power

The installed capacity of power in the state is more than 47.252 MW. The state's power supply depends upon generating stations located in the northeastern region. The state has hydropower potential amounting to 2,000 MW, the majority of which has been left untouched. This figure is more than enough to cover its power requirement of 170 MW during peak hours. Manipur's power department has identified potential sites for hydro power plants and have launched projects. The government has been active in devising policies to attract private investors to the sector.

Resources

Official Website of Manipur
http://manipur.gov.in/
Official Website of Department of Commerce & Industries, Manipur
http://dcimanipur.gov.in/
Investment Opportunities in Manipur, INDIA
http://investinmanipur.nic.in/default.htm

MEGHALAYA

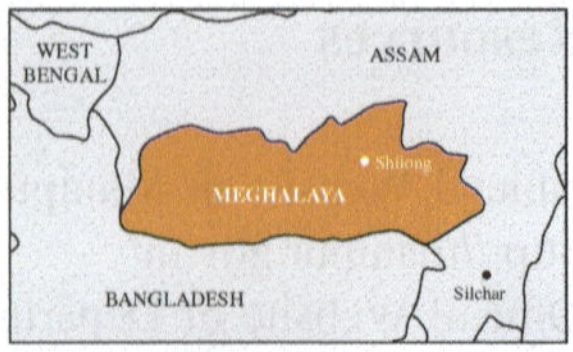

Area	22,429 sq km
Population	2.96 million
Capital	Shillong
NSDP at current prices	US$1.9 billion (2008-09); 14.31% Y/Y growth
Per capita NSDP at current prices	US$760 (2008-09); 12.96% Y/Y growth
Literacy rate	75.48 percent
Principal religions	Hinduism and Christianity
Principal languages	Khasi, Garo, Pnar and English

- Mild climate and diverse terrain is favorable to a variety of cash and plantation crops, as well as non-food plants
- The southern region of the state is rich with natural resources including coal and limestone
- This hilly state has been called "the Scotland of the East"

Overview

Meghalaya is situated in northeastern region of the country, bordered on the south and west by Bangladesh, and is mostly populated by the tribes of Khasi, Garo, and Jaintia. Meghalaya is characterized by a hilly terrain with abundant rainfall, sunshine, virgin forests, high plateaus, waterfalls, clear rivers, and a variety of soil types. It also has substantial deposits of natural resources such as uranium and coal. Meghalaya's rich landscape and climate are suitable for developing tourism, health resorts, and cultivating a variety of agricultural and horticultural plants. Given this, the Government of Meghalaya has undertaken several policy measures and incentives in order to encourage the inflow of investment into these sectors of the economy.

The state's economic growth rose 14.4% in 2010, and per capita income rose 13% in the same period. The state's economic activity is predominately agricultural, with 70% of its population dependent on farming. However, this industry only contributes to about 27% of the state's GSDP. East-Khasi Hills, West-Garo Hills, and Jainita Hills together create more than 70% of Meghalaya's gross state domestic product. In 2010, over 50% of total investments in the state were made in power, particularly hydroelectric power.

Business Opportunities

The state government, as well as the central government, in order to attract investment, provide a favorable environment for doing business and investment in Meghalaya, including several industrial zones and financial incentives on costs of infrastructure, transportation, training, power, and so on. Opportunities for investment in sectors like minerals, horticulture, agro processing, tourism, electronics, and IT have been identified by the state as focus sectors. The state's budget speech for 2011/2012 also indicates sustainable living and energy efficiency as a major initiative for future developments. Tertiary and secondary sectors are currently Meghalaya's main contributors to economic growth, with signs of decline in primary sectors.

Minerals

The natural resource deposits in Meghalaya are substantial. The opportunities for increasing the industrial production of the state's coal, limestone, granite, and clay are favorable. Coal deposits are scattered throughout the state but mainly those found in the southern region are suitable for use in the power, fertilizer, cement, textile, rubber, firing, and pottery-based industries. Limestone, also found predominately in the southern region of the state, range from low to high quality and can be used in the steel, fertilizer, and chemical industries. Granite, found in the east and west regions, is of high quality and can be found in a range of colors. Clay is found throughout the state and used in industries such as ceramics, paper, and rubber. The state's 2009 Mining Policy encourages cooperation between mining, mineral industries, and power generation industries, better methods for identifying deposits and minimizing waste, and the promotion of private sector investment.

Horticulture and Agriculture

The potential for horticulture and agriculture in the state of Meghalaya is phenomenal. With the majority of its population involved in agricultural cultivation or processing, the state produces a wide catalogue of tropical fruits, roots, tea, seeds, spices, grains, and nuts. Turmeric, particularly that grown in the Jaintia Hills, is known to be some of the world's best, and plantation and cash crops are gaining state support for development and expansion. The climate conditions of Meghalaya are also very suitable for medicinal, aromatic, and other non-food crops, which include some high-value products for exports.

Tourism

The state's hilly terrain and cool climate offers good potential for the development of tourism. The State Government has announced an industry policy which aims to market the state as a place for nature, adventure, cultural, relaxation, golf, business, sports and arts tourism. In addition, the government wants to make the state one of the best tourist destinations of the country by capitalizing on its natural assets, managing them properly and creating a consistent, competitive advantage. The state also seeks to promote public private partnerships and develop training centers in hospitality.

Infrastructure

Roadways

The state has approximately 8,371 km of roadways and access to 4 national highways.

Railways

Guwahati, 103 km from Shillong, is the closest railway station that connects northeast India to other parts of the country. Future development plans are likely to include stations within the state.

Aviation

The state has two airports at Umroi and Balajek. The Umroi airport has facilities for small aircraft and connects to Kolkata, Aizawal and Silchar. Balajek airport is still under construction. Additionally, the airport in Borjhar, located 124 km from Shillong, is a significant transportation hub in the northeast and is able to handle large capacity aircrafts. Helicopter services are also available for connection between Shillong, Guwahati, and Tura.

Power

Meghalaya has the largest hydroelectric potential in Northeast India. The generation transmission, transformation and distribution of electricity is controlled by the Meghalaya State Electricity Board. As of March 2010, the state had an installed power capacity of 289.6 MW. The state is also extremely rich in thermal power potential. It has vast coal reserves. This coal is high in sulfur and calorific value with low ash content, which makes it suitable to thermal power projects. The state is set to provide all villages with access to electricity by 2012, up from 74% access in 2008. In conjunction with the Central Government's commitment to increase cooperation with the private sector, the state is looking to alternative energy sources to generate supply.

Resources

Government of Meghalaya
http://meghalaya.nic.in/
Commerce and Industries Department
http://megindustry.gov.in/
TP Division, Ministry of External Affairs
http://www.indiainbusiness.nic.in/know-india/states/meghalaya.htm

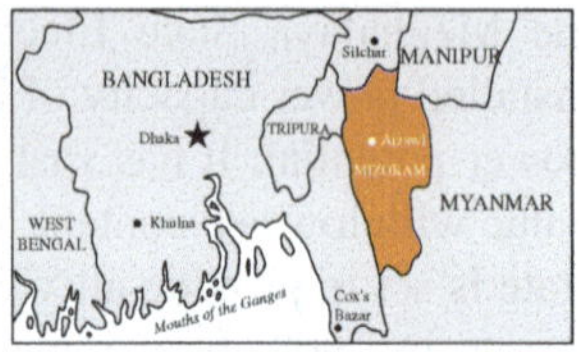

MIZORAM

Area	21,081 sq km
Population	1.1 million
Capital	Aizawl
NSDP at current prices	US$735.9 million (2008-09); 10.31% Y/Y growth
Per capita NSDP at current prices	US$683 (2008-09); 7.53% Y/Y growth
Literacy rate	91.58 percent
Principal religions	Christianity
Principal languages	Mizo and English

- Bamboo is a major contributor to Mizoram's economic output
- Almost all of the state's crops are organic due to a lack of heavy pesticide and fertilizer use
- Investments in IT development are highly encouraged
- 80 percent of total investments in infrastructure have gone towards power generation

Overview

Mizoram is one of the newest states in the Indian Union, officially established in 1987. Its landscape is characterized by steep hill ranges and narrow valleys. Mizoram has a mild climate and falls under the regular influence of monsoons. It rains heavily from May to September with little or no rainfall in the winter months.

The state borders Tripura, Assam and Manipur. Its international neighbors are Myanmar to the east and Bangladesh to the west, which positions the state in a strategic location for developing international trade.

In recent years, the state has encouraged business opportunities and growth in industries such as bamboo, agro-horticulture, tourism and information technology. In order to attract investors, particularly in the sectors just mentioned, the government of Mizoram has taken up several policy measures and incentive programs such as allowing joint ventures at all levels of industry—small, medium, and large.

The Economic Survey of Mizoram estimated the state's economic growth in 2009/2010 to be 7.2%, similar to that of India as a whole for the same period. The services sector in the state in the same period comprised 66% of the state's economy, followed by the industries sector at 19.5% and the agriculture sector at 14.5%. The secondary sector is the fastest growing sector in the state, with a compound annual growth rate of 13.6% between 2000 and 2009. On the other hand, the tertiary sector makes up the largest segment of the state's economy, mostly headed by trade, hotels, real estate, transport, and communications.

Business Opportunities

The abundance of bamboo, crops, and minerals in Mizoram affords investors numerous opportunities, especially in food processing, bottled water, fruit juice processing, preserved food canning, stone quarries, and handicrafts. With one of the highest literacy rates in the country, Mizoram has the potential to become a strong IT player. In addition, its beautiful landscape and rich cultural heritage make it an attractive tourist destination. Investment opportunities exist in several sectors including bamboo production, agro-horticulture, information technology and tourism.

In the 2010/2011 Budget Speech of the Mizoram Legislative Assembly, the Honorable Chief Minister of the state emphasized the importance of nurturing a friendly environment for investment in the private and public sectors, and named sustainability as a driving force for developments in agriculture, horticulture, irrigation, soil and water conservation, animal husbandry, fisheries, forests, sericulture, cottage and small scale industries. State-government backed initiatives in IT, power generation, sports infrastructure, low-cost housing, improvements in utilities, transportation infrastructure construction, and investment in Public Sector Enterprises and industry will receive further development.

Bamboo

Mizoram has an abundant reserve of bamboo forest that contributes to 14% of India's total bamboo output. More than 20 different species of bamboo can be found in Mizoram, of which the melocanna baccifera species accounts for 95%. Bamboo produced from Mizoram is used as a raw material in various other industries, including agricultural irrigation, construction scaffolding, handicrafts, water transportation, household goods, and exports. The 2002 Bamboo Policy aims to promote bamboo as a cash crop and expand the number of plantations in the state. The state is also in the process of developing an SEZ in its northeast region, with bamboo products forming the focal point of industrial activity in the development zone.

Agriculture and Horticulture

The use of fertilizer and pesticides is not common in the state, and as such much of Mizoram's produce is organically cultivated, giving its output a high-value in both domestic and international foods markets. The climatic condition of the state and its location in a tropical and temperate zone has contributed to the occurrence of a wide spectrum of rich and varied plant growth. Profitable crops in Mizoram include mandarin oranges, passion fruit, papaya, bananas, tomatoes, garlic, turmeric, black pepper, ginger, potatoes, sweet potatoes, coffee and coconuts. Further development in farming around these crops and others is likely to bring many more investment opportunities. Mizoram produces 12% of the total fruit output in northeast India.

Information Technology

Recognizing the potential for Mizoram's high literacy rate to contribute positively to economic growth in IT, the state government in 2001 passed the IT Policy of Mizoram. This policy emphasizes IT development in sectors such as industry, education, government, health, tourism, agriculture and provides incentives to entrepreneurs and investors. Development plans include a hi-tech complex for software development, the North Eastern Institute of Information Technology for IT education and research, the Software Technology Park for exporting services such as technology consulting, market analysis, and marketing, and IT enabled services for creating call centers, medical transcriptions, websites, and back-office operations.

Tourism

Mizoram's landscape provides ample points of interest for a vibrant tourism industry. Developing the necessary infrastructure to support it is therefore a key focus for the state government. Areas of opportunity include the following:

- Large resorts, hotels, and convention centers
- Paved roads
- Transport services
- Amusement parks

Infrastructure

The Government of Mizoram has undertaken several infrastructure projects to attract investment. Infrastructure in the state includes railways, roadways, aviation, telecommunications and power.

Roadways

The state has efficient road-connectivity, totaling 5,783.3 km. There are three national highways in the state: the NH 54 which connects it with other parts of the country through Silchar, Assam; the NH 150 connects it with Seling, Mizoram, Imphal, Manipur, and Kohima, Nagaland; the NH 40A links it with Tripura and also Bangladesh.

Aviation

Mizoram's main airport is Lengpui Airport, located near Aizawl. It services daily flights via Alliance Air Service, and flights to Kolkata, Guwahati, and Imphal are just all under 2 h.

Railways

The state's closest access to rail is located in Bairabi, which is about 110 km from Aizawl. There is also access via Silchar, Assam, about 180 km from Aizawl.

Telecommunications

By 2009, there were 56,816 landline and over 280,000 mobile phone connections and over 2,000 broadband connections in the state. Wireless and broadband internet across the state is expected to be installed by 2011.

Power

The state is dependent mainly on electricity imported from the central sector generation and from other states through grid lines. As of March 2010, the total installed power of the state was 130.9 MW, with more than 80% of the electricity used in the state imported from neighboring states.

Resources

Government of Mizoram
http://mizoram.nic.in/
Government of Mizoram—Invest in Mizoram
http://investinmizoram.nic.in/
India in Business, ITP Division, Ministry of External Affairs, Government of India
Mizoram
http://www.indiainbusiness.nic.in/know-india/states/mizoram.htm

NAGALAND

Area	16,579 sq km
Population	1.98 million
Capital	Kohima
NSDP at current prices	US$1.2 billion (2006-07); 8.43% Y/Y growth
Per capita NSDP at current prices	US$471 (2006-07); 3.14% Y/Y growth
Literacy rate	80.11 percent
Principal religions	Christianity
Principal languages	Nagamese, English, Hindi and local dialects

- IT development is a top priority for the state government
- Proximity to the Himalayas gives Nagaland great potential for adventure and outdoor tourism
- Festivals, handicrafts, and traditional agricultural practices characterize the livelihood of the numerous tribes that populate the state

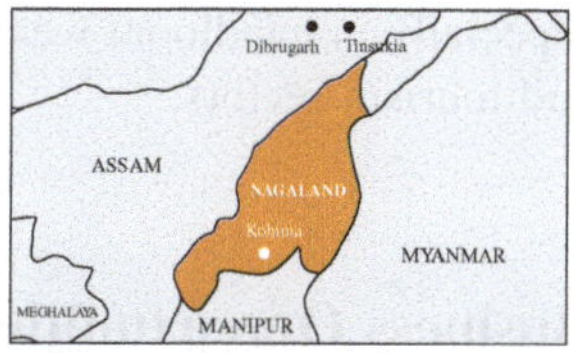

Overview

Nagaland, with a total land area of 16,579 km^2, is one of the mountainous states located in the extreme northeastern part of India. The state is bounded by Myanmar in the east, Arunachal Pradesh in the north, Assam in the west, and Manipur in the south. Mount Saramati is the highest peak in Nagaland at a height of 3,840 m, and its range forms a natural barrier between Nagaland and Myanmar. The numerous tribes that live in Nagaland are of the Indo-Mongoloid group, and their languages fall under the Tibeto-Burma family. Due to its strategic location, the state has the potential to develop into an international business and trading hub for the East Asian region.

The state is endowed with a prosperous and varied cultural heritage. It is very rich in biodiversity and has several types of forest. Nagaland has a favorable climate for growing different varieties of crops, vegetables, fruits and medicinal herbs. The labor force is mainly skilled in basketry, pottery, spinning, weaving, carving and metal work. Traditional village industries based on local forest products form the backbone of the manufacturing sector in the state.

Its proximity to the Himalayas gives Nagaland a terrain that is ideal for trekking, rock climbing, and jungle camping and other adventurous activities, increasing the numbers of tourists that visit the state each year. It also possesses rich reserves of hydrocarbons minerals such as petroleum, natural gas, coal, nickel, cobalt and chromium.

These advantageous features provide a conducive climate for attracting significant investment into the state. The government of Nagaland has announced several policies and schemes to motivate entrepreneurs to set up their industrial units in the state. Numerous opportunities exist in various sectors of the economy, especially in handloom weaving, handicrafts, sericulture, information technology, and tourism sectors.

Business Opportunities

Nagaland has increasingly become a preferred investment destination in India. It has abundant fertile soil, plentiful rainfall, a good climate, a large number of plant and animal species, and an availability of vacant land for plantation purposes. All of these have created favorable conditions for producing various types of agricultural products. In addition, the state's policies for industry and IT growth stipulate the creation of investment-friendly business environments for attracting both domestic and foreign investors.

Between 2000 and 2007, the industrial sector was the main driver of economic growth in Nagaland, which includes the construction, manufacturing, electricity, gas and water supply industries. In the same period, the secondary sector grew the fastest at 17% compounded annual growth rate, with primary and tertiary sectors following with 15.1 and 11%, respectively. Key industries in the state include natural resources, bamboo, horticulture, sericulture, tourism, agro-processing, paper and pulp processing, minerals and mining, and petrochemicals.

As of March 2010, the services sector, excluding financial services, contained 57.9% of total outstanding investment in the state, with the energy sector close behind with 39.9%. In Dimapur, there is currently an industrial growth center (IGC), and two development zones in the works, namely the Export Promotion Industrial Park (EPIP) for agro and food processing and a multi-product SEZ.

Agriculture

Major crops for the state include maize, sugar, paddy, potato, pineapple, and ginger. Slash and burn is still the most common technique used for agricultural farming in Nagaland. With these crops, development in processing industries has a good potential for success with improvements in technology and facilities.

With subtropical climates and fertile soils, Nagaland cultivates thousands of hectares of fruits and vegetables, including garlic, chili, tomato, potato, cabbage, banana, orange, passion fruit, pears, plum and sweet potato. But with basic transportation infrastructure and weak food processing industries, much of the food produced becomes wasted surplus if left unsold at local markets.

Planting of new orchards is encouraged by the Department of Horticulture to support the development of a preserved and processed fruits and vegetables industry, as well as for export. Many species of orchids are available in Nagaland, which has tremendous commercial potential. With the declaration of Guwahati as an international airport, cut flowers can also be exported from the state. Several medicinal herbs and plants are available in abundance in the hilly regions of the state; ginseng, in particular, is a medicinal root with high export value.

The state's climate is favorable for the development of Sericulture. The main four varieties of silk worms which are produced in Nagaland are Eri, Mulberry, Oak Tasar and Muga. Sericulture exhibit farms and spinning units have been set up in the state to promote the sector.

The Nagaland Bamboo Policy of 2005 strives to develop bamboo as an economic product, with research and development leading the effort. The state contains about 5% of India's total bamboo growth.

Minerals

Nagaland is rich in mineral resources. The studies conducted by the state geology and mining departments as well as by other central agencies such as the Geological Survey of India, the Oil and Natural Gas Corporation Ltd have located several mineral reserves. Some of these include petroleum and natural gas, coal, high grade limestone, nickel–cobalt-chromium bearing magnetite ore, marble and decorative stones, basalt, serpentine and quartzite. Further development in exploration and mining will require both domestic and foreign investments and advanced technology.

Handloom Weaving and Handicrafts

In light of the cultural traditions of the population of Nagaland, the handloom and handicrafts industry has great potential for growth. Basket weaving, pottery, spinning, weaving, carving, dying, and metalwork are just some of the products that are made. These products have widespread appeal and demand in the domestic as well as offshore markets.

Animal Husbandry and Meat Processing

The consumption of meat in the state is fairly high, yet because of the lack of modern technology and processing facilities, the production of meat and dairy is scattered and insufficient. Development opportunities lie in bringing advanced technology, expertise, and facilities into the state.

Tourism

The landscape of Nagaland is filled with green forests and deep valleys, coupled with a mild climate throughout the year; it is conducive to a successful tourism industry. The government is involved in the development of amusement parks, large resorts and hotels in order to ensure the right infrastructure for all types of tourists. Furthermore, with the opening of the state to international tourism following the relaxation of restricted area permits, a growing number of foreign tourists as well as domestic tourists visit Nagaland every year. Nicknamed "Land of Festivals," Nagaland hosts several festivals throughout the year as a part of tribal traditions, including Sekrenyi, Moatsu, Tokhu Emong, and Tuluni. Additionally, the Tourism Department of the state created the Hornbill festival, held annually in December, which gathers all the tribes of Nagaland together to celebrate and share in the festivities. The major tourists hotspots in the state are Dimapur, Kiphire, Kohima, Longleng, Mokokchung, Mon, Peren, Phek, Tuensang, Wokha and Zunheboto.

Infrastructure

The Government of Nagaland has recognized that adequate and sound infrastructure services are necessary to integrate the state with the rest of the nation and improve the quality of life of the people. Accordingly, it has undertaken several infrastructure projects in the state to attract foreign investors. State infrastructure includes railways, roadways and aviation, telecommunication and power.

Roadways

Nagaland has a reliable road network, which connects it to the rest of the country. The total length of the roads in the state is 13,395.9 km which includes national highways, state highways, district and village roads.

Railways

Train service is accessible in Dimapur, which is on the main line of the Northeast Frontier Railway. It is well connected to Guwahati, with a number of trains that shuttle between the two stations every day. Guwahati, on the other hand, has direct train lines with most of the major Indian cities and states. The passenger reservation system available at Kohima has been upgraded and an on-line reservation service from Kohima has been made available. Additional access to rail in the state is being developed.

Aviation

Nagaland has only one airport in Dimapur. Direct flights connect the airport to Guwahati and Kolkata. Efforts are being made to connect it to the major airports in India. Another airport at Kohima is planned.

Power

By 1981, electricity was available in 100% of villages in the state. As of March 2010, total installed power generation capacity in the state is 103.2 MW. It is estimated that Nagaland has 1,000 MW of hydro power generation capabilities, which is a huge investment opportunity.

Telecommunications

Telecommunications services are improving in the state, especially with the introduction of internet service. The Dimapurr Telecom District has now been upgraded to a Telecom Circle.

Resources

Government of Nagaland
http://nagaland.nic.in/
ITP Division, Ministry of External Affairs
http://www.indiainbusiness.nic.in/know-india/states/nagaland.htm

ORISSA

Area	155,707 sq km
Population	41.9 million
Capital	Bhubaneshwar
NSDP at current prices	US$30 billion (2009-10); 12.65% Y/Y growth
Per capita NSDP at current prices	US$740 (2009-10); 11.37% Y/Y growth
Literacy rate	73.45 percent
Principal religions	Hinduism
Principal languages	Oriya

- Orissa is an important maritime state with a coastline of 480 kilometers and strategic and natural port locations
- More than half of investments go towards large and medium industries, whereas over 95% of industries in the state are in handicrafts and cottage industries
- The government is encouraging investments in all sectors, especially IT, and infrastructure

Overview

Orissa, situated in the northeastern part of the Indian peninsula, covers an area of 155,707 km^2. It is bounded by the Bay of Bengal in the east, Chhattisgarh in the west, Jharkhand in the north; Andhra Pradesh in the south, and West Bengal in the northeast. The state is divided into five major regions, namely, the Orissa coastal plain in the east, the middle mountainous and highlands region; the central plateaus; the western rolling uplands and the major flood plains. It has a long coastline of about 500 km, with many beautiful beaches. The Chillika Lake is a brackish water lagoon located in the southern part of the Orissa's coastal plain which provides a haven for millions of birds. The lush green forests that cover much of Orissa are host to a wide variety of flora and fauna, including the Bengal tiger.

Orissa has a rich cultural heritage and is endowed with vast natural and mineral resources, which have helped to build its substantial industrial base. There are a large number of medium and small scale industries offering the foundation for the development of a strong corporate sector. The major industries in the public sector include a steel plant at Rourkela, an alumina refinery near Koraput, an aluminum smelter at Angul—a unit of Indian Rare Earth Ltd manufacturing heavy metals—a phosphate fertilizer plant at Paradeep and an urea plant at Talcher. In the private sector, there are several major groups which have set up medium to large industries in paper, automobile, synthetic fiber, cement, sugar, electronics, aluminum extrusions and sponge iron.

Business Opportunities

Orissa is considered to be one of the most preferred destinations for investors. It provides many advantages in regards to networks, natural resources, and sound government policies. It has a well-qualified and professional workforce skilled in IT and bio-technology. Mineral deposits, coastlines, agriculture, fishing, bio-technology and chemicals, and software IT offer vast scope for establishing new industries in Orissa. In addition, the state also has attractive tourism potential in the form of culture and ancient heritage. Development zones in the state include the Inland Container Depot, Agriculture Export Zone, and other Special Economic Zones.

Ninety five percent of Orissa's economy is made up by handicrafts and cottage industries. Small-scale industries come in second with almost 4% of the state's economy and large and medium industries constitute less than 1%. More than half of investments, however, go towards large and medium industries, while roughly 35 and 15% go into small-scale industries and handicrafts and cottage industries, respectively. The tertiary sector made up the most of GSDP in 2009–2010, at 46.9%.

Agriculture

Agriculture plays a large part in Orissa's economy as most of the state's total workforce directly or indirectly engages in it. The state places great emphasis on the continued growth of agriculture-based and food processing industries. The government has framed an agricultural policy to increase investment in agriculture; bringing about a shift from subsistence to commercial agriculture and thus providing a status of industry to agriculture. Investment opportunities in the sector include the provision of infrastructure like cold storage, lift irrigation and marketing; the setting up of agriculture-based industries for value addition to agricultural produce; seed production and quality planting material; agriculture-service centers; production of organic tea, coffee, ginger, turmeric, cashew, and aromatic rice; and increase of information technology.

Priority has been accorded to agriculture development through the application of high-end crop production technologies as well as adoption of integrated nutrient management and best management practices. Orissa is also involved in the production of horticulture and sericulture.

Fish and Livestock

Orissa's coastline and freshwater resources support a developing fishing industry. In addition, meat and dairy production in the state is looking to increase production output by attracting modern technology and techniques. New employment schemes and investments of better technology are potential indicators for growing opportunities in this sector.

Biotechnology

Given the rich bioresources base, the state offers several opportunities for investment in the sector. In particular, the sectors of tissue culture, herbal products, biofertilizers, biopesticides, and aqua-culture, as well as pharmaceuticals, are ripe for investment opportunities.

Handloom Weaving and Handicrafts

Orissa is known for its traditional handloom weaving and handicrafts. To continue output from this sector and to encourage entrepreneurship and self-employment among its population, the government has established assistance programs in areas such as sourcing raw materials, marketing, facilities, and financial support. This sector is particularly important to rural area communities.

Minerals

The state has vast and diverse mineral deposits amounting to almost 16.9% of India's total reserves. Mineral reserves in Orissa include chromate, nickel ore, graphite, bauxite, iron ore, manganese and coal. These reserves are a source of further investment and development for extraction and processing.

Information Technology

The government of Orissa has placed a lot of emphasis on developing its IT usage in the state and its industry sector strength. Several IT centers have been developed in the state, including a 3.12 acre area in Rourkela, a 53.229 acre bio-pharma IT park in Andharua, an information technology investment region in Bhubaneswar, and a 500 acre info valley in Jatin Tahasi.

Infrastructure

The government of Orissa has undertaken several infrastructure projects in order to attract investors and promote overall development of the state. Infrastructure in the state includes a well connected road and rail network, airports, ports, power and telecommunications.

Recognizing the crucial role played by infrastructure in economic development of a state, the government has announced an infrastructure policy. According to the policy, for rapid industrialization and balanced growth of the state, adequate facilities are a necessity. The policy aims to facilitate investments in the sector, by providing a framework for private participation in financing, construction, operation and maintenance of infrastructure projects.

Roadways

Orissa boasts a relatively well-developed network of roadways. A national highway connects to Kolkata and Chennai, in addition to the main line of transportation between east and south India. The state government is also encouraging investment in new road development and construction to increase connectivity in the state, particularly to rural areas. In total, Orissa has 242,736 km of roads.

Railways

Orissa is connected to other regions of India via the East Coast Railway, and is an important transfer post between east and west India. By the end of 2009, the state had a total of 2,439 km of rail.

Ports

Orissa is an important maritime state with a coastline of 480 km and strategic and natural port locations. Paradeep Port is one of India's 11 major ports, and is the main port area along the eastern coast of India, serving the states of Orissa, Andhra Pradesh, Madhya Pradesh, Uttar Pradesh, Bihar and West Bengal. The port is capable of handling almost all types of cargo. The facilities available at the port include iron and ore berths, cargo berths and equipment storage. It offers tremendous opportunities for international trade and is being expanded constantly.

Aviation

Bhubaneswar is home to Biju Patnaik airport with daily service to other major cities in India. The aviation facilities in the state currently also include 17 airstrips and 16 helipads, and is in the process of expansion and upgrading.

Power

In 2010, the state upgraded their total installed power generation capacity to 4,059.3 MW. With its vast water resources, Orissa also produces significant outputs of hydroelectricity power and is known for having surpluses of electricity. The state is also known for pioneering several sector reforms, and the state government continues to encourage private investment in the generation, transmission, and distribution of electricity in the power industry.

Telecommunications

The state has made rapid strides in the telecommunications sector. The network has spread to the remotest corners of the state, linking them to the information super highway.

Resources

Government of Orissa
http://www.orissa.gov.in/Portal/default.asp
Department of Industries, Government of Orissa
http://www.orissa.gov.in/industries/index.htm
ITP Division, Ministry of External Affairs
http://www.indiainbusiness.nic.in/know-india/states/orissa.htm
Team Orissa
http://www.teamorissa.org/

PUDUCHERRY

Area	479 sq km
Population	1.2 million
Capital	Puducherry
NSDP at current prices	US$2.6 billion (2009-10); 10.69% Y/Y growth
Per capita NSDP at current prices	US$2011 (2009-10); 5.32% Y/Y growth
Literacy rate	86.55 percent
Principal religions	Hinduism, Islam and Christianity
Principal languages	Tamil, Telugu, Malayalam, English and French

- Puducherry, once a French colony, still possesses much of its French-influenced architecture
- Leather is a major export
- The government is encouraging investments in all sectors, especially agro processing, textiles, leather products, auto components, and marine products

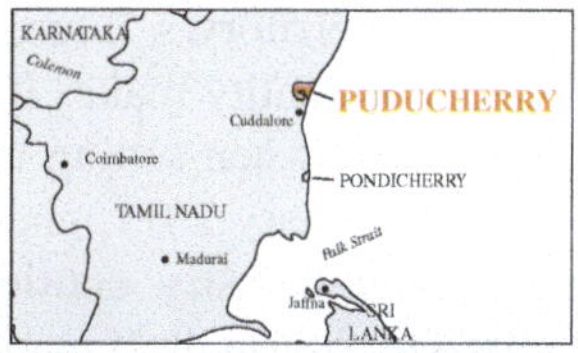

Overview

Puducherry, also known as Pondicherry, with a total area of 480 km^2, lies in the southern region of India. It is bounded by Tamil Nadu on three sides and by the Bay of Bengal in the east. It is on the east coast of India, about 160 km south of Chennai. It was once a French colony, and the French influence is still evident in the region's architecture.

In addition to Puducherry, the union territory of Puducherry is also comprised of three other coastal regions: Karaikal, Mahe and Yanam. Karaikal lies about 150 km south of Puducherry on the east coast. Mahe is situated on the Malabar Coast on the Western Ghats, surrounded by Kerala, and is about 647 km from Puducherry. Yanam adjoins the East Godavari district of Andhra Pradesh and is about 870 km from Puducherry and about 200 km from Visakhapatnam Airport.

Business Opportunities

Puducherry is fast becoming a preferred destination for investors. It is well-linked to almost all the southern states of India, and there exists immense business potential in the various sectors of the economy; main products of export are leather, chemicals, textiles, and metal goods. Puducherry's large labor force spans various skill levels and the availability of a variety of agricultural crops is key to the union territory's future and prosperity. In addition, its unique cultural and ecological identity makes it an attractive tourist spot. All of these advantages can be exploited when setting up business in the union territory.

As of January 2011, chemicals and chemical products were the most strongly represented industry entities with 1714, while repairing and personal services comprised the smallest number, with 261 and 282, respectively, according to data compiled by the Puducherry Department of Industries and Commerce. Small sized industries, by far, are the majority type of businesses in the state. Industries labeled for expansion by the state government include textiles, leather products, auto components, marine products, and agro processing.

Agriculture

Marine product processing is an important component of the territory's agro-processing industry. Puducherry's long coastline provides good opportunities for the growth and development of its fisheries sector. Great opportunities exist in the shrimping culture and crab farming. The modern fishing harbors are at Thengaithittu, Puducherry and Karukalacheri, Karaikal.

The state government hopes to expand Puducherry's agricultural industries into floriculture and tropical fruit pulp and processing such as guava.

Textiles

Textiles are the traditional industries of Puducherry. Availability of specialized skilled manpower in the territory is an advantage for the growth of the textile industry. The fabric produced is of high quality, and there is a huge demand in the overseas market. Textiles, thus, are one of the most important exports from Puducherry.

Leather

The leather industry is one of Puducherry's top industries. It has considerable expansion potential and is an export-oriented industry. Skilled craftsmen are manufacturing leather products at international standards. As a result, leather makes up the bulk of exports from Puducherry. The government has been making considerable efforts to expand the indigenous base of the leather industry as well as promoting leather products of the union territory in foreign markets.

Information Technology

Information technology is an ascendant industry in Puducherry and may hold the key to the state's future success. A large pool of IT professionals and state-of-the-art communication facilities are available. The IT sector provides ample employment opportunities in the territory. Accordingly, the government of Puducherry has formulated an IT policy aimed at accelerating the growth of IT industries in terms of hardware, software, services and training.

Tourism

As a traditionally popular tourist spot in India, Puducherry offers a variety of incentives for investors to improve its tourism infrastructure. Investment opportunities exists in developing hotels, amusement parks, multiplexes, beach resorts, eco-tourism sites, health spas, arts and craft villages, and other tourism-related products.

Puducherry is a blend of both French and Tamil cultural heritage and known for its town planning. It is close to many southern Indian towns and cities, which are known for their art, religious and cultural heritage as well as great natural beauty.

Infrastructure

The government of Puducherry has been making considerable efforts to attract large investments into the state. It has undertaken several infrastructure projects to integrate the union territory with the rest of the nation and improve the quality of life of the people.

Puducherry is easily accessible through airways, roadways, railways and waterways, and is well-connected to all districts and major towns of various states like Tamil Nadu, Karnataka, Kerala and Andhra Pradesh. The existence of an efficient power supply system and excellent telecommunications network in the union territory makes it a preferred destination for investors.

Roadways

Puducherry boasts a wide network of roadways, 2,552 km in total, connecting every village in the state. National Highway NH-45A connects Puducherry to major areas of southern India including Chennai, Bangalore and Tiruchirapalli. Puducherry and Chennai are linked via the East Coast Road, and there are frequent buses from Puducherry to Chennai, Chidambaram, Thanjavur, Coimbatore, and other locations.

Railways

Puducherry has a limited railway network. Villupuram, Villianur, is the nearest railway junction, which is fairly well-connected to places like Chennai, Madurai and Trichy.

Aviation

There is a regional airport within Puducherry, and the nearest international airport is in Chennai, which is around 162 km from Puducherry. The airport at Chennai has flights to almost all the states and cities in India as well as countries in Europe, the Middle East, Southeast Asia and the Americas.

Waterways

Puducherry has a minor port on the east coast of India, located between two major Indian ports, namely, Chennai and Tuticorin. This minor port is an open roadstead anchorage port situated about 170 km south of Chennai and is suitable for light operations during fair weather months (February to September). This is being modernized with container handling facilities and storing infrastructure. Also, Puducherry is situated close to several other ports including Nagapattinam, Kakinada, Vishakapatnam and Cochin.

Power

Being a part of the southern grid, adequate power is allocated to Puducherry. The power demand of the territory, including that of the four regions of Puducherry, Karaikal, Mahe and Yanam, is 382.9 MW during peak periods. This requirement is met through power from the Central Generating Stations, by purchasing power from the neighboring State Electricity Boards, namely, Tamil Nadu Electricity Board and Kerala State Electricity Board, and from the Pondicherry Power Corporation Limited, Karaikal.

Telecommunications

Adequate telecommunications infrastructure including cellular, pager, ISDN, and internet services are available in Puducherry. The territory has recorded 92,730 telephone lines and holds 31 telephone exchanges.

Resources

Government of Puducherry
http://www.pon.nic.in/
Department of Industries & Commerce, Government of Puducherry
http://www.industrypuducherry.com/index.shtml
Department of Tourism, Government of Puducherry
http://tourism.puducherry.gov.in/
India in Business, ITP Division, Ministry of External Affairs, Government of India
Puducherry
http://www.indiainbusiness.nic.in/know-india/states/pondicherry.htm

PUNJAB

Area	50,362 sq km
Population	27.7 million
Capital	Chandigarh
NSDP at current prices	US$39.3 billion (2009-10); 17.56% Y/Y growth
Per capita NSDP at current prices	US$1377 (2009-10); 15.42% Y/Y growth
Literacy rate	76.68 percent
Principal religions	Hinduism and Sikhism
Principal languages	Punjabi, Hindi and English

- Punjab is known as the granary of India
- The state has some of the best transportation infrastructure in India
- Investment-friendly initiatives and tax benefits have helped to accelerate Punjab's economic development and strength

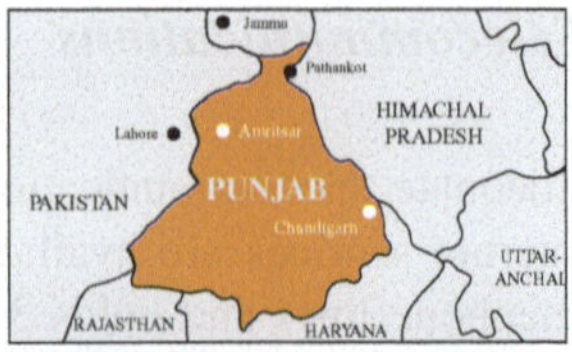

Overview

Punjab is known for its hard working, energetic, enthusiastic and adventurous people. It is a highly fertile state and has five rivers. Culturally, it is a state divided into three regions, namely, Malwa, Majha and Doaba. It is well known for its performing and visual arts, as well as literature, music, dance, drama, poetry and paintings.

The total area of Punjab is 50,362 km^2, which is 1.54% of the country's total geographical land. It is bound in the west by Pakistan, in the north by Jammu and Kashmir, in the northeast by Himachal Pradesh, and in the south by Haryana and Rajasthan.

To increase investments in various sectors of the state, the government has instated many policies and incentives that have resulted in Punjab's rapid growth in agriculture, industry, services, education, social welfare, and rural development. Punjab currently boasts one of the best qualities of life for a state in India.

Business Opportunities

Punjab has made remarkable progress in the field of agriculture and is recognized as the granary of India. The state has also made improvements in industrialization through the coordinated development of small, medium and large scale industries. It has a predominance of small-scale industries; these units produce bicycle parts, sewing machines, hand tools, machine tools, auto parts, electrical items, sports goods, surgical instruments, leather goods, hosiery, knitwear, nuts and bolts, textiles, sugar and vegetable oil. Punjab has also taken up several investment-friendly policies and incentives for developing further growth in the state, including a "single window service" program for entrepreneurs, tax benefits, and power guarantees. In 2009, Ludhiana, Punjab, was named one of the best places for doing business in India by the World Bank Study. Agriculture and services are the main drivers for the state's economic growth; the primary and tertiary sectors make up 78% of GSDP.

Agriculture

Punjab is a land of boundless opportunity for agriculture. Punjab, with only 1.5% geographical area of the country, produces 22% of India's wheat; 12% of its rice and 12% of its cotton. Other agricultural activities include sugarcane, oil seeds, horticulture and forestry. The cropping intensity of the state is more than 186%, earning it the moniker of India's food basket and granary. The investment potential in the agriculture sector lies in the following areas:

- Integrated Pest Management
- Bio-fertilizers
- Crop diversification
- Bee keeping
- Floriculture

Information Technology

Punjab is one of the favored IT destinations in India. SAS Nagar, Mohali in the vicinity of Chandigarh, has emerged as an attractive hot spot for IT and IT-enabled industries. The state government aims to deploy IT as a catalyst for economic growth, efficient governance and human resource development.

Tourism

Punjab is a destination for religious pilgrimages and wildlife sanctuaries. The major places of tourist interest include the Golden Temple, Durgiana Mandir, Jallianwala Bagh in Amritsar, Takhat Sri Kesgarh Sahib, the Khalsa Heritage Complex at Anandpur Sahib and Bhakra Dam. Tourism in the state is a source of substantial revenue, employment generation, and infrastructure.

Infrastructure

Punjab has one of the best infrastructure networks in India in terms of rail, road and transportation. Mohali-Chandigarh and Amritsar are connected to the rest of India and the world by fast trains, domestic and international flights.

Roadways

The Punjab Roads and Bridges Development Board is the main agency for improving road infrastructure in the state. All villages in the state are linked by all-weather roads and major towns of all the adjoining states are connected by national highways.

Railways

Punjab is well-connected by rail to other areas of India, with over 2,098 km within the state. The major rail networks that pass through the state are: Amritsar-Ambala-Delhi; Sriganganagar-Ambala-Delhi; Ferozepur-Ludhiana-Ambala; Pathankot-Rupnagar-Fatehgarh Sahib; and Sriganganagar-Bathinda-Narwana. Chandigarh, Ludhiana, Amritsar, Ferozepur and Jalandhar are on the main line and have excellent daily train services to New Delhi including convenient overnight trains.

Aviation

The state has a domestic airport at Chandigarh, an international airport at Rajasansi, and two aerodromes at Patiala and Sahnewal, Ludhiana. There are also four civil aviation clubs located at Ludhiana, Patiala, Amritsar and Jalandhar.

Power

The three main sources of power in the state are thermal, hydroelectric and solar power. At the end of 2010, the state's installed power generation capacity was 6,921.9 MW. By 2012, Punjab is geared to be a power surplus state based on the major government-backed projects in Gidderbaha, Talwandi Sabo, Rajpura, and Goindwal Sahib.

Telecommunications

Telephone and allied facilities are available to all cities and small towns of the state. International direct dial facilities are available from the majority of villages. The various service providers are BSNL, Reliance, HSCL, Spice Telecom, Airtel, Hutch and Tata.

Resources

Government of Punjab
http://www.punjabgovt.nic.in/index.html
Department of Industries, Government of Punjab
http://pbindustries.gov.in/index.htm
Department of Information Technology, Government of Punjab
http://www.doitpunjab.gov.in/index.html
India in Business, ITP Division, Ministry of External Affairs, Government of India
Punjab
http://www.indiainbusiness.nic.in/know-india/states/punjab.htm

RAJASTHAN

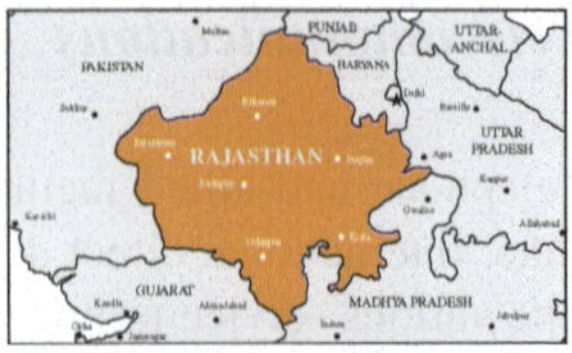

Area	342,239 sq km
Population	68.62 million
Capital	Jaipur
NSDP at current prices	US$43.2 billion (2009-10); 8.80% Y/Y growth
Per capita NSDP at current price	US$652 (2009-10); 6.98% Y/Y growth
Literacy rate	67.06 percent
Principal religions	Hinduism, Islam, Jainism and Sikhism
Principal languages	Hindi, Rajasthani and English

- Rajasthan is the largest state in India by land area
- The state is aggressively increasing its emphasis on attracting private sector investment in all industry sectors
- Rajasthan is a large producer in India of minerals, herbs, and spices

Overview

In terms of land size, Rajasthan is the largest state in India, covering 342,239 km^2. It is bounded by Pakistan in the west and northwest, Punjab in the north, Haryana in the northeast, Uttar Pradesh in the east, Madhya Pradesh in the southeast, and Gujarat in the southwest. The southern part of the state is 225 km from the Gulf of Kutch and 400 km from the Arabian Sea.

The state is rich in natural diversity, ranging from dense forests and hills to deserts and valleys. The Aravali Mountain Range and the Great Indian Desert are both located in Rajasthan. The state's cultural history includes forts, palaces, carved temples, museums, archaeological sites and art galleries, as well as a diversity of peoples, customs, culture, costumes, music, dialects and cuisine. It is a resource-rich state, with the second largest mineral deposits in India, both metallic and non-metallic. It is a large provider of wollastonite, zinc, and copper, as well as a major producer of agricultural products.

Business Opportunities

Rajasthan possesses many opportunities for growth, especially in its agricultural and mineral industries. Leather, wool, dairy, meat, textiles, tourism, automobiles, consumer goods, and IT are just some of the growth industries present in Rajasthan. In 2009–2010, the tertiary sector accounted for 45.2% of GSDP.

The state has shown significant industrial activity, based on the exploitation of its agriculture and rich mineral deposits. It is manufacturing a wide range of products, including synthetic and cotton yarn, cement, marble and granite slabs, edible oils, chemicals, rubber and plastic based items, fertilizers, electrical and electronics goods, ceramic and glass. In addition, its landscape diversity has made tourism in the state a preferred sector for investment. It is also the second largest mineral producing state in India and one of the largest producers of cement.

Agriculture

Rajasthan has a varied climate ranging from arid western regions to humid southeastern regions. It is able to produce a wide variety of products from arid fruits to scented rice. It is a leading producer of bajra, barley, pulses, coriander, cummin, and other herbs. The state alone contributes 50% towards the country's spice production, offering numerous opportunities for the development of agro-based industries. Additional industries include solvent extraction, oleo-resins, orange juice, malt extracts, floriculture, mushrooms, tomato processing as well as other processing industries based on fruit and vegetables. Industries based on herbal and medicinal plants, poultry products and non-edible oil have good exporting potential.

Tourism

Rajasthan is known for its exotic landscape, rich cultural heritage, wildlife, sand dunes, green forests and biodiversity. Some of the prominent tourism locations are Jaipur, Jodhpur, Udaipur, Bikaner, Mount Abu, Sariska Tiger Sanctuary in Alwar, Keoladeo National Park at Bharatpur, Ajmer, Jaisalmer, Pali and Chittorgarh. Rajasthan's fairs and festivals have assumed international prominence.

Information Technology

Rajasthan is one of the front-runner states in India in the use of IT in government functions. The state government is making a huge effort to leverage the benefits of IT to improve the quality of life in the state. It has undertaken several steps to promote Rajasthan as an attractive location for investment in the IT industry. The Rajasthan State Industrial Development and Investment Corporation (RIICO) has established IT parks in Jaipur, Kota, Udaipur, and Jokhpur to promote IT investment and exports. Incentive policies are also present to help attract investment into the state's IT sector.

Biotechnology

Bio-technology is an industry that Rajasthan is focusing on for future investments. Various opportunities are present in areas including research and development, bio-pesticides, genetic improvements of seeds and animals, dry farming, recycling of bio-products, waste management, bio fuels, and energy.

Infrastructure

The state government has recognized the need for efficient infrastructure and is developing the state's facilities to cater to increasing investment. The entire state is well connected to other parts of the country through rail, road and air transport. In order to further strengthen its infrastructure, the state government is encouraging private investment into construction and the improvement of roads.

Roadways

Thirteen major national highways pass through Rajasthan and connect the state to major industrial hubs in other areas of India. Further investment is planned to expand the network of roads in the state to support a growing economy.

Railways

The state has a well-established railway network, totaling 5,683 km. Jodhpur, Jaipur, Bikaner, Kota, Sawai Madhopur and Bhagalpur are some of the main railway junctions. Most of the important towns and cities are connected by regular rail services to New Delhi, Mumbai, Kolkata, Bangalore, Chennai, Hyderabad and Ahmadabad.

Aviation

Rajasthan is easily accessible by air, with commercial airlines offering services to the cities of Jaipur, Jodhpur and Udaipur. Indian Airlines and other airlines provide regular flights from New Delhi, Mumbai and Ahmadabad. In addition, Bikaner, Kota and Jaisalmer have been included in the list of cities open for private investment in air taxi services.

Power

More recently, the state government has increased its focus on promoting private sector investment in power generation in the state. Many incentives and tax breaks have been put in place to attract investors, which will only require private sector projects to sell at minimum 50% of its generated power within Rajasthan.

Resources

Government of Rajasthan
http://www.rajasthan.gov.in/
ITP Division, Ministry of External Affairs Rajasthan
http://www.indiainbusiness.nic.in/know-india/states/rajasthan.htm

SIKKIM

Area	7,096 sq km
Population	607,688
Capital	Gangtok
NSDP at current prices	US$504 million (2008-09); 14.10% Y/Y growth
Per capita NSDP at current prices	US$847 (2008-09); 12.61% Y/Y grow
Literacy rate	76.6 percent
Principal religions	Hinduism, Christianity and Buddhism
Principal languages	Nepali and English

- Sikkim has an abundant supply of water, which gives the state enormous hydropower potential
- Due to its natural endowments, Sikkim has great potential to flourish into a popular eco-tourism destination
- The government is actively promoting IT industry in the state with special emphasis on e-governance

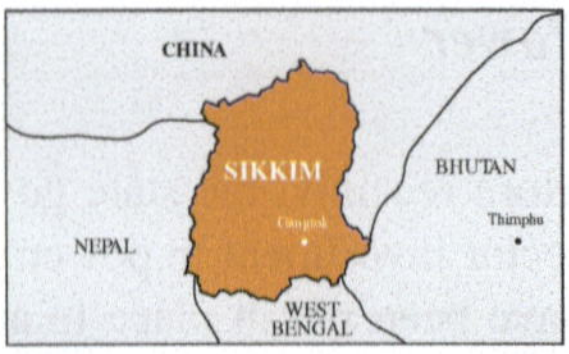

Overview

Sikkim is situated in the eastern Himalayan stretch of the Indian subcontinent. It is bounded by vast stretches of the Tibetan Plateau in the north; the Chumbi Valley of Tibet and the Kingdom of Bhutan in the east, Nepal in the west, and Darjeeling (West Bengal) in the south. Mount Kanchenjunga, the world's third highest mountain, dominates this tiny Himalayan state. Sikkim is rich with biodiversity. It includes nearly one third of the total species of angiosperm found in India, around 4,000 species of flowering plants, 300 species of ferns, 144 species of mammals, and 600 species of birds. Such natural beauty along with ideal climatic conditions make it an attractive tourist and investment destination.

Ethnically, the people of Sikkim can be divided into three groups: Nepalis, Bhutias and Lepchas. They are mainly engaged in tourism, horticulture and agriculture.

Given these opportunities, the government of Sikkim has made several efforts to attract investment into the various sectors of the state. Investors can establish various industrial units by optimally utilizing the numerous resources as well as the incentives and schemes available in the state.

Business Opportunities

Sikkim, in spite of its hilly terrain, has several advantages and opportunities for investment. It has a rich resource base which can be utilized to set up industrial units in the state. There is immense unharnessed potential in the various sectors of its economy. For instance, it is the largest producer of cardamom and utilizes huge areas to cultivate many crops. Its traditional handloom weaving and handicrafts are in demand internationally.

Agriculture

Sikkim is an agrarian state, such that agriculture is the major economic activity practiced on its terraced fields. Maize, rice, wheat, potato, large cardamom, ginger and turmeric are the principal crops; while mandarin orange, guava, passion fruit and banana are the principal fruits grown in the state. As far as floriculture is concerned, the state produces a variety of orchids, gladioli and rhododendrons, the commercial cultivation of which is picking up rapidly. Even medicinal and aromatic herbs are seeing an expanding market both nationally and internationally.

There are several limitations in terms of productivity, irrigation and the scope for extending cultivation due to the practice of terrace farming. Investment is needed in the fields of horticulture, floriculture and in innovative practices of land management. Also, due to the availability of all the necessary raw materials, there is enormous untapped potential to set up various agro-based industries in the state.

Handloom Weaving and Handicrafts

The traditional handicrafts and handloom products of the state are of high quality and enjoy huge demand, both nationally and internationally. These include carpet weaving, cane and bamboo crafts, spinning wool, handmade paper and Thanka paintings, which are world famous. The industry has great potential to generate income and employment in the state. In order to give a boost to the sector, the government of Sikkim has been making several efforts, which include providing training to upgrade the quality and designs of the products, and bringing expertise and professionals for their marketing and supply.

Information Technology

The state has already seen many achievements in the knowledge-based industries such as information technology. The government of Sikkim has placed IT high on its agenda. The Department of Information Technology has been set up to prepare extensive projects, particularly aimed at e-governance; promoting IT enabled services like medical transcription and computerized Braille. The real potential of the IT industry lies in its skilled manpower resource. The government has framed an IT policy with the aim of transforming Sikkim into an IT state.

Tourism

Sikkim, due to its spectacular natural beauty, cultural uniqueness and religious mysticism, is emerging as one of the premier tourist destinations in the Eastern Himalayas. It includes a wealth of natural resources, the third highest mountain in the world, rich flora and fauna, as well as cultural festivals. The government of Sikkim is encouraging private participation in the developmental and commercial activities of the tourism sector. There are tremendous opportunities for investment to meet the demands for resorts, hotels, restaurants, surface and air transportation and, entertainment outlets.

Infrastructure

The government of Sikkim has undertaken several infrastructure projects in order to attract investment and ensure overall welfare of the state. Because the roadway is the only method of transportation in Sikkim, the government is planning to launch projects to establish airports and to explore waterways through its vision statement for the development of roads and bridges up to 2020.

Roadways

Sikkim has a wide network of roads, which is its only means of transportation. The total length of roads amount to 1,983.62 km. The National Highway 31A connects Siliguri to Gangkok with an all-weather metaled road stretching along the Teesta River. Through its vision for the development of roads and bridges by 2020, the state government aims to connect all village areas, improve roads, upgrade all national highways to four-lane roads and all state roads to two-lane roads.

Railways

The closest railway stations are Siliguri (114 km away) and New Jalpaiguri (125 km away) connecting Kolkata, Delhi, Guwahati, Lucknow and other important cities.

Power

Sikkim is a state with abundant hydropower potential with capacity of 8,000 MW untapped. The total installed capacity of power in the state is 100.70 MW. The state was also able to generate additional revenue by selling its power surplus.

Resources

The Official Website of the Government of Sikkim
http://www.sikkim.gov.in/
Official Portal of NIC Sikkim State Center
http://www.sikkim.nic.in/

TAMIL NADU

Area	130,058 sq km
Population	72.14 million
Capital	Chennai
NSDP at current prices	US$67.5 billion (2008-09); 11.33% Y/Y growth
Per capita NSDP at current prices	US$1017 (2008-09); 10.55% Y/Y growth
Literacy rate	80.33 percent
Principal religions	Hinduism
Principal languages	Tamil and English

- Tamil Nadu is the third most urbanized state after Maharashtra and Gujar
- Tamil Nadu is a leader in the field of technology with numerous leading companies settled in the state; they include leaders in the Indian IT sector Tata Consultancy Services (TCS), Infosys, Wipro, and Satyam, among others

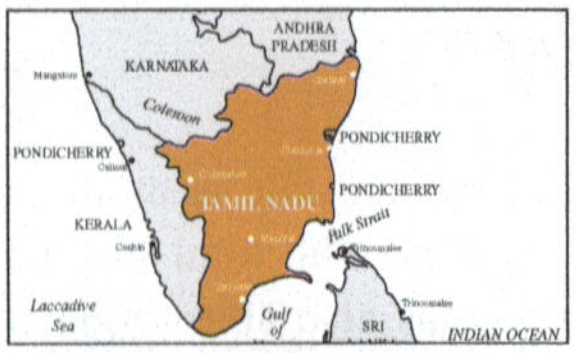

Overview

Tamil Nadu is the 11th largest state in India and the third most urbanized state next to Maharashtra and Gujarat. It is located in the southeastern part of the Indian peninsula. Tamil Nadu has a long eastern coastline dotted with beaches on the Bay of Bengal in the east. It is bounded in the north by Andhra Pradesh and Karnataka, in the west by Kerala, in the east by the Bay of Bengal, and in the south by the Indian Ocean.

Chennai, the capital city of Tamil Nadu, is the gateway to South India with an international airport, sea port and good rail and road network connectivity. Coimbatore, Madurai and Tiruchirappalli, Salem and Tirunelveli are some of the other major towns. The state has a large number of educational institutions and is a leader in the field of science and technology and particularly in information technology.

Tamil Nadu is one of the most developed states in India. Literacy levels in the state are some of the highest of all Indian states.

The state is experiencing rapid industrialization with overall economic development and has grown as a manufacturing powerhouse, especially in automobiles and textiles. The state's capital city, Chennai is often called "The Detroit of India."

Business Opportunities

Tamil Nadu is also one of the most developed states in terms of industrial development. The state government is focused on stimulating further industrial development, attracting investment, facilitating new manufacturing capacity and enabling global manufacturing competence and the competitiveness of local industry. Tamil Nadu has emerged as a front ranking state in attracting investments. Between the year 2000 and the year 2009, Tamil Nadu attracted the fifth highest value of foreign direct investment in India.

Software and Electronics

Tamil Nadu has witnessed substantial growth in IT, ITES, BPO and IT hardware manufacturing sectors. The presence of leading technology companies such as Dell, Nokia-Siemens, Samsung and Moser Baer in the Tamil Nadu has helped strengthen the state's computer and electronic hardware sectors. The number of software units in the state is also growing rapidly and the state is now India's second-largest software exporter by value. The rapid rise in the number of national and international players that have chosen to establish their business premises and manufacturing facilities as well as the expansion of the activities of the established firms in this state is a firm indication that Tamil Nadu has emerged as a preferred destination for domestic as well as foreign direct investment. Leaders in the Indian IT sector such as Tata Consultancy Services (TCS), Infosys, Wipro, Satyam, HCL, Patni Computers, I-Flex, Polaris and Hexaware as well as many international companies including Accenture, Verizon, Xansa, Office Tiger, and Cognizant Technology have established their operations in Tamil Nadu. The state's IT sector accounted for an 11% share of India's total investment in IT and is aiming to increase this number to 25% by 2013.

Agriculture and Food Processing

Tamil Nadu has a rich resource endowment. Fruit such as mango and banana, and vegetables and spices are abundantly available. Owing to the ideal climatic conditions a strong agro-based food industry has emerged in the state. The state is a world leader in agricultural production with a high yield per hectare of sugarcane, rice and groundnut.

Textile Industry

Tamil Nadu is called the "yarn bowl" of the country with 47% of India's spinning capacity and 60% of the yarn exports originating in the state. Tamil Nadu's textile industry, which includes handloom, power loom, textile and spinning, is the largest employer, after the agricultural sector. The Coimbatore, Erode and Tirupur districts are known collectively as the "Textile Valley of India." Tirupur and Erode are India's largest exporters of knitwear with 56% of India's total knitwear exports originating from Tirupur. Tirupur is also known collectively as "knitting city" and is home to about 3,000 exporters.

Automotive Industry

Tamil Nadu's capital city, Chennai, is growing as a major export hub for vehicles in the Southeast Asian markets. The state has a 30% share in the India automotive industry. Its automotive sector contributes significantly to the state's economy as it accounts for 8% of GSDP and provides direct employment to about 300,000 people. Some of the major companies in the industry have a presence in Tamil Nadu including Ford Motor Company, Hyundai Motor India Limited, Mitsubishi Motors Corporation and Nissan Motor India Private Limited.

Chemicals and Petrochemicals

The chemicals industry has grown rapidly in India and overseas. The state traditionally has a strong base in the chemicals industry. Manali, situated on the outskirts of Chennai, has emerged as a major petrochemical complex. The petrochemical industry here is on the threshold of rapid expansion.

Biotechnology

Tamil Nadu is rich in bio-resources. The variety of topography provides tremendous biodiversity rarely seen in any other single state. The forest, agricultural and plant resource base of the state are both large and diverse and represent great market opportunity for biotechnology products.

Infrastructure

Tamil Nadu has made tremendous progress in infrastructure development which has been rated as "one of the best" by several independent studies. The state is at the forefront of the Indian subcontinent in providing an efficient transport service.

The government has encouraged private sector participation in the process of infrastructure development. This has resulted in the rapid expansion of railways, roadways and the capacity enhancement of ports. The road network of the state has considerably influenced economic development, population distribution, size of cities and towns, environmental quality, energy consumption, and access to social infrastructure.

Ports

Tamil Nadu has 3 major ports and 15 minor ports. There are three major ports in Chennai, Ennore and Tuticorin, which handle approximately 12.3% of the total traffic at all major ports in India. The major ports fall under the control of the government of India whereas the minor ports fall under the control of the state government. The Tamil Nadu Maritime Board is responsible for administering, controlling, regulating and managing the minor ports.

Aviation

There are six airports in Tamil Nadu. There are two international airports in Chennai and Trichy and four domestic airports located in Chennai, Coimbatore, Tuticorin and Madurai. Chennai International Airport is the largest in southern India. It is the main center of airline routes in southeast India.

Roadways

Tamil Nadu is at the forefront for developing road infrastructure. The total length of roadways in the state is 198,642 km. It consists of 4,873 km of 24 national highways, 9,384 km of state highways, 11,288 km of major district roads and 34,293 km of other district roads. The state's road connectivity improved significantly with surfaced road reaching 80.8% of total roadways. The single lane roads are being expanded to multi-lane roads and bypass roads are being constructed for major towns.

Railways

The total length of the railroad is 3,926.99 km, of which 70.65% of the length is broad gauge and 29.35% is meter gauge. The main junctions are Chennai, Madurai, Tiruchirapalli, Coimbatore and Salem. Installing additional lines between Karur and Salem, Tindivanam and Tiruvannamalai, Erode and Palani, and Attipattu and Puttur is under consideration. The Chennai Metro Rail Project is being carried out at a rapid pace to address the traffic congestion on the roads. Under phase I of the project, a railroad from Washermenpet to the Airport extending 23.1 km and a railroad connecting Chennai Central to St. Thomas Mount extending 45.1 km will be established with the completion target of 2014–2015. Aside from 41% contribution from the Government of India and the State Government, the project will be taken on by private companies.

Power

Tamil Nadu's power is generated by the Tamil Nadu Electricity Board (TNEB) and by other independent power producers. The total installed capacity for electricity in the state is 14,410 MW. Tamil Nadu's power generation from renewable energy sources increased to as much as 4,790 MW. Of this, 99.6% came from the private sector. Wind power accounts for about 90% of the renewable power generating capacity in the state. Tamil Nadu has renewable energy generating potential also in biomass, solid wastes and solar sources. The state's power sector received more than half of all infrastructure related investments in 2010. Tamil Nadu is aiming to become power sufficient by 2011 and a power surplus state after 2012.

Telecommunications

The state offers state-of-the-art telecommunications infrastructure for high-speed large volume data transfers. Wireless connections in Tamil Nadu amount to an estimated 53.7 million, with 3.6 million wire-line connections, according to the Telecom Regulatory Authority of India (TRAI). The proportion of phone availability is 48.12% for Tamil Nadu ranking its tele-density the 8th highest in India.

Resources

Government of Tamil Nadu
http://www.tn.gov.in/

TRIPURA

Area	10,492 sq km
Population	3.67 million
Capital	Agartala
NSDP at current prices	US$2.3 billion (2007-08); 4.83% Y/Y growth
Per capita NSDP at current prices	US$650 (2007-08); 3.56% Y/Y growth
Literacy rate	87.75 percent
Principal religions	Hinduism, Islam and Christianity
Principal languages	Bengali and Kokborak

- Tripura has a strategic location as a potential gateway between Bangladesh and the northeast
- The state has vast reserves of natural gas, offering a great opportunity to set up gas-based industrial units or to utilize gas as a cheaper source of energy
- It is the second largest rubber producing state

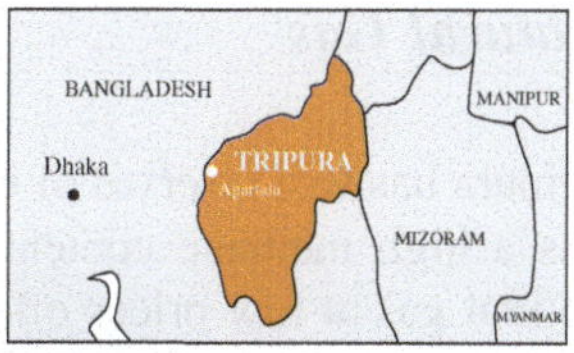

Overview

Tripura is one of the seven states in the northeastern part of India. It is bounded in the north, west, south and southeast by Bangladesh and in the east it has a common boundary with Assam and Mizoram. Tripura's location is strategic in the context of international trade, as it sits between Bangladesh and Southeast Asia.

It is the second largest state in northeastern India in terms of population. The state is rich in natural and human resources. It has vast reserves of natural gas with a high methanol content. There is potential for setting up projects in gas-based fertilizer, methane, PVC, compressed natural gas and other related projects. The state has a large variety of fruit crops including pineapples, oranges and jackfruit.

The Government of Tripura has made the effort to attract investment into the various sectors of the state. Investors can set up various industrial units by optimally utilizing the numerous resources as well as the incentives and schemes available in the state.

Business Opportunities

Tripura offers an investor-friendly environment. The government welcomes investments into the state, from both domestic and foreign investors. The Tripura Industrial Development Agency was established to provide a single-window service to investors in facilitating all necessary government clearances.

Natural Gas

Tripura has vast reserves of natural gas in non-associate form. The high quality gas has a high methane content of up to 97%. The availability of superior quality natural gas at low prices offers a great opportunity to prospective investors to set up gas-based industrial units, such as using natural gas as feedstock to produce urea, methanol, PVC and other projects. Natural gas can also be utilized as a cheaper source of energy for various energy-intensive industrial projects. Natural gas is available at the Baramura hills and in Rokhia, where gas-based power plants have been set up.

Rubber

Tripura is known as the second largest rubber producing state. It has a total plantation potential of 1 million ha. Its vast potential allowed Tripura to develop as a state with great potential for rubber-based industries. Tripura was the first to set up a rubber-wood factory in northeastern India in 2009 and a rubber park will be established in the state.

Food Processing

The State Government has identified food processing as a major investment area and there is vast potential in food processing. Tripura's climate is ideally suited for producing a large variety of horticultural crops. The "Queen" and "Kew" varieties of pineapple, jampui oranges, litchis and cashews from Tripura are well known in the rest of the country. A food park and a pineapple agri-export zone is being developed in the state to foster its growth in food processing industry.

Information Technology

Tripura is considered the second best IT destination in the northeast. The IT sector, including IT-enabled services, has been identified as one of the major potential growth sectors by the state. The high literacy rate of the state provides an additional advantage for the development of the sector. The State Government has also accorded special status to this industry and special incentives have been announced.

Tourism

Tripura is an attractive tourist destination. The state has a rich cultural heritage. There are number of historical Hindu and Buddhist sites. The state also has rich flora and fauna. In Tripura, hotels have been considered as industry, with a view to promote tourism. All incentives available to other industrial activities are also available for setting up hotels.

Handicrafts

A large variety of handicrafts using bamboo and cane are made by different ethnic groups in Tripura. The State Government has initiated steps in view of the vast potential of the industry to grow, both in domestic as well as international markets.

Infrastructure

With one of the lowest power tariffs in India, the state has developed a fairly good industrial infrastructure. There are five existing industrial estate areas. In addition, a growth center project is under way. The government is constructing an export promotion industrial park and is also in the process of setting up an IT park at Agartala.

Roadways

The total length of roads in the state is 15,551 km, of which major district roads constitute 90 km, smaller district roads amount to 1,274 km, and state highways account for 545 km. Tripura is connected to Guwahati by National Highway. Its road network will be stretched to the southernmost point of the state at Sabroom, which is only 75 km from Chittagong Port of Bangladesh.

Railways

Tripura's major railway stations are located at Agartala, Dhamanagar and Kumarghat. Tripura is expected to witness massive improvement in its railroad network in the coming years with many projects being implemented. Agartala is currently linked by railway to Siliguri and it will be extended to Sabroom located on the southern part of Tripura by 2012. A railway connecting Kumargaht and Agartala covering 119 km is also under construction.

Aviation

Singerbhil domestic airport located in Agartala is the single main airport of Tripura. It is the second busiest airport in northeastern India. It operates flights connecting to major cities such as Kolkata, Delhi, Mumbai and Guwahati.

Power

The total installed power generation capacity is 244.1 MW. Tripura has reached the power-surplus state during non-peak period. Its tarrifs on power are also much lower than other states.

Telecommunications

Tripura has total number of 5,519,150 cellular subscribers, 88 telephone exchanges and 84,207 telephone connections installed as of 2009. All telecom services including landline, mobile, WLL, 3G, Broadband/WiMAX internet are available in Tripura.

Resources

Official Website of Government of Tripura
http://www.tripura.nic.in/

UTTAR PRADESH

Area	240,928 sq km
Population	199.58 million
Capital	Lucknow
NSDP at current prices	US$96.6 billion (2009-10); 19.05% Y/Y growth
Per capita NSDP at current prices	US$493 (2009-10); 16.91% Y/Y growth
Literacy rate	69.72 percent
Principal religions	Hinduism and Islam
Principal languages	Hindi, Urdu and English

- Uttar Pradesh leads in production of wheat and sugarcane; the government is paying special attention to sugar industry to promote investment in the sector.
- Uttar Pradesh is growing as one of the biggest market for IT and e-governance solutions in India
- The state's abundant source of minerals provides excellent potential in mineral-based industries

Overview

Uttar Pradesh, situated in the northern part of India, covers a total area of 240,928 km^2. It is bounded by Uttarakhand and Himachal Pradesh in the north, Aryana and Delhi in the west, Madhya Pradesh in the south, and Bihar in the east. It can be divided into two distinct regions: the Southern Hills and Gangetic Plain. Nepal also touches the northern borders of Uttar Pradesh. Due to its location, Uttar Pradesh is of strategic importance to India's defenses.

Agriculture is a major industry in Uttar Pradesh. The main agricultural commodities are wheat, sugarcane, rice, fruit and vegetables. Textile production, sugar production, food processing and mining have become backbone industries of the state's economy. It is also an important tourist destination and is dotted with various holy shrines and pilgrimage locations. In addition, there are the integrated townships of Noida and Greater Noida, adjacent to New Delhi, with fully developed infrastructure.

Uttar Pradesh has abundant land, water, minerals and forest resources. It also has a skilled, educated and technical human resource base. A large number of bank branches has been established in the state, including major foreign banks, providing good financial services to the local communities and investors. Well-developed special purpose modern industrial areas are also prevalent. Given such advantages, the state government has undertaken several policy measures and incentives. These measures aim to utilize fully Uttar Pradesh's available resources and generate adequate employment opportunities.

Business Opportunities

In recent years, Uttar Pradesh has attracted a high percentage of investment proposals. Some of the largest international companies have set up their industrial units in the state. The main traditional industries of the state are the sugar industry, the mineral-based industry, information technology, handlooms weaving and textile production. A wide variety of agricultural and horticultural crops are produced in the state, which also have huge export potentialities. The state's main strength lies in its skilled, educated and hardworking workforce.

Agriculture and Food Processing

Agriculture is the main occupation of majority of the population in Uttar Pradesh. Uttar Pradesh is among the largest producers of agricultural commodities within the country. It accounts for about 32.7% of India's wheat production and 35.8% of its sugarcane production. It is also a leading producer of rice, jowar, bajra, maize and groundnuts.

It also has the largest livestock population and highest milk production in India, offering excellent opportunities to set up various food processing units. Uttarakhand also has potential in floriculture and horticulture based industries.

Information Technology

Uttar Pradesh has always been a proactive state and is today one of the most sought after IT destination in the country. In Uttar Pradesh, Noida takes the lead as the most preferred IT destination for its robust infrastructure, excellent social values, educational institutes of excellence and world class health facilities.

Under the state's information technology policy, provisions have been made to computerize all the government departments and connect their computers through networking. This helps in ensuring easy availability of information to the people, besides bringing about efficiency and transparency in the government functioning.

Sugar Industry

The state of Uttar Pradesh is one of the largest producers of sugarcane in India. Sugar, molasses and bagasse are main derivatives of sugarcane. Molasses is further used for manufacturing industrial alcohol, potable alcohol and other chemicals. Bagasse is used for cogeneration of power and paper manufacturing. The state has the potential to produce about 35.8% of the country's sugar production. Given the importance of the sugar industry, the state government has formulated a comprehensive sugar policy to promote investment in this sector.

Minerals

The mining of limestone, coal, rock phosphate, dolomite and silica-sand is carried out in the public sector. The bulk production of most minor and some of the major minerals like limestone, silica-sand, pyrophyllite and diaspore is mostly carried out in the private sector. Important mineral based industries in the state include large cement plants in Sonbhadra.

Tourism

Known for its ancient traditions, Uttar Pradesh has many places of religious importance. The state is specially known for its cultural centers. It has varied attractions for all kinds of tourists. Important ancient places of pilgrimage are Varanasi, Vindhyachal, Ayodhya, Chitrakoot, Prayag, Naimisharanya, Mathura, Vrindavan, Dewa Sharief, Dargah of Sheikh Saleem Chishti in Fatehpur Sikri.

To encourage tourism and the foreign exchange that flows from it, the government of Uttar Pradesh has made tourism a priority industry.

Infrastructure

The state government is focused on infrastructure development and has undertaken several infrastructure projects to attract investment and promote overall development of the state. Infrastructure in the state includes roadways, railways, airways, power and telecommunication networks.

Roadways

Uttar Pradesh is well connected to its neighboring states through 42 National Highways (6,774 km) that run through the state. The highway network of the state accounts for 9.6% of the country's total national highway network.

Railways

Uttar Pradesh has a good network of intra-state railway through which the towns and the district headquarters of Uttar Pradesh are connected. Uttar Pradesh has the largest railway network in the country extending over 8,890 km. Lucknow is the main junction of the northern rail network.

Aviation

There are six airports in Uttar Pradesh located at Agra, Allahabad, Gorakhpur, Kanpur, Luckmnow and Varanasi International flights are available at Chaudhary Charan Singh International Airport in Lucknow and Lal Bahadur Shastri Airport in Varanasi. There are additional airports to be built at Gautam Buddha Nagar, Shrawasti and Kushinagar districts as well as the Taj International Airport at Jewar village in Gautam Buddha Nagar district pending.

Power

The total installed power capacity in Uttar Pradesh is 9,983.7 MW of which 4,621.2 MW is state share, 862.6 MW private share and 4,499.9 MW central share. Uttar Pradesh has the lowest per capita energy consumption in the nation at 340 kWh. More than 75% of Uttar Pradesh's infrastructure-related investments have been allotted to power generation and distribution and the state plans to increase power capacity by 10,500 MW by 2012.

The state has a reliable telecommunications network with both government and private players. Bharat Sanchar Nigam Limited (BSNL) is the main telecommunications service provider in the state. Better customer services like STD, ISD, Telex, Fax, online billing and broadband Internet are being made available.

Resources

Official Website of Government of Uttar Pradesh
http://upgov.nic.in/

UTTARAKHAND

Area	53,484 sq km
Population	10.11 million
Capital	Dehradun
NSDP at current prices	US$9.2 billion (2009-10); 16.34% Y/Y growth
Per capita NSDP at current prices	US$948 (2009-10); 14.60% Y/Y growth
Literacy rate	79.63 percent
Principal religions	Hinduism and Islam
Principal languages	Hindi, Garhwali and Kumaoni

- Uttarakhand is located close to the national capital region of Delhi and has good connectivity with neighboring states
- The state has the potential to become a preferred destination for IT and ITES along with hardware production
- Uttarakhand has excellent potential for hydroelectric power generation with only 9% of total hydro power potential currently in use

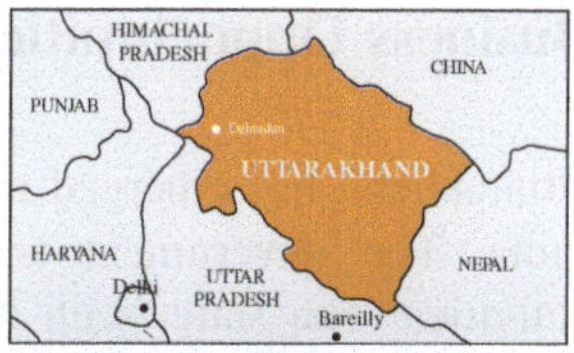

Overview

Uttarakhand was formed on November 9, 2000 as the 27th state of India when it was carved out of northern Uttar Pradesh. Located in the foothills of the Himalayan mountain ranges, it is largely a hilly state, sharing international boundaries with China in the north and Nepal in the east. To its northwest lies Himachal Pradesh, while in the south is Uttar Pradesh. It is rich in natural resources especially water and forests with many glaciers, rivers, dense forests and snow-clad mountain peaks.

The state possesses a rare biodiversity and is home to 175 rare species of aromatic and medicinal plants. It has almost all major climatic zones, making it amenable to a variety of commercial opportunities in horticulture, floriculture and agriculture. The tourism sector has particularly good potential, especially in adventure, leisure, and eco-tourism.

Uttarakhand is rich in mineral deposits like limestone, marble, rock phosphate, dolomite, magnetite, copper and gypsum. Small scale industries number over 35,000 providing employment to over 142,000 people.

With levels of literacy higher than the national average, the state has abundant availability of quality human resources. Within the short span of its existence, Uttarakhand has emerged as a significant destination for investments in manufacturing, tourism and infrastructure. The government's emphasis is on stimulating all three sectors of its economy—agriculture, industry and services—to their fullest potential. The Government of Uttarakhand has undertaken several policy measures and incentives in order to encourage the inflow of investment into the various sectors of its economy.

Business Opportunities

Uttarakhand has emerged as one of the most attractive industrial destinations in India. The government is encouraging private participation in all industrial activities. The state, with its vast natural resource base, large forest cover and enormous power generating capability, holds the potential to be one of the most prosperous states in India. Given the terrain of the state and favorable climatic conditions, agriculture continues to be the major source of income for more than three-quarters of the state's population. The major interest areas for the state of Uttaranchal are the development of the tourism, IT and biotechnology fields, particularly industries based on herbal and medicine plants and hydroelectric power generation. Significant opportunities are available for the construction of industrial parks and specialized production zones for IT. The government has established the State Infrastructure and Industrial Development Corporation of Uttarakhand to conceptualize and formulate the state's industrial development.

Information Technology

Given the state's high literacy rate and concentration of high quality educational institutions across the districts, Uttarakhand has the potential to become a preferred destination for IT and ITES along with hardware production. With the establishment of an STPI Earth Station at Dehradun and proposed Earth Stations at other locations, the state offers high-speed connectivity. The state has come up with incentives for the industry like exemption from electricity duty on generator sets, stamp duty concessions and rationalization of land use and conversion charges.

Handloom Weaving and Handicrafts

Uttarakhand is host to several handicrafts industries such as carpet weaving, woodcarving, brassware and copper based industries. The state plans to revive these industries to ensure adequate backward and forward linkages by way of centrally sponsored schemes. The handloom weaving industry is critical for employment generation in rural areas. The state plans to tap the potential of these skills-intensive industries by way of infrastructure support, training, design development, new techniques, packing, marketing events and exhibitions. Wool and wax based industries and khadi and village industries are some of the key traditional industries operating in the state. The wax-based industry is an important handicraft employer in the hill regions of the state and a large section of the population in the state is associated with the wool based industry. The state has assigned due priority to develop these industries to their full potential.

Biotechnology

Biotechnology is emerging at the global level and is poised to make significant contributions in agriculture, human and animal health care, environment management and process industries. Being host to a vast diversity of flora and fauna and rare species of plants and animals, Uttarakhand has a natural advantage in the sector. A high-level biotechnology board is being set up to pursue initiatives in the field of research. The state will accord the units coming under this sector with industry status and aims to establish an internationally competitive business infrastructure and environment for the industry in the state. A biotechnology park is to be developed that will integrate resources and provide a focused institutional set up for accelerated commercial growth of biotechnology and bioinformatics. The government is also in the process of creating an exchange for medicinal and aromatic plants to serve as a common platform for research institutions, technology developers and producers.

Agriculture and Food Processing

The State Government will assist in establishing small and medium size agriculture and food processing parks which will provide common infrastructure facilities for storage, processing, grading and marketing, thus ensuring that surplus fruit and vegetables do not go to waste as at present. Four agri-export zones have already been declared under the AEZ scheme of the Government of India for litchi, horticulture, herbs, medicinal plants and basmati rice. Further, efforts will continue to promote production for export and provide access to domestic and export markets for products from the state.

Tourism

Uttarakhand is an important tourist destination, especially for religious pilgrims. Sacred pilgrimages of different religions including: Haridwar and the world famous Char Dham—the four Hindu pilgrimage destinations of Shri Badrinath, Kedarnath, Gangotri and Yamunotri—and the sacred Sikh pilgrimages of Hemkund-Lokpal, Nanakmatta and Meetha-Reetha Sahib have drawn pilgrims and seekers of spiritual fulfillment to Uttarakhand for centuries. The rich cultural traditions, the rare natural beauty and the cool and invigorating climate of this land where the Holy Ganga and Yamuna rivers originate have been its main attractions.

Infrastructure

Uttarakhand compares favorably with the rest India in terms of the spread of basic infrastructure facilities. The creation of higher level infrastructure within the state offers tremendous potential for private investment. For a potentially power-rich state, generation, transmission and distribution of power provides vast investment opportunities.

Roadways

The state has good transport and communication networks. It also has a total length of 1,375.76 km of national highways and 1,575.50 km of state highways running through it.

Railways

The total length of railways in Uttarakhand is 345 km. The main railway stations are located in Dehradun, Hardwar, Roorkee, Kotdwar, Kashipur, Udhamsingh Nagar, Haldwani, Ramnagar and Kothgodam. A railway project to establish monorails at Dehradum, Haridwar and Rishikesh is underway.

Aviation

Uttarakhand has two domestic airports at Jolly Grant in the Dehradun district and Pant Nagar in the Udham Singh Nagar district. Delhi is well-connected by all flights at the airport. Jolly Grant airport is being upgraded to handle international traffic.

Power

The state has excellent potential for hydroelectric power generation. The total installation capacity in Uttarakhand is 2,405 MW of which 1,385.1 MW is controlled by the State Government, 400 MW is controlled by the private sector and 61.9 MW controlled by the Union Government. Uttarakhand is aiming to raise this level to 5,000 MW by 2011–2012. The state is seeking renewable energy as an alternative source of power generation. Many private companies are participating in various projects to develop the energy potential of Uttarakhand. Uttarakhand is growing as an "energy state" and aims to develop its hydroelectric power potential to more than 20,000 MW. Currently only 9% of its power potential has been realized.

Telecommunication

Uttarakhand has a well-developed communication network. The number of exchanges using the telephone in Uttarakhand is 458, with 372,051 telephone connections by BSNL and 748,027 mobile phone by BSNL.

Resources

Uttarakhand Government Portal
http://uk.gov.in/

WEST BENGAL

Area	88,752 sq km
Population	91.34 million
Capital	Kolkata (Calcutta)
NSDP at current prices	US$71.7 billion (2008-09); 14.38% Y/Y growth
Per capita NSDP at current prices	US$819 (2008-09); 13.28% Y/Y growth
Literacy rate	68.6 percent
Principal religions	Hinduism and Buddhism
Principal languages	Bengali

- Abundance of natural resources gives the state an advantage in the iron and steel industry
- West Bengal is the second largest tea growing state in India
- The IT industry has achieved significant growth in recent years, in areas including software development, hardware manufacturing, IT real estate, IT-enabled services and IT security

Overview

West Bengal, with a total geographical area of 88,752 km^2, is located in northeast India. It is bordered by Bihar and Jharkhand in the west, Orissa in the south, and Sikkim in the north. It is strategically positioned with three international frontiers: Bangladesh in the east; Nepal in the west; and Bhutan in the northeast. The land frontier of West Bengal stretches for about 700 km, from the Bay of Bengal in the south to the Himalayas in the north.

Business Opportunities

Major industries in West Bengal include agriculture (including jute and tea), leather, and information technology. In addition, significant investment has been made in iron and steel.

Agriculture and Horticulture

West Bengal is an agrarian state (the tertiary sector contributes to about 55% of the gross state domestic product) and offers tremendous potential for investment in agriculture-related businesses. The state has fertile soil, an excellent climate and aggressive land reform programs.

Rice, vegetables, sugarcane and wheat are the key agricultural products of West Bengal, while the state is also a major center for tea and jute. West Bengal is the second largest tea growing state in India—the two major districts in this industry are the northern Darjeeling and Jalpaiguri—and contributes about 24% of the total production of tea in India. West Bengal is the largest jute-producing state in India, producing 2/3 of the country's total jute supply. In addition, West Bengal is also the country's leading exporter of flowers.

Biotechnology is receiving large government support. With extremely simple methods of processing and scientific handling and storage, the entire sector provides a range of opportunities for investors in a host of areas, from grain handling and storage to the construction of food processing facilities or the building up of cold chain infrastructure.

Leather

With easy availability of raw materials and skilled manpower, the leather industry in West Bengal is quite significant and the state is India's leading exporter of finished leather goods. In 2008–2009, the state accounted for around 16% of the country's exports of leather and leather products. Kolkata Leather Complex, at 1,100 acres, is India's largest consolidated leather park.

Information Technology

West Bengal has prioritized growing its IT industry, specifically looking at developing second-tier cities like Haldia, Durgapur and Siliguri and also suburban areas around Kolkata into IT hubs. The IT industry has achieved significant growth in recent years, with major development areas including software development, hardware manufacturing, IT real estate; IT-enabled services and IT security. The state has 14 IT parks and a 16-acre SEZ has been approved for Tata Consultancy Services.

Infrastructure

West Bengal has ports at Kolkata and Haldia, efficient networks of railways, roadways and airports, a stable power grid and a recently improved telecommunication system.

Roadways

West Bengal has 92,023 km of roads, with 14 national highways running through the state, according to the Ministry of Road Transport & Highways. National Highway 2 connects Kolkata to New Delhi and is part of the national Golden Quadrangle. A number of road development projects have been taken up under public private partnerships, including the Kolkata-Durgapur expressway, the Palsit-Dankuniroad project and the Panagarh-Palsitroad project.

Railways

The total length of railway track in the state is around 4,500 km. Howrah Asansol, Sealdah, Bandel, Bardhaman, Kharagpur and New Jalpaiguri are the main railway junctions.

Aviation

West Bengal presently has two commercial airports: Netaji Subhas International Airport in Dum Dum and Bagdogra Airport in Darjeeling. The former is being modernized in 2011 and will quadruple the airport's handling capacity from 2009.

Waterways

The state of West Bengal has two modern seaports in Kolkata and Haldia. Together they handle over 60 million tons of cargo and their throughput ranks among the highest among the major ports of India. The West Bengal Government also plans to construct a container port at Kulpiand, at the mouth of the Hooghly River.

Power

West Bengal had a total installed power generation capacity of 8,149.5 MW, which comprised 6,013.6 MW under state utilities, 1,361.7 MW under the private sector and 774.3 MW under the central sector as of March 2010, according to the Central Electricity Authority. The state is encouraging developments in renewable energy and has significant generation capacity in thermal power, hydropower, and other such sources.

Telecommunications

The state telecommunications industry offers vast potential for investment with the penetration of optic fiber cables and the expansion of broadband services all over the state. Mobile cellular services and e-mail services are also available from a host of operators.

Resources

Official Site of Government of West Bengal
http://www.wbgov.com/
West Bengal Industrial Development Corporation
http://www.wbidc.com/

Chapter 7
India and China Compared

Looking Ahead: The Next Two Decades

Despite the fanfare surrounding India's rapid development, many are starting to question just how well the emergent power can compete against its much larger and much more developed rival next door: China.

In some respects, India's rise has been overshadowed by what has been happening in China over the past two decades. If development in China had not occurred, India would be the rising star of global economic growth. On the upside, the lack of media attention has allowed India to continue growing without being the subject of harmful media speculation that can often be disruptive to capital markets in an emerging economy. China's rise, moreover, may have provided an example of what to follow in some respects and, in other respects, an example of what to avoid.

Over much of the past decade, India's growth has begun to mirror that of China's. Both nations have been growing at roughly 9% annually, though, India's growth proceeds from an economy roughly one-third the size of China's (meaning, in an absolute sense, China's economy expands three times as much per year as India's).

And yet, India is ranked as the 10th largest economy in the world by organizations such as the World Bank, International Monetary Fund, and the CIA. Many predict that it will soon be the world's 3rd largest economy, and only lag behind China and the United States in gross domestic product. The United Nations Industrial Development Organization also ranks India in the global top ten for its contribution to the world's total manufacturing output and its share of manufacturing is greater than that of many already-industrialized nations. Members of the global community—businesses and foreign governments alike—are starting to take notice of India's rise and recognize the opportunities such development brings. This is particularly true in China. Chinese businesses are starting to move to India, Indian businesses are increasingly moving to China. Dezan

Dezan Shira & Associates and C. Devonshire-Ellis (eds.), *Doing Business in India*, India Briefing, DOI: 10.1007/978-3-642-27618-7_7,

Shira & Associates, Asia Briefing's parent company, handles many firms' turn-key investment from both countries into either side.

	2010		2030 (forecasted)	
	China	India	China	India
Size of economy in global terms[a, b]	3rd	12th	2nd	4th
Global position in purchasing power parity[c, d]	2nd	4th	2nd	3rd
Global ranking among fastest growing economies	1st	2nd	20th	12th
Per capita income (US $)	3,180	1,032	10,700	8,900
World per capita income ranking	104th	139th	80th	88th
Number of workers (millions)	250	500	175	600
Population growth rate	0.63%	1.55%	0.82%	1.01%
Total population in global terms	21%	17.50%	19%	21.50%
Percentage of global trade	8%	1.50%	8%	5.50%
Global trade (US $bn, 2010)[e, f]	2,972.8	528	9,824	4,500
Total rail track (km)	86,000	63,140	200,000	130,000
Total highway length (km in millions)	1.43	0.07	1.8	0.9
Total number of English speakers (millions)	10	232	10	250

[a] International monetary fund
[b] Goldman sachs
[c] Price water house coopers
[d] CIA World fact book
[e] U.S. China business council
[f] CIA World fact book

India's demographics also indicate room for growth that is yet to come. India's available workforce is twice the size of China's, and while China is aging, India is growing younger. India's birthrate also is three times that of China's, suggesting that the future of labor-intensive industry may lie on the Indian subcontinent. As wages continue to skyrocket in coastal China, China's chief propeller of economic growth—cheap labor—will likely be on the move. India also has 800,000 km^2 more arable land than China and roughly ten times the fresh water resources—two natural inputs critical for the development of sectors whose growth will reverberate nation-wide; agriculture and textiles.

Much has been made of India's lack of infrastructure, but by the numbers, India's 4.2 million km of road isn't too far behind China's 3,829,200 km. Furthermore, over the next three years, India's government will spend US $500 billion in an effort to improve the nation's infrastructure. Some major projects to be implemented in the coming years include the National Highways Development Project and the Mumbai-Pune Express. Goldman Sachs has said, over the next decade, India would need to raise US $1.7 trillion to spend on its roadways to improve growth. It is well on its way, but the government will also provide incentives to encourage foreign investment such as toll rights for developers to fund these projects. In aspects such as power generation, rail connectivity, internet access and highway length, however, India still lags significantly behind its peer.

Within the next few years, India is expected to clock a faster annual growth rate than China, according to Morgan Stanley and its population is widely expected overtake China's by 2030. With double the amount of available workforce, a younger population, and a consumer-driven economy that relies on its own demand, India's tortoise may catch up with China's hare much sooner than expected. When that happens, the two countries will have reached their rightful place as regional partners and usher in what then may be henceforth referred to as "the Asian century."

India-China Trade

Sino-India trade during 2010 reached over US$60 billion, the same level it was at before the global financial crisis. Premier Wen in Q4 2010 said in Delhi that the two nations will increase trade to US$100 billion by 2015.

Due to their respective positions on the global value chain, in many industries, China imports inputs from India and exports finished goods back to India. By volume, the main Indian items intended for Chinese markets are iron ore, slag and ash, iron and steel, plastics, organic chemicals, cotton and textile fabrics; whereas Chinese items that enter Indian markets tend to be electrical machinery and equipment, cement, organic chemicals, machinery and oils.

India's government has been attempting to reposition the country's output further up the value chain into the export of specialized services, including biotechnology, IT and ITES, health, education and financial advisory as a way to decrease the ever-growing trade defict. But the trade deficit is at this point still growing and India has successfully appealed to the WTO on several occasions to block the export of Chinese products.

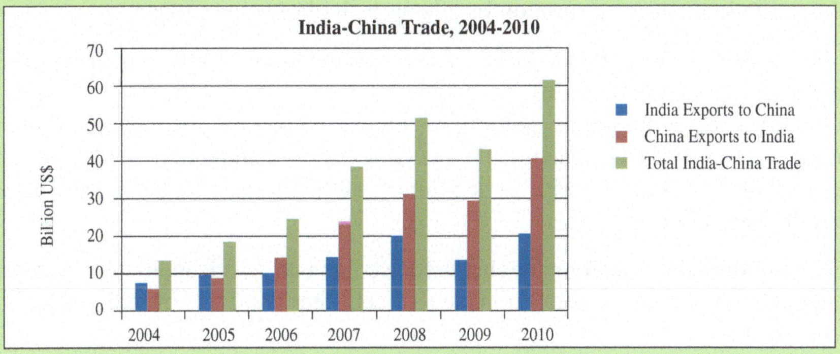

China Project Offices Versus India Project Offices

Establishing project offices (POs) in a country allow foreign investment and participation in a specific project, and are usually linked to a high value contract that may take two to 3 years to complete. They negate the need for the foreign participant to establish a more permanent presence, as the life of the PO is linked to the contract's life cycle, but POs still provide flexibility in terms of hiring labor, acquiring funds for the project, and remitting profits overseas. As China developed and required particular skill sets to complete specific, usually construction based projects, the China PO enjoyed a relatively successful period of popularity in the late 1990 and early 2000s. Recently, they have fallen out of favor, mainly as Chinese contractors are now able to take the lion's share of construction work and do not need foreign short-term sub-contractors to assist. When discussing the matter with authorities in Beijing, it appeared no PO licenses have been granted for a number of years, and that applications would probably no longer be approved.

This policy is in sharp contrast to India's, where the project office remains a viable vehicle for foreign investors to participate in infrastructure- and construction-related projects. Foreign investors planning to execute specific projects in India can set up a temporary project site office in India to handle the contract. The Reserve Bank of India provides approval and grants general permission for foreign entities to establish project offices, but such entities are subject to certain conditions. One such stipulation is that before getting approval for a PO, the foreign investor must have secured a contract from an Indian company to execute a project in India.

In addition, the project needs to adhere to one of the following conditions:

- The project is funded directly by inward remittance from abroad
- The project is funded by a bilateral or multilateral international financing agency
- The project has been cleared by an appropriate authority
- A company or entity in India awarding the contract has been granted term loan by a public financial institution or a bank in India for the project.

If at least one of the above criteria is not met, the foreign entity has to approach the RBI to obtain approval.

In terms of remittances, authorized Indian banks can permit intermittent remittances by the PO, pending the winding up or completion of the project provided they are satisfied with the legitimacy of the transaction, but are subject to the following criteria:

- The PO submits an auditors or chartered accountants certificate to the effect that sufficient provisions have been made to meet other liabilities in India including income tax
- An undertaking from the PO that the remittance will not, in any way, affect the completion of the project in India and that any shortfall of funds for meeting any liability in India will be met by inward remittance from abroad.

Any inter-project transfer of funds requires prior permission of the pertinent regional office of the RBI under whose jurisdiction the PO is situated. In the financial circumstances described above, readers familiar with China-based transactions involving foreign currency should note the Reserve Bank of India in such circumstances fulfills much the same role as China's State Administration of Foreign Exchange.

In order to take advantage of India's massive reconstruction projects, foreign investors may well find the Indian project office a suitable vehicle to use as it affords relatively easy market entry and exit upon project completion. This contrasts greatly with China, where the project office is now largely seen as having had its day.

China FICE Versus India Branch Offices

There are some legal differences between China's foreign-invested commercial enterprises and India's branch offices (BO), not least amongst them being that Indian BOs are not independent legal entities, whereas China FICEs are. However, in terms of use, both fulfill pretty much the same criteria for foreign investors: they permit the import and export of goods, can buy and sell goods, can trade or offer consulting services, and can remit profits back overseas. Branch offices differ in that they are still considered part of a foreign entity based overseas, and are not limited liability companies. By contrast, foreign invested commercial enterprises are independent, limited liability companies. Accordingly, BOs do not require capitalization whereas FICEs do. A downside of the India BO is the high level of corporate income tax—41.86% against India's norm of 33.99%—and the standard income tax rate of 25% in China.

Other differences exist for FICEs and BOs engaged in the service sector. Branch offices do not attract turnover tax, whereas in China, FICEs involved in the service industry face a monthly rate of 5% tax. Service industry BOs are subject to a service tax against invoice value at a rate of 10.3%. For trading however, the applicable tax burden is the VAT, which in China is 17% and in India is 12.5%. Though it may not be possible to reclaim all VAT upon export in China, in India VAT can be reclaimed in full upon the export of product.

The advantage of the BO over the FICE is the ease of establishing and exiting it as an entity. For this reason it may make sense to set up a BO despite the initial higher income tax burden to test the Indian market without having to commit to major capitalization costs in India. For longer term trading and manufacturing, a private limited company incorporation would be more suitable.

Chinese foreign invested commercial enterprises versus Indian branch offices

Requirement	China	India
Limited liability	Yes	No
Minimum capital investment	According to company law:	N/A
• multiple shareholder	US $4,614	
• single shareholder	US $15,381	
Permissible activities	Wholesale, retail, franchising, commission agency	Retail
Income tax	25%	41.86%
VAT	17%	12.5%
Average gross hourly pay	US $3	US $1.20
Employee welfare (% of salary)	45–50%	10.3%

China WFOE Versus India Private Limited Companies

China's wholly foreign-owned enterprise (WFOE) has become the investment vehicle of choice for the international investor wanting to manufacture, provide a service or trade in China. In addition to the WFOE's expansive business scope, its unrivaled popularity arises from multiple other factors, including 100% foreign ownership and control, security of technology and intellectual property rights, a self-developed internal structure, the insertion of existing company culture, and ability to sell to China's domestic market, and the ability to repatriate profits. In this regard, India's private limited companies (IPLC) are the same animal, with the exception that whereas China has a specific set of regulatory considerations for Sino-foreign joint ventures, an IPLC can also be an Indo-foreign JV, and both 100% foreign-owned IPLCs and IPLC JVs are governed by the same regulations.

For the purposes of this analysis, we shall concentrate on the 100% foreign-owned IPLC. The need for such a company to have either 100% foreign ownership or whether it requires an Indian investor is dependent, in a similar fashion to China, upon the scope of the business's intended activities. The intended scope of business activities in India needs to be studied first to assess the suitability of the business as being a 100% foreign-owned entity.

On the assumption that the scope of activities does not require Indian investment, then an IPLC may be established with 100% foreign ownership in India. Investment may proceed under what is known as the "automatic route" and does not require additional approvals.

Unlike in China, application procedures for 100% foreign ownership of IPLC may sometimes fall into a second category, which does require specific approval from India's Foreign Investment Promotion Board (FIPB). These categories are identified by the Reserve Bank of India, and comprise two lists concerning approval required (List A), and limited eligibility (List B) that affect foreign investment in India. All items and activities that are not mentioned in List A and List B are eligible for foreign investment under the automatic route up to 100%. Items in List A require approval from the FIPB. List B prescribes the limits on the foreign investments for which automatic approval will be granted by RBI. The lists are quite specific and generally do not cover standard manufacturing or trading operations which are usually under the purview of the automatic route. Most India investors entering the market to manufacture trade and sell standard products will not fall into either List A or B restrictions. Similar to the China WFOE, an IPLC requires a minimum of two directors, and has from two to 50 shareholders with limited liability related to the amount of paid up capital. Both directors and shareholders can be other legal entities. As is the case in China, the amount of paid up capital required should be a financial exercise to determine the business's start up and cash flow needs.

Interestingly, when all taxes are considered, in terms of repatriating profits from India, the IPLC is more tax efficient than the China WFOE. Although India's profits tax is higher, it does not levy a tax on profits repatriated overseas, which China does impose. The additional costs of labor welfare are also considerably more in China, making the IPLC more financially viable than its Chinese counterpart—a fact which might warrant some further consideration if weighing the benefits of one market over those of the other.

Chinese wholly foreign owned enterprises versus Indian private limited companies

Requirement	China	India
Limited liability	Yes	Yes
Minimum capital investment	According to company law:	Rs 100,000
• multiple shareholder		
• single shareholder		
Regulatory status	US $4,614	Two tier
Income tax	US $15,381	30%
VAT	17%	12.5%
Profits repatriation tax	10%	Nil

China Versus India Corporate Income Taxes

Both China and India have fairly well developed tax structures, both with the authority to levy taxes divided between the central and regional governments. Both countries are going through an extended period of tax reform at present, with India especially doing so as it seeks to pass legislation to update its tax base for the first time in 50 years.

Top amongst these changes is likely to be the introduction of a goods and services tax (GST) at varying rates amongst internal purchase and sales, although 100% refund upon export is expected. The GST is expected to amount to 16% of invoice value. This system is expected to partially replace VAT in some states, although in others it will be a new introduction. VAT is not uniformly applied by all states in India. For certain "sin" goods, such as tobacco and petrol, VAT may be applied on top of GST.

On the other hand, India does score better in the application of VAT (and future GST) refunds against exports. China levies a tiered system of VAT refunds against exports, and in some sectors, such as garments, does not permit refunds at all.

India however permits VAT refunds against all categories of goods and services upon export. It should be noted that China does not currently levy VAT on services, while India does.

Corporate income taxes, China versus India

Tax	China	India
Corporate income tax	25%	30–40%
Education surcharge	3%	3%
Business (turnover) tax	5%	Nil
Wealth tax	Nil	1% (if t/o above US $65,000)
Dividend tax to overseas parent	10%	15%
Transaction-based taxes	China	India
VAT	17%	12.5%
GST	Nil	Rollout pending
Withholding taxes on royalties charge from overseas	0–45% depending on service, average 20%	10–40% depending if permanent establishment is in India or not

Note: While every effort has been made to ensure accuracy of tax data, readers are asked to bear in mind that in both cases, regional variations occur and that the tax regimes in both countries are evolving rapidly. The figures above are as a general guideline only, and may be subject to change. Accurate and industry specific tax data should be obtained directly from professional advisers

Tax Incentives

With China unifying its tax base in 2008, it did away with preferential tax incentives largely available to foreign investors, and especially those in free trade zones and special economic zones. China now tends to levy or provide refunds against a variety of taxes depending upon the industry. In doing so the Chinese Central Government tries to manage balances between domestic sales of certain products and exports of certain products, and varies these from time to time or as circumstances dictate. China is still very much a centrally planned economy. Specific tax incentives therefore are usually applicable in certain industries only, occasionally regionally based, and typically involve a manipulation of business tax, profits tax or VAT.

India on the other hand wishes to develop its special economic zones and free trade zones, and accordingly provides highly attractive tax incentives to do so. These can include 100% corporate income tax breaks for up to 10 years. These can be applicable to certain development projects to be carried out in India, mainly with infrastructure. Incentives also exist for businesses involved in the 100% export of products manufactured in an Indian SEZ or FTZ. These are typically 100% for the first 5 years of profitability, and 50% for an additional 5 years, although there are regional and eligibility variations. Nevertheless, the boom in manufacturing that China enjoyed with the tax incentives it used to offer in its development zones are now being recreated in India, and this should spur foreign investors familiar with the China model to consider India as an alternative manufacturing base, as these incentives provide a clear impetus for doing so.

It should be noted that China engages a calendar year audit cycle, January 1 to December 31. India uses the fiscal period from April 1 to March 31.

Summary

From the global manufacturing perspective, China and India now offer similar, yet also differing opportunities. The main thrust of China's development is to create an equality of wealth within its borders, and to do this it needs to both improve upon some of its infrastructure, education and housing options and facilities that are currently available in rural areas. China's growth will come increasingly from the rural population and it is this sector that the government wishes to develop into becoming a consumer class. Today's opportunities for China are largely about being able to service this sector. China is also moving up the value chain and wants to move away from its traditional low cost, export-driven manufacturing base. In doing so, opportunities exist in adding value—research and development, innovation and design are all going to be developing services that China increasingly needs.

For India, this is also partially true. Indians are receptive to international brands and a wealthy middle class, and with English being so widely spoken, India has huge and yet still untapped potential for global manufacturers looking for sales overseas. This is true of everything from auto components to fashion, and in this aspect the two countries share similarities in their major urban markets. India has also taken up the mantle, recently discarded by China, of offering cheap manufacturing. As China has wound down its free trade zones and special economic zones for the purposes of export manufacturing, India has ramped its own offerings up. China has become too dependent upon export manufacturing to the detriment of its overall economy, while India does not have enough manufacturing capability and is too dependent upon services. It is these realignments that are creating opportunities to be realized. Accordingly, India may now be considered as a viable and serious contender for export-driven manufacturing to markets abroad.

In truth, the China versus India debate is a no-brainer. It's neither one, nor the other, and although some competition in capabilities will undoubtedly emerge, it is quite apparent to this house at least, that global strategy, in terms of getting growth onto balance sheets of parent companies elsewhere, must now embrace China and India as two unique, but complimentary, destinations to achieve dynamism and development for the next two decades.

Directory

Government Offices, Trade Associations and Chambers of Commerce

Department of Commerce
Ministry of Commerce and Industry
Udyog Bhawan
New Delhi, 110107
Tel: (11) 2306 2261
www.commerce.nic.in

Public Private Partnerships in India
Ministry of Finance, Department of Economic Affairs
67, North Block
New Delhi, 110001
Tel: (11) 2309 3881
www.pppinindia.com

All India Association of Industries
New Excelsior Building
6th Floor, A.K. Nayak Marg
Mumbai, 400001
Tel: (22) 2201 9265
www.aiaiindia.com

The Associated Chambers of Commerce and Industry of India
1 Community Centre
Zamrudpur, Kailash Colony
New Delhi, 110048
Tel: (11) 4655 0555
www.assocham.org

Confederation of Indian Industry
Mantosh Sondhi Centre
23 Institutional Area, Lodi Road
New Delhi, 110003
Tel: (11) 2462 9994
www.cii.in

Federation of Indian Chambers of Commerce and Industry
Federation House
Tansen Marg
New Delhi, 110001
Tel: (11) 2373 8760
www.ficci.com

Federation of Indian Export Organizations
Niryat Bhawan, Rao Tula Ram Marg
New Delhi, 110057
Tel: (11) 4604 2222
www.fieo.org

India Brand Equity Foundation
249-F Sector 18 Udyog Vihar
Phase IV Gurgaon
Haryana, 122015
Tel: (124) 401 4060
www.ibef.org

Indian Chamber of Commerce
ICC Towers
4, India Exchange Place
Kolkata, 700001
Tel: (33) 2230 3242
www.indianchamber.org

India Trade Promotion Organization
Pragati Bhawan
Pragati Maidan
New Dellhi, 110001
Tel: (11) 2337 1540
www.indiatradefair.com

Institute of Chartered Accountants of India
ICAI Bhawan
Indraprastha Marg, Post Box. No. 7100
New Delhi, 110002
Tel: (11) 3989 3989
www.icai.org

SME Export Promotion Council of India
3 & 4, Upper Ground Floor
Samruddhi Venture Park, Marol
MIDC Industrial Area
Mumbai, 400093
Tel: (22) 6677 0218
www.smeepcofindia.com

American Chamber of Commerce in India
PHD House, 4th Floor, 4/2, Siri Institutional Area, August Kranti Marg
New Delhi, 110016
Tel: (11) 2652 5201
www.amchamindia.com

British Business Group
Victor House
1st Floor, 142/C. N.M. Joshi Marg
Mumbai, 400013
Tel: (99) 8706 6623
www.bbgmumbai.org

The Council of EU Chambers of Commerce in India
3rd Florr, Y.B. Chavan Centre
Gen.J. Bhosale, Marg
Mumbai, 400021
Tel: (22) 2285 4563
www.euindiachambers.com

European Business Group in India
65, Golf Links,
New Delhi, 110003
Tel: (11) 2463 6675
www.europeanbusinessgroupindia.com

India China Chamber of Commerce and Industry
54-A, Elite Auto House
Andheri-Kurla Road, Andheri East
Mumbai, 4003
Tel: (22) 2825 9484
www.indiachinachamber.com

Indo-American Chamber of Commerce
PHD House Opp. Asian Games Village
New Delhi, 110016
Tel: (11) 2696 3387
www.iaccindia.com

Indo-French Chambers of Commerce and Industry
B-5, Venkatesh Chambers, Prescot Road
Mumbai, 400001
Tel: (22) 2206 4660
www.ifcci.org.in

Indo-German Chambers of Commerce and Industry
Maker Tower E, 1st Floor, Cuffe Parade
Mumbai, 400005
Tel: (22) 6665 2121
www.indo-german.com

Indo-Italian Chamber of Commerce and Industry
502, Bengal Chemicals Coumpound
Veer Savakar Marg Prabhadevi
Mumbai, 400025
Tel: (22) 2436 8186
www.indiaitaly.com

Indo-Japanese Chamber of Commerce and Industry
Oricon House, Kalaghoda Hutatma Chowk (Flora Fountain)
Mumbai, 400023
Tel: (22) 2284 4772
www.ijcci.com

German Centre for Industry and Trade
Building No. 9, Tower B, Level 12
DLF Cyber City Phase III,Gurgaon
Haryana, 122002
Tel: (12) 4463 6000
www.gurgaon.germancentre.com

The UK India Business Council
UKIBC Mumbai Level 9
Platina, G- Block, Plot C - 59
Bandra Kurla Complex
Mumbai, 400051
Tel: (22) 3953 0722
www.ukibc.com

Dezan Shira & Associates and C. Devonshire-Ellis (eds.), *Doing Business in India*, India Briefing, DOI: 10.1007/978-3-642-27618-7,

Embassies

Australian High Commission
1/50 G Shantipath, Chanakyapuri
New Delhi, 110021
Tel: (11) 4139 9900

Embassy of Austria
EP 13, Chandergupta Marg Chanakyapuri
New Delhi, 110021
Tel: (11) 2688 9050

British High Commission
Shantipath, Chanakyapuri
New Delhi, 110021
Tel: (11) 2419 2100

Embassy of Chile
146 Jor Bagh,
New Delhi, 110003
Tel: (11) 2461 7123

Embassy of People's Republic of China
50-D, Shantipath, Chanakyapuri
New Delhi, 110021
Tel: (11) 2611 2345

Canadian High Commission
7/8, Shantipath, Chanakyapuri
New Delhi, 110021
Tel: (11) 5178 2000

Embassy of the Czech Republic
50-M, Niti Marg, Chanakyapuri
New Delhi, 110021
Tel: (11) 2611 0205

Embassy of Denmark
11, Aurangzeb Road
New Delhi, 110011
Tel: (11) 4209 0700

Embassy of the Democratic People's Republic of Korea
D-14, Maharani Bagh
New Delhi, 110065
Tel: (11) 2682 9644

Embassy of Egypt
1/50 M, Niti Marg Chanakyapuri
New Delhi, 110021
Tel: (11) 2611 4096

Embassy of Germany
6/50 G, Shanti Path, Chanakyapuri
New Delhi, 110021
Tel: (11) 2687 1831

Embassy of Finland
E 3, Nyaya Marg Chanakyapuri
New Delhi, 110021
Tel: (11) 4149 7500

Embassy of France
2/50 E, Shantipath Chanakyapuri
New Delhi, 110021
Tel: (11) 2419 6100

Embassy of Luxembourg
730. Gadaipur Road Branch
Post OfficeGadaipur
New Delhi, 110030
Tel: (11) 2680 1954

Embassy of Greece
EP 32, Dr. S Radhakrishnan
Marg Chanakyapuri
New Delhi, 110021
Tel: (11) 2688 0700

Embassy of Japan
50 G, Shantipath Chanakyapuri
New Delhi, 110021
Tel: (11) 2687 6581

Embassy of Jordan
30, Golf Links
New Delhi, 110003
Tel: (11) 2465 3318

Embassy of the Republic of Korea
9, Chandragupta Marg
Chanakyapuri Extension
New Delhi, 110021
Tel: (11) 2412 1389

Embassy of Kuwait
5 A, Shantipath Chanakyapuri,
New Delhi, 110021
Tel: (11) 2411 8008

Embassy of Ireland
230, Jor Bagh,
New Delhi, 110003
Tel: (11) 2462 6733

Embassy of Italy
50 E, Chandragupta Marg Chanakyapuri
New Delhi, 110021
Tel: (11) 2611 4355

Malaysian High Commission
50-M Satya Marg Chanakyapuri
New Delhi, 110021
Tel: (11) 2611 1291

Mauritius High Commission
EP 41, Jesus & Mary Marg Chanakyapuri
New Delhi, 110021
Tel: (11) 2410 2161

Embassy of Mexico
C8 Anand Niketan
New Delhi, 110021
Tel: (11) 2411 7180, 81/82

Embassy of Mongolia
34, Archbishop Makarios Marg
New Delhi, 110003
Tel: (11) 2463 1728

New Zealand High Commission
Sir Edmund Hillary Marg Chanakyapuri
New Delhi, 110021
Tel: (11) 2688 5622

Embassy of Oman
EP 10 & 11, Chandragupta
Marg Chanakyapuri,
New Delhi, 110021
Tel: (11) 2688 5622

Embassy of Poland
50 M, Shantipath Chanakyapuri
New Delhi, 110021
Tel: (11) 4149 6900

Embassy of Qatar
EP 31 A, Chandragupta
Marg Chanakyapuri,
New Delhi, 110021
Tel: (11) 2611 7988

Embassy of the Russian Federation
Shantipath Chanakyapuri
New Delhi, 110021
Tel: (11) 2687 3799

Embassy of Saudi Arabia
2, Paschimi Marg, Vasant Vihar
New Delhi, 110057
Tel: (11) 2614 4073

Embassy of Sweden
Nyaya Marg Chanakyapuri
New Delhi, 110021
Tel: (11) 2419 7100

Embassy of Switzerland
Nyaya Marg Chanakyapuri
New Delhi, 110021
Tel: (11) 2687 8372

Embassy of Spain
12, Prithvi Raj Road
New Delhi, 110011
Tel: (11) 2435 9004

Embassy of Turkey
N-50, Nyaya Marg Chanakyapuri
New Delhi, 110021
Tel: (11) 2688 9053

Embassy of United States of America
Shantipath, Chanakyapuri
New Delhi, 110021
Tel: (11) 2419 8000

ASIA BRIEFING
Regional Business Intelligence
From the Asia Foreign Direct Investment Practice
Dezan Shira & Associates
www.asiabriefingmedia.com
CHINA BRIEFING
www.china-briefing.com
INDIA BRIEFING
www.india-briefing.com
RUSSIA BRIEFING
www.russia-briefing.com
MONGOLIA BRIEFING
www.mongolia-briefing.com
VIETNAM BRIEFING
www.vietnam-briefing.com
2point6billion.com
www.2point6billion.com
DEZAN SHIRA & ASSOCIATES
Business Advisory · Corporate Establishment · Tax · Accounting · Payroll · Due Diligence · Audit
CHINA
INDIA
VIETNAM
SINGAPORE
www.dezshira.com

The manufacturer's authorised representative in the EU is Springer Nature Customer Service Centre GmbH, Europaplatz 3, 69115 Heidelberg, Germany. If you have any concerns regarding our products, please contact ProductSafety@springernature.com

Printed and bound by CPI Group (UK) Ltd, Croydon, CR0 4YY
22/09/2026
02220981-0008